3-6574

Politics and Literature in the Eighteenth Century

Edited, with an introduction by
H. T. Dickinson

Dent, London
Rowman and Littlefield, Totowa, NJ

Politics and Literature in the Eighteenth Century

Edited, with an introduction, by
H. T. Dickinson
Reader in History
University of Edinburgh

Dent, London
Rowman & Littlefield, Totowa, N.J.

© Introduction, selection and commentary,
J. M. Dent & Sons Ltd, 1974

J. M. DENT & SONS LTD
Aldine House · Albemarle Street · London
First published 1974
First published in the United States 1974
by ROWMAN AND LITTLEFIELD, Totowa, New Jersey

Dent edition
Hardback ISBN: 0 460 10197 8
Paperback ISBN: 0 460 11197 3

Rowman and Littlefield edition
Library of Congress Cataloging in Publication Data
Dickinson, H T comp.
  Politics and literature in the eighteenth century.

  Bibliography: p.
  1. Political science—Literary collections.
2. English literature—18th century. 3. Great
Britain—Politics and government—18th century—
sources. I. Title.
  PR1111.P6D5   820'.8'03   73-11109

ISBN 0-87471-405-2;
ISBN 0-87471-400-1 (pbk)

Contents

1791614

v

Introduction

The work of Sir Lewis Namier and his disciples has had an immense impact on the study of eighteenth-century British politics. It has done much, for example, to dispel myths about the absolutist aims of George III and about the existence of organized Whig and Tory parties in the mid-eighteenth century. This 'Namierite' preoccupation with the structure of politics, however, with its emphasis on the mechanical and manipulative aspect of politics, has sometimes been taken too far. In less skilful hands than those of Namier it has led to a failure to understand the operative force of political ideas. Robert Walcott, for example, was able to write *English Politics in the Early Eighteenth Century* (Oxford, 1956) without reference to the works of such political writers of the day as Swift, Defoe, Addison or Steele. Even Namier himself paid scant attention to the writings of Bolingbroke or Burke when writing about mid-eighteenth-century politics. The Namierite approach, while undeniably offering valuable insights into the nature of the eighteenth-century political system, neglects the political climate which influences or restricts what politicians do. It reveals much about political actions and ambitions, but it ignores what politicians and commentators of the time actually thought and felt about what was happening. For a full understanding of eighteenth-century politics we need to appreciate not just what historians now believe to be the objective reality, but how men at the time regarded the situation. This kind of understanding can only be achieved by studying the whole range of political ideas and political literature of the period.

x   *Introduction*

Much of this evidence may exaggerate or distort, it may be
prejudiced or blind to reality, but, without it, we cannot
really understand why men responded to political events in
the ways in which they did.

There is a wealth of political literature that can be studied
by the historian interested in the political ideas and the
climate of opinion in eighteenth-century Britain. It extends
from the partisan polemics of Junius and Wilkes to the philosophical and sociological works of David Hume and Adam
Ferguson; from the turgid pamphlets of Grub Street hacks to
the lasting literary works of Swift and Gay. All of this evidence
repays careful study, though it is not always easy to interpret
its meaning or to assess its value. The historian has to calculate,
for example, to what extent the writings of Bolingbroke and
Burke were distorted and exaggerated by their personal political ambitions. He also has to determine the ways in which
the political situation in eighteenth-century Britain influenced
such works as the sociological studies of Adam Ferguson or the
historical writings of Edward Gibbon. Such questions are not
easy to answer, but at least historians are trained to study such
problems. It is more difficult for them to assess the value of
imaginative literature as historical source material, but it is
precisely this kind of evidence which is so plentiful and so
essential to the historian of eighteenth-century politics. Such
a historian cannot regard imaginative literature simply as a
mirror of its time, as a collection of historical documents, or as
an illustration of the history of political ideas. The originality
of the individual writer and the art form he adopts inevitably
means that his work is not an objective picture of external
reality. The greater the writer, the greater is his capacity to
express more than just the ideas, attitudes and standards of
his own day. Even if the author of a piece of imaginative
literature is directly influenced by the real political world that
surrounds him, the form or style he chooses, as the means of
expressing his ideas, will distort or modify reality. Thus, for
example, the use of satire will inevitably lead to exaggeration.
Political realities were also distorted when writers imagined
the political situation in Britain being described by foreigners
visiting the country for the first time, as in George Lyttelton's

Persian Letters (1734), or by an Englishman in a strange land, as in Swift's *Gulliver's Travels* (1726). Furthermore, the ideas and opinions expressed by characters in a work of imaginative literature may not be those of the author. This distinction is made quite clear in parts of *Tom Jones* (1749). In book 12, chapter 12, Tom is much attracted to the absolute and arbitrary authority of the gypsy king, but, in case his readers should misunderstand him, Henry Fielding makes it clear that he personally has no liking for absolute rulers or the theory of divine right. In this instance, Fielding forewarns the historian about the careless use of imaginative literature as historical source material. The same caution is needed in evaluating all imaginative literature, but this provides such important evidence of political opinions in the eighteenth century that it must be studied.

The Namierite approach to the study of eighteenth-century politics results in a stress on the stability and harmony of the period. By studying the whole range of political literature the historian becomes more aware of the existence of political tensions and controversies. In the middle decades of the eighteenth century, the period most studied by Namier himself, Britain enjoyed unparalleled political stability. There was no serious threat to the 'Whig' constitution or the political authority of the men of property. This was not the case, however, if we move away from these years. In the early eighteenth century there was a bitter conflict between Whigs and Tories about some of the consequences of the constitutional settlement apparently reached after the Glorious Revolution. The Revolution Settlement had laid down general guidelines for establishing a limited monarchy and securing the Protestant succession, but it did not clearly define the relationship between crown and parliament. It even created new political problems because of its impact on the country's religious, financial and foreign policies. The political tension created by these problems did not ease before the 1720s. Fifty years later new demands for constitutional changes began to be made. There was an increasing number of reformers, both moderate and radical, who wished to see a diminution of the crown's power and alterations in the parliamentary representation and franchise. These demands were not met to any significant extent, but the fact that they were made reveals the existence of a serious political debate. Even between these major debates of the early and late eighteenth century, there was much political discussion about the constitutional value of parliamentary parties and the right to form an organized opposition to the ministers of the crown.

It cannot be denied, however, that, throughout the eighteenth century, there was widespread support for what were regarded as the underlying principles of the British constitution. There was general agreement that the constitution was a limited monarchy which sought to combine political stability with a respect for individual liberty. Britain enjoyed a mixed form of government which gave her the benefits of monarchy, aristocracy and democracy in the institutions of Crown, Lords and Commons. The vices of these forms of government in their pure form, namely absolutism, oligarchy or anarchy, were prevented by balancing the power of Crown, Lords and Commons. Each of these institutions had its own independent rights and privileges to counterbalance those of the other two, but all three had to co-operate as the legislative power. It was this intricate balance, rather than any separation of powers, that created stability while defending liberty.

Many commentators, both British and foreign, praised the constitution for these virtues. Probably the most famous and certainly the most extended defence of the constitution was made by William Blackstone in his *Commentaries upon the Laws of England* (4 vols, 1765–9). In the first volume, he wrote:

And herein indeed consists the true excellence of the English government, that all the parts of it form a mutual check upon each other. In the legislature, the people are a check upon the nobility, and the nobility a check upon the people; by the mutual privilege of rejecting what the other has resolved: while the king is a check upon both, which preserves the executive power from encroachments. And this very executive power is again checked and kept within due bounds by the two houses, through the privilege they have of enquiring into, impeaching, and punishing the conduct (not indeed of the king, which would destroy his constitutional independence; but, which is more beneficial to the public) of his evil and pernicious counsellors.

Thus every branch of our civil polity supports and is supported, regulates and is regulated, by the rest: for the two houses naturally drawing in two directions of opposite interest, and the prerogative in another still different from them both, they mutually keep each other from exceeding their proper limits; while the whole is prevented from separation, and artificially connected together by the mixed nature of the crown, which is a part of the legislative, and the sole executive magistrate. Like three distinct powers in mechanics, they jointly impel the machine of government in a different direction from what either, acting by itself, would have done; but at the same time in a direction partaking of each, and formed out of all; a direction which constitutes the true line of the liberty and happiness of the community. [I, 154-5]

While the political nation was almost unanimous in its support for these constitutional principles, there were many who pointed out that existing political practices fell far below the standards envisaged in the constitutional theories described by Blackstone. In his *Fragment on Government* (1776), Jeremy Bentham strongly criticized Blackstone for failing to distinguish between theory and reality. Blackstone himself occasionally gave indications that he was aware that some political abuses did exist. When discussing parliamentary elections he felt moved to confess: 'This is the spirit of our constitution: not that I assert it is in fact quite so perfect as I have here endeavoured to describe it; for, if any alteration might be wished or suggested in the present frame of parliaments, it should be in favour of a more complete representation of the people.' [I, 172]

This admission provides the clue to a major theme of the political debate of the eighteenth century that is neglected when there is too much emphasis on the structure of politics and on the widespread support for the existing general constitutional framework. This theme was the fear that the balance of the constitution was being seriously, perhaps fatally, disturbed by the power of the crown. Royal patronage, it was often claimed, was being so extended and abused that it was creating a new threat of arbitrary power. In the seventeenth century the Stuarts had failed to destroy the nation's liberties by their misuse of the crown's prerogative powers, but it now seemed that the Hanoverians might achieve the same end by different means: the widespread use of the crown's powers of patronage. This was being exploited by ambitious ministers to corrupt public life and, in particular, to undermine the independence of parliament. Secret service money was being used to bribe electors, while places, pensions and sinecures were offered as rewards for those M.P.s who could support the ministry's policies in the Commons. If this situation were allowed to go unchecked, parliament might continue to exist, but its power to influence and restrain the crown would be destroyed. As a result, the spirit of resistance in the nation at large would be sapped by the corrupting effect of money and ambition. Patriotism and the love of liberty would be replaced by a vicious pursuit of personal and material gain.

The researches of Namierite historians have shown that these fears were either exaggerated or unfounded. The crown could never rely on a subservient majority in parliament and royal ministers had to make every effort to persuade or cajole the independent country gentlemen, who held the key to the control of the Commons. These conclusions may convince the modern historian, but they do not prove that these fears did not exist or that they had no effect on political actions. There is an abundance of evidence to show how widespread was the concern about arbitrary power and corruption. This was not just confined to ambitious or factious politicians like Bolingbroke and Junius. Adam Ferguson was not an active partisan in the struggle for power and did not concern himself directly with the political stituation in Britain, but his *Essay on the History of Civil Society* (1767) devoted considerable space to the threat posed by political corruption and to the need to combat this danger by a spirited resistance. By using the example of Rome, Edward Gibbon, in his *Decline and Fall of the Roman Empire* (6 vols., 1776–88), also deliberately sought to instruct his contemporaries on the dangers of arbitrary power and corruption. The same themes pervade a great deal of imaginative literature. Both Gay's *The Beggar's Opera* (1728) and Fielding's *Jonathan Wild* (1743) used bands of thieves as a means of condemning the corruption of society and the abuse of power. Addison's play, *Cato* (1713), and Swift's third voyage of *Gulliver's Travels* (1726) praised the destroyers of tyrants in the ancient world, while David Mallet's *The Masque of Alfred* (1740) and Alexander Bicknell's *The Patriot King: or Alfred and Elvida* (1788) turned to examples of patriotism in English history. Even in such works as Richardson's *Clarissa Harlowe* (1747–8) and Godwin's *Caleb Williams* (1794), where few comments were made on politics, the authors were clearly concerned with how the exercise of arbitrary power could corrupt personal relationships.

This widespread concern with the dangers of political corruption accounts for the popularity and the frequency of measures to end electoral abuses and to exclude placemen from sitting in the Commons. It also forced ministers to hire writers to counter this hostile climate of opinion by asserting that the crown had to have supporters in parliament in order to make the balanced constitution work. Modern historians, particularly the Namierites, have accepted this argument, but it is surely significant that in the eighteenth century it carried little weight outside the ranks of active government supporters. Two notable exceptions were David Hume and Bernard Mandeville, whose comments give an added dimension to the debate on corruption. Hume, in contrast to most of his contemporaries, believed that the greatest threat to the balanced constitution came from the exorbitant power of the House of Commons, which was in the position to usurp the authority of the crown if it so wished. It was therefore essential that the crown could and should restrain the Commons by using the royal patronage to create a strong body of supporters among its members. In his essay, *Of the Independence of Parliament* (1741), Hume wrote of the crown's hold over some M.P.s: 'We may therefore give to this influence what name we please; we may call it by the invidious appellations of *corruption* and *dependence*; but some degree and some kind of it are inseparable from the very nature of the constitution and necessary to the preservation of our mixed government.' Bernard Mandeville was not just concerned with the debate about political corruption, but with the clamour against the dangerous influence on society of materialism and luxury. In his poem, *The Grumbling Hive* (1705), the first part of *The Fable of the Bees*, he maintained that such abuses were the natural and inevitable consequence of living in a prosperous and civilized society. The moral of his poem concluded that those who would eradicate the love of money must be prepared to live in a poor and backward society:

> Then leave Complaints: Fools only strive
> To make a Great an honest Hive.
> T'enjoy the World's Conveniencies,
> Be famed in War, yet live in Ease
> Without great Vices, is a vain
> Eutopia seated in the Brain.
> Fraud, Luxury, and Pride must live
> Whilst we the Benefits receive.
> Hunger's a dreadful Plague, no doubt,
> Yet who digests or thrives without?
> Do we not owe the Growth of Wine
> To the dry shabby crooked Vine?
> Which, whilst its Shutes neglected stood,
> Choak'd other Plants, and ran to Wood;
> But blest us with its Noble Fruit;
> As soon as it was tied, and cut:
> So Vice is beneficial found,
> When it's by Justice lopt, and bound;
> Nay, where the People would be great,
> As necessary to the State
> As Hunger is to make 'em eat.
> Bare Virtue can't make Nations live
> In Splendour; they, that would revive
> A Golden Age, must be as free,
> For Acorns, as for Honesty.

The literature on the themes of corruption and arbitrary power provides a valuable corrective to the work of those commentators like Blackstone who praised the virtues of the British constitution. It shows that there was greater debate and less agreement on the working of the constitution than is implied by historians primarily concerned with explaining the structure of eighteenth-century politics. If we probe further into the literature of the period, however, we can discover important differences of opinion about constitutional *theories* and not merely about political *practices*. There was a philosophical debate about the nature of the social contract, and about the balance between liberty and authority, which can be seen to underlie the more frequent discussions about the power of the crown and the freedom of parliament. It has been too readily assumed that the political theories of John Locke reigned supreme in the eighteenth century. Locke's *Second Treatise on Civil Government* (1690) is often regarded as an exposition of the political theory underpinning the British constitution, and it was certainly appealed to as such by many Whig politicians, but a study of the political literature of the eighteenth century soon shows that Locke's work was not always accepted uncritically. Some of Locke's theories were accepted or rejected according to whether they supported or opposed the particular views put forward by later writers. In general, the conservative strand in Locke's political theory was seized upon by those anxious to consolidate their hold on political power, while Locke's support for the natural rights of all men to their life, liberty and property was seized upon by radical thinkers who were determined to challenge the political establishment. Throughout the eighteenth century the conservative interpretation of Locke prevailed, but by the 1790s the radical interpretation was mounting a serious challenge.

Bolingbroke, even though he was hostile to those in power, was among those who feared the radical implications of Locke's views on the natural rights of man. He preferred to emphasize a paternalistic view of society and he maintained that the original political contract had not been an agreement assented to by every individual, but an agreement between the heads of families and the prince. David Hume went further and rejected the whole notion of an original political contract. Governments had usually been established by conquest or usurpation, but this in itself did not make them illegitimate. Even the Revolution of 1688 had been carried through by a tiny fraction of the nation. This defence of minority rule, while implicit in much of Locke's own political thought, was not easily reconciled to Locke's justification of the people's right of resistance to an executive power which broke its trust.

William Blackstone was only one of many conservative Whigs who wanted to justify the unique example of the Glorious Revolution, while playing down the abstract right of resistance. In Blackstone's view Locke's political theory might be used to defend the attack on the crown in 1688, but it should not be used to justify subsequent resistance to the constitutional system established by that revolution. This would be a dangerous attack on duly constituted authority and would give the people too much political power. In his *Commentaries upon the Laws of England*, therefore, Blackstone took Locke to task on this point:

> It must be owned that Mr Locke, and other theoretical writers, have held, that 'there remains still inherent in the people a supreme power to remove or alter the legislative, when they find the legislative act contrary to the trust reposed in them: for, when such trust is abused, it is thereby forfeited, and devolves to those who gave it.' But however just this conclusion may be in theory, we cannot adopt it, nor argue from it, under any dispensation of government at present actually existing. . . . No human laws will therefore suppose a case, which at once must destroy all law, and compel men to build afresh upon a new foundation; nor will they make provision for so desperate an event, as must render all legal provisions ineffectual. So long therefore as the English constitution lasts, we may venture to affirm, that the power of parliament is absolute and without control. [I, 161-2]

This kind of stress on the importance of obedience to established authority and this fear of disorder are most clearly found in Burke's *Reflections on the Revolution in France* (1790). In order to preserve the British constitution, Burke now invested it with the kind of sanctity previously attributed to absolute monarchy. He appealed to history and experience as means of proving the virtues of the constitution and he cast doubts upon the notion that further improvements were possible. Burke took up this conservative stance in the 1790s because by then radical thinkers had begun to stress the theory of natural rights and the doctrine of popular sovereignty. Ironically, the radicals, though directly stimulated by events in France, traced their ideas back to Locke. They stressed those abstract general rights which Locke had claimed were inherent in the people as a whole. Many of these radicals maintained that these rights had in fact existed in Saxon times, before the 'Norman yoke' had been imposed on the people. Others, like Tom Paine, began to abandon this historical and empirical argument. They chose instead to rest their claims on an appeal to reason. They maintained that man had an inalienable right to freedom which could not be challenged by the evidence of history. Because of this right, men could justify their desire to change the constitution and assert their claim to political liberty.

The more conservative political theories were accepted by the majority of those able to sit in parliament because these ideas reinforced a political system which protected their particular interests. Nevertheless, the fact that these theories came under increasing attack is further proof of the existence of serious political debate in the eighteenth century. To understand how this challenge was made and how effective it was, we need to do more than look at what went on at court or in parliament. This debate was carried on in the press and by extra-parliamentary movements such as the Yorkshire Association and the London Corresponding Society. The more conservative Whigs dominated parliament and defeated most of the measures aimed at reforming the constitution, but those who wanted to change the existing system were able to mobilize public opinion outside parliament. All extra-parliamentary organizations and interests used the press in their campaigns to persuade those in power to change their policies. The press was not merely a vehicle for expressing a wide spectrum of political opinions and for voicing opposition to the political establishment. As it grew in strength it altered the actual nature of the political debate. It created an informed public which was increasingly interested in parliamentary and political affairs. This politically educated public opinion began to make parliament, even in its unreformed state, more sensitive to that opinion. Moreover, while reformers and radicals were free to propagate their ideas, the great Whig connections were prevented from establishing a narrow and static oligarchy. Thus, the freedom of expression enjoyed in the eighteenth century acted as a brake on the conservative tendencies of the Whig oligarchs. It was also a safety valve which prevented the development of a strong revolutionary movement. The stability of the political system depended therefore not just on the conservative opinions of those in power, but on the ability of those outside this narrow circle to influence political events without needing to destroy the actual constitutional framework. The constitution showed itself capable of being amended in response to strong political pressure from outside parliament.

The press went from strength to strength in the eighteenth century. The first regular newspapers began in the late 1690s and within a few years London had several newspapers with circulations of over 3,000 copies per issue. By mid-century there were over forty provincial newspapers and the annual sale of newspapers had reached nearly ten million copies. Both these figures had doubled by the end of the century. Since newspapers were provided in coffee houses, inns and ale-houses, or were read aloud in societies and clubs, political news reached a very large audience, including people fairly low in the social scale. Political news was a major item in all the newspapers, but political ideas and opinion were often expressed more effectively in periodicals and pamphlets. *The Spectator*, *The Craftsman*, *The Gentleman's Magazine*, etc., were probably more politically influential than newspapers, at least among the educated public, while individual pamphlets such as Swift's *The Conduct of the Allies* (1711) and Price's *Observations on the Nature of Civil Liberty* (1776) sold in tens of thousands and had a considerable impact. The audience for imaginative literature, which, as we have seen, often carried a political message, also increased throughout the eighteenth century. The demand from the expanding middle classes for something interesting and instructive to read encouraged writers, publishers, booksellers and circulating libraries to increase the output and improve the distribution of all forms of literature.

This dissemination of political information and exchange of political ideas defended and indeed extended political liberty in Britain. The press became a virtual fourth estate of the realm. The strict censorship of the press had ended with the lapsing of the Licensing Act in 1695, but successive governments attempted to muzzle the press in the eighteenth century. They tried to restrict the political freedom of the press in three ways, but these all ultimately failed. First, there were regular attempts to increase the price of newspapers by levying stamp duties. These acts usually had a temporary effect on circulations, but they all failed in the long run as the sale of newspapers steadily grew. Second, attempts were made to harass printers and publishers by taking judicial action against them, often by charging them with seditious libel. The storm over general warrants in the Wilkes affair of the 1760s finally curtailed the government's ability to harass journalists. Juries, moreover, were often reluctant to convict in libel cases involving the press and, after Fox's Libel Act of 1792, juries were charged with not only deciding whether the offending item had been printed but with deciding whether it in fact amounted to libel. This prevented conservative judges making the expression of views distasteful to authority a hazardous undertaking. Third, there were frequent attempts to prevent the press reporting parliamentary debates. These restrictions were ignored, but journalists were undoubtedly hampered in their attempts to give detailed and accurate accounts of parliamentary business. It was not until 1771 that the Commons finally abandoned its right to prohibit parliamentary reporting after the stormy conflict with Wilkes and the printers of London newspapers. Thereafter, although there were still no official or comprehensive reports of the debates in parliament, and the task of the newspaper reporters was not made easy, newspapers were able to carry increasingly lengthy accounts and employed specialist parliamentary journalists.

Thus, as the eighteenth century progressed, the liberty and the power of the press were extended. Very large numbers of people, who lacked any direct influence on parliament, were kept informed about political news and opinions. There was a large and increasing demand for information about public affairs and the press not only catered for it by providing news, but also presented the public with vigorous political propaganda. Much of this propaganda was hostile to the government of the day. In the earlier eighteenth century this propaganda was usually directed by the parliamentary opposition to the voters in the constituencies. With increasing frequency, however, it began to be aimed at politicians, especially the independent majority in the Commons, by extra-parliamentary groups and interests. At no stage during the century was government or parliament immune from the storms of public opinion, but they undoubtedly became more responsive to it later in the century. Governments, having failed to curb the power of the press, were forced to use the same weapons as their critics. They too joined in the battle to inform, educate and harness public opinion. Any attempt therefore to understand eighteenth-century politics must involve more than just a study of the structure of politics. It needs to examine both the content of the political debates of the period and the ways in which the public participated in these debates.

HARRY DICKINSON

Edinburgh University, 1974

Select Bibliography

This list is divided into two sections: one dealing primarily with political ideas and theories, the other with the politics of imaginative literature. The place of publication is London, unless otherwise stated.

I. B. Bailyn, *The Ideological Origins of the American Revolution* (Cambridge, Mass., 1967); E. C. Black, *The Association* (Cambridge, Mass., 1963); D. J. Boorstin, *The Mysterious Science of the Law* (Cambridge, Mass., 1941); I. R. Christie, *Wilkes, Wyvill and Reform* (1962); I. R. Christie, *Myth and Reality in Late Eighteenth-Century British Politics* (1970); A. Cobban (ed.), *The Debate on the French Revolution 1789–1800* (1950); C. B. Cone, *Torchbearer of Freedom: The Influence of Richard Price on Eighteenth-Century Thought* (Lexington, 1952); C. B. Cone, *Burke and the Nature of Politics* (2 vols, Lexington, 1957, 1964); G. A. Cranfield, *The Development of the Provincial Press 1700–1760* (Oxford, 1962); H. T. Dickinson, *Bolingbroke* (1970); H. T. Dickinson, 'Walpole and His Critics', *History Today* (June 1972); J. Dunn, 'The politics of Locke in England and America in the eighteenth century', in *John Locke: Problems and Perspectives*, ed. John Yolton (Cambridge, 1969); W. H. Greenleaf, *Order, Empiricism and Politics* (1964); J. A. W. Gunn (ed.), *Factions No More* (1972); L. Hanson, *Government and the Press, 1695–1763* (Oxford, 1936); E. Halévy, *The Growth of Philosophical Radicalism* (1928); R. W. Harris, *Politics and Ideas, 1760–1793* (1963); R. W. Harris, *Reason and Nature in 18th Century Thought* (1968); G. S. Holmes and W. A. Speck, *The Divided Society: Party Conflict in England 1694–1716* (1967); I. Kramnick, *Bolingbroke and His Circle* (Oxford, 1968); H. J. Laski, *Political Thought in England: From Locke to Bentham* (1955); H. C. Mansfield, *Statesmanship and Party Government* (Chicago, 1965); C. Parkin, *The Moral Basis of Burke's Political Thought* (Cambridge, 1956); J. G. A. Pocock, 'Machiavelli, Harrington and English Political Ideologies in the Eighteenth Century', *William and Mary Quarterly* (1965); J. G. A. Pocock, 'Burke and the Ancient Constitution—a Problem in the History of Ideas', *Historical Journal* (1960); J. R. Pole, *Political Representation in England and the Origins of the American Republic* (1966);

C. Robbins, *The Eighteenth-Century Commonwealthsman* (Cambridge, Mass., 1959); R. R. Rea, *The English Press in Politics 1760–1774* (Lincoln, Nebr., 1963); W. A. Speck, 'Political Propaganda in Augustan England', *Trans. Royal Hist. Soc.* (1972); L. Stephen, *English Thought in the Eighteenth Century* (2 vols, 1876); D. H. Stevens, *Party Politics and English Journalism 1702–1742* (Menasha, 1916); J. B. Stewart, *The Moral and Political Philosophy of David Hume* (New York, 1963); E. N. Williams, *The Eighteenth Century Constitution* (Cambridge, 1960).

II.   M. R. Adams, *Studies in the Literary Background of English Radicalism* (Penn., 1947); W. J. Bate, *From Classic to Romantic* (Cambridge, Mass., 1946); J. T. Boulton, *The Language of Politics in the Age of Wilkes and Burke* (1963); J. T. Boulton, *Arbitrary Power: An Eighteenth-Century Obsession* (Nottingham, 1967); C. Brinton, *The Political Ideas of the English Romanticists* (Oxford, 1926); J. Butt, 'Pope and the Opposition to Walpole's Government', in *Pope, Dickens and Others: Essays and Addresses by John Butt* (Edinburgh, 1969); J. L. Clifford (ed.), *Eighteenth-Century English Literature* (New York, 1959); J. L. Clifford (ed.), *Man versus Society in 18th-century Britain* (Cambridge, 1968); A. Cobban, *Edmund Burke and the Revolt against the Eighteenth Century* (1929); B. Dobrée, *The Theme of Patriotism in the Poetry of the Early Eighteenth Century* (1949); C. H. Firth, *The Political Significance of 'Gulliver's Travels'* (1920); P. Fussell, *The Rhetorical World of Augustan Humanism* (Oxford, 1965); D. J. Greene, *The Politics of Samuel Johnson* (New Haven, 1960); P. Hartnoll, 'The Theatre and the Licensing Act of 1737', in *Silver Renaissance*, ed. Alex Natan (1961); A. R. Humphreys, *The Augustan World* (1954); A. N. Jeffares (ed.), *Fair Liberty was all his Cry* (1967); J. Loftis, *The Politics of Drama in Augustan England* (Oxford, 1963); M. Mack, *The Garden and the City* (Toronto, 1969); K. Maclean, *John Locke and English Literature of the 18th Century* (New Haven, 1936); A. D. McKillop, *The Background of Thomson's 'Liberty'* (Houston, 1951); C. A. Moore, *Backgrounds of English Literature 1700–1760* (Minneapolis, 1953); M. Percival (ed.), *Political Ballads illustrating the administration of Sir Robert Walpole* (Oxford, 1916); P. Rogers, *Grub Street* (1972); G. Sherburn and D. F. Bond, *The Restoration and Eighteenth Century*, vol. III of *A Literary History of England* (2nd edn, 1967); L. Stephen, *English Literature and Society in the 18th Century* (1904); C. L. Thomson, *English History in Contemporary Poetry: Part V* (1914); E. R. Wasserman (ed.), *Aspects of the Eighteenth Century* (Baltimore, 1965); I. Watt, *The Rise of the Novel* (1957); B. Willey, *The Eighteenth Century Background* (1940); K. Williams, *Jonathan Swift and the Age of Compromise* (Kansas, 1959).

PART ONE
A 'Whig' or 'Tory' Constitution?

The early years of the eighteenth century saw the political nation more clearly divided over issues of principle and more effectively organized into national political parties than at any time during the remainder of the century. These divisions, into Whig and Tory, extended beyond the narrow confines of court and parliament. General elections were not simply a contest of local forces over local issues, but generally took the form of straight party fights between Whigs and Tories on questions of national importance. Whereas in the mid-eighteenth century many constituencies were uncontested and general elections were only held every seven years, relatively few seats remained uncontested during the first fifteen years of the century and there were no fewer than eight general elections during these years. The electorate entitled to take part in these contests was less than five per cent of the total population, about 250,000 out of a population of just less than six millions, but this still meant that a higher proportion of the population could vote than at any time before the widening of the franchise by the Reform Act of 1832.

Many of the great writers of the day were deeply involved in political issues, and leading politicians of both parties sought to enlist their aid in converting parliament and the electorate to their particular opinions. Indeed, the relationship between politics and literature has scarcely ever been closer than in the early eighteenth century. Politics was the main topic and theme of countless pamphlets and periodicals, prints, poems and plays. Many of the leading politicians wrote their own political literature, but both parties were also the patrons or paymasters of numerous writers. These included not only the hacks of Grub Street, but the great writers of the age. Addison and Steele were on intimate terms with the leading Whigs of the Kit Cat Club, while Swift and Arbuthnot were closely connected with important Tory members of the Scriblerus Club. Daniel Defoe actually managed to make his living as a political writer and secret agent. For many years he sold his services to Robert Harley, but, like most of the writers of the day, he expressed his own, not merely his paymaster's, political principles.

The Revolution Settlement, reinforced by the Act of Settlement of 1701, had established a limited monarchy in Britain and had sought to guarantee the Protestant succession to the throne. Since Whigs and Tories had combined, however reluctantly, to secure these advantages, it might have been expected that political stability and harmony would be established at the beginning of the eighteenth century. Certainly many writers and politicians lamented the continued division of the nation into Whig and Tory camps. Yet their own activities make it clear that men still bitterly disagreed on the nature of the political and constitutional settlement apparently accepted by a majority on both sides. Writers such as Defoe and Addison might plead for unity [see extracts 3 and 6], might seek to argue that their own particular views were those which men of sense and moderation maintained [Nos. 3, 6 and 7], or might use a satirical approach in an effort to disarm their opponents [No. 9 and Defoe's *The Shortest Way with the Dissenters*]. Nevertheless, whatever their stylistic approach, they were far from impartial. There was still a great political gulf between, for example, the Dissenter, Defoe, and the high-Church parson, Sacheverell [Nos. 3 and 2], and between the radical Whig, Lord Molesworth, and the high-Tory, Bishop Atterbury [Nos. 5 and 8].

The bitter disputes between Whigs and Tories continued, in part, because the Revolution Settlement had not entirely solved the political and constitutional problems which had divided the political nation in the seventeenth century, but also because this very settlement had created new sources of friction. The Glorious Revolution had dealt a hard blow to the Tory doctrines of divine right, indefeasible hereditary succession and non-resistance, but these principles did not die overnight. As late as 1709 Dr Henry Sacheverell, in his famous sermon on *The Perils of False Brethren* [No. 2], was still preaching such notions. The Whigs felt impelled to impeach him in order to justify the principles of the Revolution Settlement, while Defoe urged parliament to commit itself more firmly to the doctrine that subjects had the right to resist and overthrow an arbitrary ruler [No. 3]. While men held such different views on the nature of monarchy and the political contract between ruler and subjects, it is not surprising that the problem of the Protestant succession was not solved until the defeat of the Jacobite rebellion of 1715. Despite the terms of the Act of Settlement the conflict between Hanoverians and Jacobites was a constant theme of political debate and political literature in the reign of Anne.

Important though the issue of the Protestant succession undoubtedly was, there were other major political issues which had arisen as a consequence of the Revolution Settlement and which divided Whigs and Tories far more sharply. Most Tories did, after all, accept the Hanoverian succession, but most of them were deeply disturbed by the implications of the financial revolution, the revolution in foreign policy, and the change in the relationship of church and state, that had occurred after the Glorious Revolution. The accession of William III saw the country embark on what was to prove a long series of costly wars against France, wars which were to be at the heart of many political disputes throughout the eighteenth century. The government's need for huge sums of ready cash to meet the expense of these wars initiated a far-reaching financial revolution. The most important innovation was the development of a completely new system of public credit, the national debt. Financiers, often connected with the Bank of England (launched in 1694), the East India Company and, later, the South Sea Company, raised massive loans for the government in return for rates of interest whose payment was guaranteed by specific parliamentary taxes. Country gentlemen became alarmed at this powerful new interest based on paper money rather than land. The financiers appeared to be able to conjure money out of thin air and to prosper during an expensive war, whereas the landed interest had to pay a land tax of four shillings in the pound to pay the interest on the national debt to these public creditors. The protests of Tory squires reached their peak in the later years of Anne's reign when they demanded an end to the enormously costly War of the Spanish Succession and a prompt reduction both of the land tax and the rate of interest on the national debt. It was to give vent to such feelings and to justify the Tory government's determination to make peace with France, if necessary by a separate treaty which left the allies in the lurch, that Swift wrote his celebrated pamphlet, *The Conduct of the Allies* [No. 4].

Swift did not only complain about the sufferings of the landed interest and protest at the fortunes made by those most anxious to prolong the war, but criticized the whole concept of the Whigs' foreign policy. By attacking the heavy costs of Marlborough's campaigns and lamenting the unfair burden placed on Britain because of the refusal of her Dutch and Austrian allies to bear their fair share of the war effort, Swift hoped to reverse the whole Whig policy of direct military involvement on the European continent. The Tories had always claimed that Britain's interests would be better served by a concentration of her efforts at sea, in a trade and colonial war. Throughout the eighteenth century this 'blue-water' policy was to remain popular with the backwoods squires.

The Tory opposition to the financial revolution and to expensive military campaigns in Europe did not stem solely from hostility to the land tax and the new monied interest. They were alarmed at the effect of these policies on the size and behaviour of the executive. To raise the necessary taxation and to provide the vital supplies for the much-expanded armed forces, the government had to expand most of the administrative institutions of the state, particularly the treasury and revenue departments. This expansion of the administration and its increased expenditure offered the opportunity of rich pickings, not always by honest means, to those in office. Political corruption became and remained a major grievance of the Tory squires. With some justice they believed that the Whigs had abandoned their former hostility to the executive because, after the Revolution, they were in a position to profit from involvement in government affairs and were prepared to support the innovations in financial and foreign policies in order to safeguard the new political settlement. They castigated these 'modern Whigs' for embezzling public funds, increasing government appointments in order to reward their friends, and bribing both M.P.s and the electorate. The justice of such charges, made by Charles Davenant, Swift and Atterbury, among others [Nos. 1, 4 and 8], was keenly felt by 'old Whigs' or Commonwealthsmen, like Lord Molesworth [No. 5], who also attacked standing armies, monied men and corruption in political life.

This concern with issues raised by the government's financial and foreign policies dominated most of the political debates of the eighteenth century. This was in marked contrast to the seventeenth century when the main political disputes focused on religious disagreements. In the early eighteenth century, however, the religious debate was still alive. It was chiefly concerned with the degree of toleration to be granted to Protestant Dissenters and the consequences this would have on the privileged position of the Church of England. The Toleration Act of 1689 was a very limited concession to the Dissenting minority, but the Tories, the Church party, placed no trust in the Whigs. They feared that this act might be but a prelude to such measures as the repeal of the Test and Corporation Acts [Nos. 2 and 8]. Thus, for years after the Toleration Act, there was a constant stream of sermons and pamphlets on the theme of 'the Church in danger'; and the Tories in parliament sought to curtail the concessions to the Dissenters by passing the Occasional Conformity and Schism Acts. Daniel Defoe satirized the extravagant fears of the high-Church fanatics in his famous pamphlet, *The Shortest Way with the Dissenters* (1702), but he and Whigs like Lord Molesworth had considerable difficulty in persuading the Tories to accept the idea of religious toleration [Nos. 3 and 5]. Unfortunately, some of their allies only confirmed the worst suspicions of the Tories. In 1717 Benjamin Hoadly, an active Whig pamphleteer and Bishop of Bangor, provoked a major religious controversy when he preached a sermon before George I on *The Nature of the Kingdom or Church of Christ* [No. 10]. When a bishop of the Church of England could reject the need for an established church in such forthright terms, those loyal to the concept of a State church had good cause for alarm. Their expressions of outrage forced the prorogation of Convocation for the rest of the century and warned the Whigs not to tamper too much with the privileges of the Church of England.

1 Charles Davenant:
The True Picture of a Modern Whig (1701)

A Dialogue between Mr Whiglove and Mr Double, two under-spur-leathers to the late ministry [pp. 5–6, 25–6, 32–5]

... *Double* ... 'tis the principle of us modern Whigs to get what we can, no matter how. But if the other side prevails, we must strike in with them, however this must be our last shift: in the mean while let us do what we can to keep up our party, for men of our principles can never thrive so well under any new ministry as we did by the last, our endeavours therefore must be to bring them once more into play for many reasons. They made use of none but such as were of our stamp and kidney; we had all the places and preferments, and then you know how kindly they wink'd at our cheating the publick, and if any of us were caught tripping how bravely did they defend us in the House of Commons.[1] Have they ever suffer'd any of us to be brought to condign punishment? When any of the Country-Puts had a mind to save the nation in its taxes, and to inquire into abuses, and into the expence of the mony they had granted, did not our noble friends always baffle them and their inquiries, and bring us off triumphantly?

Whiglove I know you will never see such brave times as you had under them, it rain'd gold and silver, you wallow'd in the peoples wealth, and if you could have held it ten years longer, you had bought all those country boobies out of their estates, who were wont to roar at you in St Stephen's

---

[1] Between 1691 and 1697 Commissioners of Accounts tried in vain to find evidence of the misuse of public funds. In 1701 the Whig majority in the Lords prevented the Commons reappointing Commissioners, but they were restored by the Tories in 1702.

Chappel. . . . I always understood we Whigs had been the divisers of the new taxes and remote funds, but did not know till now the share you had in it.

Double I have done my part, and think I have reason to pretend to a great deal of merit. For what had become of our party, if it had not been for these projects? 'Tis true, we have run the nation over head and ears in debt by our fonds, and new devices, but mark what a dependance upon our noble friends, this way of raising mony has occasion'd. Who is it sticks to 'em but those who are concern'd in tallies and the new stocks? The plain county gentleman, who has nothing to trust to but his estate, is for having 'em call'd to an accompt for robbing the nation; but we, who through their means, have so many years got fifteen and twenty *per cent* for our mony, and who by their help have had so many other ways of raising our selves, cry up their innocence, and long to see 'em again at the helm, that under their countenance and protection we may once more fleece the kingdom. Take this for a rule, if you see any man very hot for 'em in the country, he or his relations are engag'd in the annuities, and they whom you hear roaring so for 'em in the City, are such as have stock-jobb'd tallies at 30, or 40 *per cent* profit. For we have taken care to insinuate to all those who have dealt with the Exchequer, that the eighteen millions England now owes will never be paid unless they are restor'd to the ministry, and you must be sure to spread this about in the country as you travel.[1] . . .

Double Prithee friend *Whiglove*, leave off calling thy self an Old Whig, it will do thee hurt with the party. We reckon those men our worst of enemies. . . . What have we in us that resembles the Old Whigs? They hated arbitrary government, we have been all along for a standing army: they desir'd triennial parliaments, and that tryals for treason might be better regulated; and 'tis notorious that we oppos'd both those bills. They were for calling corrupt ministers to an accompt; we have ever countenanc'd and

[1] Some Whigs maintained that they alone could be trusted to manage the National Debt and that the Tories would repudiate the Debt if they ever got the chance.

protected corruption to the utmost of our power. They were frugal for the nation, and careful how they loaded the people with taxes; we have squander'd away their mony as if there could be no end of England's treasure. The Old Whigs would have prevented the immoderate growth of the *French* empire, we Modern Whigs have made a partition-treaty, which, unless Providence save us, may end in making the King of France universal monarch.

Whiglove I must confess we are very much departed from the principles we profess'd twenty years ago. But pray tell me of what sort of persons does our party consist at present, for we still call our selves Whigs?

Double 'Tis not so easy as you imagin to describe the strange medly of which we are now compos'd, but I shall do my best to let you into the secret. First, you must know there are some men of true worth and honour that still continue among us; why I can't guess, but those I fear we shall lose when they come plainly to discover our bad designs, and how furiously we drive to bring the kingdom into a civil war. Nor have we lost all the Old Whigs; there are still listed with us, Whig-pickpockets, Whig-gamesters, Whig-murderers, Whig-outlaws, Whig-libertines, Whig-atheists, such as in former reigns have had some note of infamy publick or private fix'd upon 'em; all these stick close to our side, nor do we apprehend that any one of 'em will forsake us, because they know crimes of no nature whatsoever are ill look'd upon among us, and that even hereafter, they may commit more, if they please, under the shelter of our wings.

Whiglove But have we no more than what you have here reckon'd?

Double O yes, or we shou'd be but weak. The bulk of our party consists of those who are of any side where they can best make their markets; such sort of men naturally like the Whigs most, because ours was a negligent weak administration. Every body did what seem'd good in his own eyes, we troubled no man with calling him to an accompt. The accompts of the army, navy, customs, and excise, are not yet made up. There are upwards of four and twenty millions of the peoples money unaccompted for to this day. Under our ministry all the officers that handled the King's business or revenue liv'd in clover. Every little scoundrel got an estate. We suffer'd 'em to drink up the people's blood till they were out of breath, and till their eyes grew red. In short, all men cheated to what degree they pleas'd, which was wink'd at in hopes to make and to secure a party. Therefore all the busy proling fellows both in town and country, who hope to advance themselves, wish to see our noble friends restor'd to their former power. And all these sort of men, while they have any hopes that way, will join with us to buoy them up, and to exclaim against the new ministers. But if they find the game lost, if they see the King resolv'd to correct abuses, and to call them to a reckoning who have so much wrong'd him and the nation, and if they find the parliament stick to their point; if they see the country-gentlemen resolute to be no longer impos'd upon by upstarts and hairbrain'd rulers of a state, like rats they will all run from a falling house, they will disown the name of Whigs, and send us and our party to the devil. . . .

2 Henry Sacheverell:
The Perils of False Brethren, Both in
Church and State (1709)

[Sermon delivered on 5 November 1709 and then printed at the request of the Lord Mayor of London. Pp. 10–15. The Whig ministry impeached Sacheverell in 1710 for this attack on the principles underlying the Glorious Revolution, but a Tory reaction in his favour saved him from serious punishment.]

. . . If, upon all occasions to comply with the Dissenters both in publick, and private affairs, as persons of tender conscience, and piety, to promote their interests in elections, to sneak to 'em for places, and preferment, to defend toleration, and liberty of conscience, and under the pretence of moderation, to excuse their separation, and lay the fault upon the true sons of the Church, for carrying matters too high; if to court the fanaticks in private, and to hear 'em with patience, if not approbation, rail at, and blaspheme the Church, and upon occasion to justify the king's murder; if to flatter both the dead and the living in their vices, and to tell the world, that if they have wit, and money enough they need no repentance, and that only fools and beggars can be damn'd; if these, I say, are the modish, and fashionable criterion of a True-Church-Man, God deliver us all from such FALSE BRETHREN. . . .

. . . Our constitution both in Church, and State has been so admirably contriv'd, with that wisdom, weight and sagacity, and the temper, and genius of each, so exactly suited and modell'd to the mutual support, and assistance of one another, that 'tis hard to say, whether the doctrins of the Church of England contribute more to authorize, and enforce our civil laws, or our laws to maintain, and defend the doctrins of our Church. The natures of both are so nicely correspondent, and so happily intermixt, that 'tis almost impossible to offer a violation, to the one, without breaking in upon the body of the other. So that . . . whosoever presumes to innovate, alter, or mispresent any point in the articles of the faith of our Church

11

ought to be arraign'd as a traytor to our state; heterodoxy in
the doctrins of one, naturally producing, and almost necessarily inferring rebellion, and high-treason in the other, and
consequently a crime that concerns the civil magistrate, as
much to punish, and restrain, as the ecclesiastical. . . . The grand
security of our government, and the very pillar upon which it
stands, is founded upon the steady belief of the subject's
obligation to an absolute, and unconditional obedience to the
supream power, in all things lawful, and the utter illegality
of resistance upon any pretence whatsoever. But this fundamental doctrin, notwithstanding it's divine sanction in the
express command of God in Scripture, and without which it
is impossible for any government of any kind, or denomination
in the world, should subsist with safety, and which has been
so long the honourable, and distinguishing characteristic of
our Church, is now, it seems, quite exploded, and redicul'd
out of countenance, as an unfashionable, superannuated, nay
(which is more wonderful) as a dangerous tenet, utterly
inconsistent with the right liberty, and property of the
PEOPLE; who as our new preachers and politicians teach us, (I
suppose by a new and unheard of Gospel, as well as laws)
have in contradiction to both, the power invested in them, the
fountain and original of it, to cancel their allegiance at
pleasure, and call their sovereign to account for high-treason
against his supream subjects, forsooth! nay to dethrone, and
murder him for a criminal, as they did the royal martyr by a
judiciary sentence. And what is almost incredible, presume
to make their court to their prince, by maintaining such antimonarchical schemes. But God be thanked! neither the constitution of our Church or State is so far alter'd, but that by
the laws of both, (still in force, and which I hop for ever will
be) these damnable positions, let 'em come either from Rome
or Geneva, from the pulpit or the press, are condemn'd for
rebellion and high-treason. Our adversaries think they effectually stop our mouths, and have us sure and unanswerable
on this point, when they urge the Revolution of this day [i.e
5 November 1688] in their defence. But certainly they are the
greatest enemies of that, and his late Majesty, and the most ungrateful for the deliverance, who endeavour to cast such black

and odious colours on both. How often must they be told, that the King himself solemnly disclaim'd the least imputation of resistance in his declaration; and that the parliament declar'd, that they set the crown on his head, upon no other title, but that of the vacancy of the throne? And did they not unanimously condemn to the flames, (as it justly deserv'd) that infamous libel, that would have pleaded the title of conquest by which resistance was suppos'd? So tender were they of the regal rights, and so averse to infringe the least tittle of our constitution! . . . Yet, if those silly pretences and weak excuses for it alledg'd, carry any strength of reason in them at all, they will equally serve to justify all the rebellions that ever were or can be committed in the world. . . . Certainly the Toleration [Act] was never intended to indulge and cherish such monsters and vipers in our bosom, that scatter their pestilence at noon-day and will rend, distract and confound the firmest and best-settl'd constitution in the world. In short, as the English government can never be secure on any other principles, but strictly those of the Church of England, so I will be bold to say, where any part of it is trusted in persons of other notions, they must be false to themselves, if they are true to their trusts; or if they are true to their opinions and interests, must betray that government they are enemies to upon principle. . . .

3 Daniel Defoe:
A Review of the State of the British Nation (1710)

[Vol. VI, no. 119.   10 January 1710]

I have, in the humblest manner possible, address'd this Paper to the present assembled Parliament, in the case of the late attack made upon our establishment and constitution from the pulpit—by advancing the absurd and exploded notions of passive-obedience, non-resistance, and hereditary succession, against the declar'd principles of parliamentary limitations ... Passive-obedience, non-resistance, and the divine right of hereditary succession, are inconsistent with the rights of the BRITISH NATION, (not to examine the rights of nature) inconsistent with the constitution of the BRITISH GOVERNMENT, inconsistent with the being and authority of the BRITISH PARLIAMENT, and inconsistent with the declar'd essential foundation of the BRITISH MONARCHY.—These abhorr'd notions would destroy the inestimable privileges of Britain, of which the House of Commons are the glorious conservators; they would subject all our liberties to the arbitrary lust of a single person, they would expose us to all kinds of tyranny, and subvert the very foundations on which we stand—They would destroy the unquestion'd sovereignty of our laws, which for so many ages have triumph'd over the invasions and usurpations of ambitious princes; they would denude us of the beautiful garment of liberty, and prostitute the honour of the nation to the mechanicism of slavery—They would divest GOD Almighty of his praise, in giving his humble creatures a right of governing themselves, and charge heaven with having meanly subjected mankind to the crime of TYRANNY, which he himself abhors.

'Tis to this honourable House the whole nation now looks

for relief, against these invaders, and honest men hope, that now is the time, when the illegitimate spurious birth of these monsters in politicks shall be expos'd by your voice—Now is the time, when you shall declare it criminal for any man to assert, that the subjects of Britain are oblig'd to an absolute uncondition'd obedience to their princes . . . Now is the time, when you shall declare it criminal for any man to assert, the illegality of resistance on any pretence whatever, &c. Or in plain English, the right of self-defence against oppression and violence, whether national or personal . . . Now is the time, when you shall again declare the rights of the people of England, either in Parliament or in Convention assembled, to limit the succession of the crown in bar of hereditary claims, while those claims are attended with other circumstances inconsistent with the publick safety, and the establish'd laws of the land ; since her Majesty's title to the crown, as now own'd and acknowledg'd by the whole nation, and the succession to the crown, as entail'd by the acts of succession in England, and the late Union of Britain, are built on the right of parliament to limit the crown, and that right recogniz'd by the Revolution. . . .

It is well known to your honourable House, that notwithstanding the self-evident testimony of the rights of the people of Britain, as above, there are not wanting men among us who broach again, and vigorously promote, both in printing, preaching, and conversation, the said exploded principles of passive-obedience, non-resistance, and divine right, with manifest design to render odious and contemptible our legal establishment, to overthrow the foundations of our present government, unravel the Revolution, and invalidate the just title, which her Majesty derives to these crowns by the principle of parliamentary limitation. . . .

These things have receiv'd a just check by the resentment your honourable House has lately express'd at one of the forward agents of this mischievous party—and it gives new life to the nation's hopes, that they may at last expect, it shall farther and most effectually be discourag'd by this step taken to punish the offender.

But may it please your Honours to consider, whether it

would not for ever silence this wicked party, strike dumb the opposer's of Britain's peace, and blast all the prospect our enemies entertain from these things, of dividing us to our destruction, if the very principles, on which these things are founded, receiv'd their just sentence from your breath? Whether the voice of the Commons of England, declaring, once for all, the undoubted rights of the people, of the crown, and of parliament, with respect to obedience, government, and limitation, would not perfectly silence the pretences, whether of one party or another, to passive, uncondition'd obedience, non-resistance, and divine right of succession.

Then we may hope to live at rest from the perpetual strife of parties, and principles of Jacobitism would wither away, for want of the vital moisture they receive from these notions —Then her Majesty's frequent exhortations to peace and union, which have hitherto been the jest and scorn of this party, tho' of the last consequence to the nation, will come to be effectual, and valued by us—Then we may see a temper spring up among us of charity, a thing almost extinct, and we may cease to be biting and devouring one another for trifles.

These doctrines are now unhappily mixt with our divinity, with our politicks, with our loyalty, and with our charity, and most fatally perplex and debauch them all; but if they are blasted by the vote of this honourable assembly, their life will be taken away, they will corrode and putrifie in their own filth, and stink in the nostrils of those that now espouse them, till, like the dead carcasses of former favourites, they will desire to bury them out of their sight. . . .

The manifest attempts of a perjur'd party among us, to divide, to disquiet, and to amuse the poor credulous people, in order to support and encourage Jacobitism and tyranny, are not conceal'd from you—If but the principle on which they act, which is visibly corrupt and mischievous, were branded by the vote of Parliament, the party will dwindle away insensibly—And the abus'd people be soon restor'd to a native rectitude both in principle and practice. . . .

1 Jonathan Swift:
The Conduct of the Allies, and of the Late Ministry, in beginning and carrying on the Present War (1711)

[Edited by C. B. Wheeler (Oxford 1916), pp. 8–9, 13, 15–16, 20–2, 47–53, 56, 68–9. Swift wrote this pamphlet to persuade the nation to support the Tory ministry's plans to make a separate peace with France. It was one of the most successful pamphlets of the age.]

... At the *Revolution*, a general war broke out in *Europe*, wherein princes joined in an alliance against *France*, to check the ambitious designs of that monarch; and here the *Emperor*, the *Dutch*, and *England*, were principals. About this time the custom first began among us of borrowing millions upon funds of interest: it was pretended, that the war could not possibly last above one or two campaigns; and that the debts contracted might be easily paid in a few years, by a gentle tax, without burthening the subject. But the true reason for embracing this expedient, was the security of a new prince, not firmly settled on the throne: people were tempted to lend, by great premiums and large interest, and it concerned them nearly to preserve that government, which they trusted with their mony. The person said to have been author of so detestable a project, is still living, and lives to see some of its fatal consequences, whereof his grandchildren will not see an end.[1] And this pernicious council closed very well with the posture of affairs at that time: for, a set of upstarts, who had little or no part in the *Revolution*, but valued themselves by their noise and pretended zeal, when the work was over, were got into credit at court, by the merit of becoming undertakers and projectors of loans and funds: these, finding that the gentlemen of estates were not willing to come into their measures, fell upon those new schemes of raising mony, in order to create a

---

[1] William Paterson (1658–1719) drew up the plans for the Bank of England and the raising of the National Debt in the early 1690's.

monied-interest, that might in time vie with the landed, and of which they hoped to be at the head.

. . . Some time after the Duke of *Anjou*'s succeeding to the monarchy of *Spain*, in breach of the partition treaty [1699], the question here in *England* was, whether the peace should be continued, or a new war begun. Those who were for the former, alledged the debts and difficulties we laboured under; . . . those whose opinion, or some private motives, inclined them to give their advice for entring into a new war, alledged how dangerous it would be for *England*, that *Philip* should be King of *Spain*; that we could have no security for our trade, while that kingdom was subjected to a prince of the *Bourbon* family; nor any hopes of preserving the balance of *Europe*, because the grandfather [Louis XIV] would, in effect, be king, while his grandson had but the title, and thereby have a better opportunity than ever of pursuing his design for universal monarchy. These and the like arguments prevailed; and so, without offering at any other remedy, without taking time to consider the consequences, or to reflect on our own condition, we hastily engaged in a war which hath cost us sixty millions; and after repeated, as well as unexpected success in arms, hath put us and our posterity in a worse condition, not only than any of our allies, but even our conquered enemies themselves.

The part we have acted in the conduct of this whole war, with reference to our allies abroad, and to a prevailing faction at home, is what I shall now particularly examin; where I presume it will appear, by plain matters of fact, that no nation was ever so long or so scandalously abused by the folly, the temerity, the corruption, the ambition of its domestick enemies; or treated with so much insolence, injustice and ingratitude by its foreign friends.

. . . we ought to have entered into this war only as auxiliaries. Let any man reflect upon our condition at that time: just come out of the most tedious, expensive and unsuccessful war that ever *England* had been engaged in; sinking under heavy debts, of a nature and degree never heard of by us or our ancestors; the bulk of the gentry and people heartily tired of the war, and glad of a peace, tho' it brought no other advantage but it self: no sudden prospect of lessening our taxes, which were grown as necessary to pay our debts, as to raise armies: a sort of artificial wealth of funds and stocks in the hands of those who for ten years before had been plundering the publick: many corruptions in every branch of our government, that needed reformation. Under these difficulties, from which twenty years peace, and the wisest management, could hardly recover us, we declare war against *France*, . . .

We have now for ten years together turned the whole force and expence of the war, where the enemy was best able to hold us at bay; where we could propose no manner of advantage to our selves; where it was highly impolitick to enlarge our conquests; utterly neglecting that part which would have saved and gained us many millions, which the perpetual maxims of our government teach us to pursue; which would have soonest weakned the enemy, and must either have promoted a speedy peace, or enabled us to go on with the war. . . .

I say not this, by any means, to detract from the army or its leaders. Getting into the enemies lines, passing rivers, and taking towns, may be actions attended with many glorious circumstances: but when all this brings no real solid advantage to us, when it hath no other end than to enlarge the territories of the *Dutch*, and encrease the fame and wealth of our *G[enera]l* [Marlborough], I conclude, however it comes about, that things are not as they should be; and that surely our forces and money might be better employed, both towards reducing our enemy, and working some benefit to ourselves. . . .

I have already observed, that when the counsels of this war were debated in the late king's time, my Lord *G[odolphi]n* was then so averse from entring into it, that he rather chose to give up his employment, and tell the king he could serve him no longer. Upon that prince's death, although the grounds of our quarrel with *France* had received no manner of addition, yet this lord thought fit to alter his sentiments; for the scene was quite changed; his Lordship and the family with whom he was engaged by so complicated an alliance, were in the highest credit possible with the Q[uee]n: the Treasurer's staff was ready for his lordship, the Duke [of Marlborough] was to

command the army, and the Dutchess [of Marlborough], by
her employments, and the favour she was possessed of, to be
always nearest her M[ajest]y's person; by which the whole
power, at home and abroad, would be devolved upon that
family. This was a prospect so very inviting, that, to confess
the truth, it could not be easily withstood by any who have so
keen an appetite for wealth or ambition. By an agreement
subsequent to the Grand Alliance, we were to assist the *Dutch*
with forty thousand men, all to be commanded by the D. of
M. So that whether this war were prudently begun or not, it
is plain, that the true spring or motive of it, was the aggrandiz-
ing a particular family; and in short, a war of the *General* and
the *Ministry*, and not of the *prince* or *people*; since those very
persons were against it when they knew the power, and consequently the profit, would be in other hands.

With these measures fell in all that sett of people, who are
called the *monied men*; such as had raised vast sums by trading
with stocks and funds, and lending upon great interest and
premiums; whose perpetual harvest is war, and whose beneficial way of traffick must very much decline by a peace. . . .

But when the war was thus begun, there soon fell in other
incidents here at home, which made the continuance of it
necessary for those who were the chief advisers. The *Whigs*
were at that time out of all credit or consideration: the reign-
ing favourites had always carried what was called the Tory
principle, at least as high, as our consitution could bear; and
most others in great employments, were wholly in the church-
interest. These last, among whom several were persons of the
greatest merit, quality and consequence, were not able to
endure the many instances of pride, insolence, avarice and
ambition, which those favourites began so early to discover,
nor to see them presuming to be the sole dispensers of the royal
favour. However, their opposition was to no purpose; they
wrestled with too great a power, and were soon crushed under
it. For those in possession finding they could never be quiet in
their usurpations, while others had any credit, who were at
least upon an equal foot of merit, began to make overtures to
the discarded *Whigs*, who would be content with any terms of
accommodation. Thus commenced this *Solemn League and*

Covenant, which hath ever since been cultivated with so much application. The great traders in money were wholly devoted to the *Whigs,* who had first raised them. The army, the court, and the treasury, continued under the old *despotick* administration: the *Whigs* were received into employment, left to manage the parliament, cry down the landed interest, and worry the Church. Mean time our allies, who were not ignorant that all this artificial structure had no true foundation in the hearts of the people, resolved to make their best use of it, as long as it should last. And the General's credit being raised to a great height at home, by our success in *Flanders,* the *Dutch* began their gradual impositions, lessening their quota's, breaking their stipulations, garrisoning the towns we took for them, without supplying their troops; with many other infringements: all which we were forced to submit to, because the General was *made easie*; because the monied men at home were fond of the war; because the *Whigs* were not yet firmly settled; and because that exorbitant degree of power, which was built upon a supposed necessity of employing particular persons, would go off in a peace. It is needless to add, that the Emperor, and other princes, followed the example of the *Dutch,* and succeeded as well, for the same reasons.

I have here imputed the continuance of the war to the mutual indulgence between our General and allies, wherein they both so well found their accounts; to the fears of the *mony-changers,* lest their *tables should be overthrown*; to the designs of the *Whigs,* who apprehended the loss of their credit and employments in a peace; and to those at home, who held their immoderate engrossments of power and favour, by no other tenure than their own presumption upon the necessity of affairs. The truth of this will appear indisputable, by considering with what unanimity and concert these several parties acted towards that great end. . . .

So when the Q[uee]n was no longer able to bear the tyranny and insolence of those ungrateful servants, who as they *wexed the fatter,* did but *kick the more*; our two great allies abroad, and our stock-jobbers at home, took immediately the alarm; applied the nearest way to the throne, by memorials and messages, jointly directing Her Majesty not to change her

Secretary [of State] or Treasurer; . . . Thus it plainly appears, that there was a conspiracy on all sides to go on with those measures, which must perpetuate the war; and a conspiracy founded upon the interest and ambition of each party; which begat so firm a union, that instead of wondring why it lasted so long, I am astonished to think how it came to be broken. . . .

Having thus mentioned the real causes, tho' disguised under specious pretences, which have so long continued the war; I must beg leave to reason a little with those persons who are against any peace, but what they call a *good one*; and explain themselves, that no peace can be *good*, without an entire restoration of *Spain* to the House of *Austria*. It is to be supposed, that what I am to say upon this part of the subject, will have little influence on those, whose particular ends or designs of any sort, lead them to wish the continuance of the war. I mean the General and our allies abroad; the knot of late favourites at home; the body of such as traffick in stocks; and lastly, that set of factious politicians, who were so violently bent, at least, upon *clipping* our constitution in Church and State. Therefore I shall not apply myself to any of those, but to all others indifferently, whether *Whig* or *Tory*, whose private interest is best answered by the welfare of their country. And if among these there be any, who think we ought to fight on till King *Charles* is quietly settled in the monarchy of *Spain*, I believe there are several points which they have not thoroughly considered.

For, first, it is to be observed, that this resolution against any peace without *Spain*, is a new incident, grafted upon the original quarrel, by the intrigues of a faction among us, who prevailed to give it the sanction of a vote in both houses of parliament, to justifie those, whose interest lay in perpetuating the war. . . .

The House of *Austria* approved this scheme with reason, since whatever would be obtained by the blood and treasure of others, was to accrue to that family, and they only lent their name to the cause.

The *Dutch* might, perhaps, have grown resty under their burthen; but care was likewise taken of that by a *Barrier-Treaty* made with the *States*, which deserveth such epithets as

I care not to bestow. . . . By this treaty, the condition of the war, with respect to the *Dutch*, was widely altered: they fought no longer for security, but for grandeur; and we, instead of labouring to make them *safe*, must beggar our selves to render them *formidable*. . . .

But the common question is, if we must now surrender *Spain*, what have we been fighting for all this while? The answer is ready; we have been fighting for the ruin of the publick interest, and the advancement of a private. We have been fighting to raise the wealth and grandeur of a particular family; to enrich usurers and stock-jobbers; and to cultivate the pernicious designs of a faction, by destroying the landed-interest. The nation begins now to think these *blessings* are not worth fighting for any longer, and therefore desires a peace.

5   Robert, Lord Molesworth:
The Principles of a Real Whig (1711)

[Published as a Preface to Francis Hotman's *Franco-Gallia* (1711) and in *The Memoirs of John Ker of Kersland* (1726), iii, 191–221.]

. . . My notion of a Whig, I mean a real Whig (for the nominal are worse than any sort of men) is, that he is one who is exactly for keeping up to the strictness of the true old Gothick constitution, under the three estates of King (or Queen) Lords and Commons; the legislature being seated in all three together, the executive intrusted with the first, but accomptable to the whole body of the people, in case of male administration.

A true Whig is of opinion, that the executive power has as just a title to the allegiance and obedience of the subject, according to the rules of known laws exacted by the legislature, as the subject has to protection, liberty and property: and so on the contrary.

A true Whig is not afraid of the name of commonwealths-man, because so many foolish people, who know not what it means, run it down: the anarchy and confusion which these nations fell into near sixty years ago, and which was falsly called a Commonwealth, frightening them out of the true construction of the word. But Queen Elizabeth, and many other of our best princes, were not scrupulous of calling our government a commonwealth, even in their solemn speeches to Parliament. . . .

It is certainly as much a treason and rebellion against this constitution, and the known laws, in a prince to endeavour to break thro' them, as it is in the people to rise against him, whilst he keeps within their bounds, and does his duty. Our constitution is a government of laws, not of persons. Allegiance

24

and protection are obligations that cannot subsist separately; when one fails, the other falls of course. . . .

Whiggism is not circumscribed and confined to any one or two of the religions now professed in the world, but diffuses itself among all. We have known Jews, Turks, nay, some Papists, (which I own to be a great rarity) very great lovers of our constitution and liberty: And were there rational grounds to expect, that any numbers of them could be so, I should be against using severities or distinctions upon account of religion. . . . And therefore all penal acts of Parliament for opinions purely religious, which have no influence on the state, are so many encroachments upon liberty, . . .

I profess myself to have always been a member of the Church of England, and am for supporting it in all its honours, privileges and revenues; but as a Christian and a Whig, I must have charity for those that differ from me in religious opinions, whether pagans, Turks, Jews, Papists, Quakers, Socinians, Presbyterians, or others. I look upon bigotry to have always been the very bane of human society, and the offspring of interest and ignorance, which has occasioned most of the great mischiefs that have afflicted mankind. We ought no more to expect to be all of one opinion, as to the worship of the Deity, than to be all of one colour or stature. . . .

But as, on the one hand, a true Whig thinks that all opinions purely spiritual and notional ought to be indulged; so on the other, he is for severely punishing all immoralities, breaches of laws, violence and injustice. A minister's tythes are as much his right as any layman's estate can be his; and no pretence of religion or conscience can warrant the subtracting of them, whilst the law is in being which makes them payable: for a Whig is far from the opinion that they are due by any other title. It would make a man's ears tingle, to hear the Divine Right insisted upon for any human institutions; and to find God Almighty brought in as a principal there, where there is no necessity for it. To affirm, that monarchy, episcopacy, synods, tythes, the hereditary succession to the crown, &c. are Jure Divino; is to cram them down a man's throat; and tell him in plain terms, that he must submit to any of them under all inconveniences, whether the laws of his country are for it or against it. . . .

A right Whig looks upon frequent parliaments as such a fundamental part of the constitution, that even no parliament can part with this right. High Whiggism is for annual parliaments, and Low Whiggism for triennial, with annual meetings. I leave it to every man's judgment, which of these would be the truest representative; would soonest ease the house of that number of members that have offices and employments, or take pensions from the court; is least liable to corruption; would prevent exorbitant expence, and soonest destroy the pernicious practice of drinking and bribing for elections, or is most conformable to ancient custom. The law that lately passed [in 1694] with so much struggle for triennial parliaments shall content me, till the legislature shall think fit to make them annual.

But methinks (and this I write with great submission and deference) that (since the passing that act) it seems inconsistent with the reason of the thing, and preposterous, for the first parliament after any prince's accession to the crown, to give the publick revenue arising by taxes, for a longer time than that parliament's own duration. I cannot see why the members of the first parliament should (as the case now stands) engross to themselves all the power of giving, as well as all the merit and rewards due to such a gift: and why succeeding parliaments should not, in their turn, have it in their power to oblige the prince, or to straiten him, if they saw occasion; and pare his nails, if they were convinced he made ill use of such a revenue. . . .

An old Whig is for chusing such sort of representatives to serve in parliament, as have estates in the kingdom; and those not fleeting ones, which may be sent beyond sea by bills of exchange by every pacquet-boat, but fixed and permanent. To which end, every merchant, banker, or other monied man, who is ambitious of serving his country as a senator, should have also a competent, visible land estate as a pledge to his electors that he intends to abide by them, and has the same interest with theirs in the publick taxes, gains and losses. I have heard and weighed the arguments of those who, in opposition to this, urged the unfitness of such, whose lands were engaged in debts and mortgages, to serve in parliament, in comparison with the monied man who had no land: but those arguments never convinced me.

No man can be a sincere lover of liberty, that is not for increasing and communicating that blessing to all people; and therefore the giving or restoring it not only to our brethren of Scotland and Ireland, but even to France itself (were it in our power) is one of the principal articles of Whiggism. . . .

A genuine Whig is for promoting a general naturalization, upon the firm belief, that whoever comes to be incorporated into us, feels his share of all our advantages and disadvantages, and consequently can have no interest but that of the publick; to which he will always be a support to the best of his power, by his person, substance and advice. . . . And this is the common calamity of most of our corporate towns, whose inhabitants do all they can to encourage plenty, industry and population; and will not admit of strangers but upon too hard terms, . . . most throughout England fall to visible decay, whilst new villages not incorporated, or more liberal in their privileges, grow up in their stead; till, in process of time, the first sort will become almost as desolate as Old Sarum, and will as well deserve to lose their right of sending representatives to parliament. For certainly a waste or a desart has no right to be represented, nor by our original constitution was ever intended to be; yet I would by no means have those deputies lost to the Commons, but transferred to wiser, more industrious, and better peopled places, worthy (through their numbers and wealth) of being represented.

A Whig is against the raising or keeping up a standing army in time of peace; but with this distinction, that if at any time an army (though even in time of peace) should be necessary to the support of this very maxim, a Whig is not for being too hasty to destroy that, which is to be the defender of his liberty. . . .

The arming and training of all the freeholders of England, as it is our undoubted ancient constitution, and consequently our right; so it is the opinion of most Whigs, that it ought to be put in practice. This would put us out of all fear of foreign invasions, or disappoint any such when attempted: this would soon take away the necessity of maintaining standing armies of mercenaries in time of peace: this would render us a hundred times more formidable to our neighbours than we are, and secure effectually our liberties against any king that should have a mind to invade them at home, which perhaps was the reason some of our late kings were so averse to it. . . .

A right Whig lays no stress on the illegitimacy of the pretended Prince of Wales; he goes upon another principle than they, who carry the right of succession so far, as (upon that score) to undo all mankind. He thinks no prince fit to govern, whose principle it must be to ruin the constitution, as soon as he can acquire unjust power to do so. He judges it nonsense for one to be the head of a church, or a defender of a faith, who thinks himself bound in duty to overthrow it. . . .

Lastly, the supporting of parliamentary credit, promoting of all publick buildings and high-ways, the making all rivers navigable that are capable of it, employing the poor, suppressing idlers, restraining monopolies upon trade, maintaining the liberty of the press, the just paying and encouraging of all in the publick service, especially that best and usefullest sort of people the seamen: these (joined to a firm opinion) that we ought not to hearken to any terms of peace with the French King, till it be quite out of his power to hurt us, but rather to die in defence of our own and the liberties of Europe are all of them articles of my Whiggish belief, and I hope none of them are heterodox. And if all these together amount to a Commonwealthsman, I shall never be ashamed of the name, though given with a design of fixing a reproach upon me, and such as think as I do.

6 Joseph Addison:
The Spectator (1711)

[No. 125. 24 July 1711]

. . . There cannot a greater judgment befall a country than such a dreadful spirit of division as rends a government into two distinct people, and makes them greater strangers and more averse to one another, than if they were actually two different nations. The effects of such a division are pernicious to the last degree, not only with regard to those advantages which they give the common enemy, but to those private evils which they produce in the heart of almost every particular person. This influence is very fatal both to men's morals and their understandings; it sinks the virtue of a nation, and not only so, but destroys even common sense.

A furious party-spirit, when it rages in its full violence, exerts it self in civil war and bloodshed; and when it is under its greatest restraints naturally breaks out in falshood, detraction, calumny, and a partial administration of justice. In a word, it fills a nation with spleen and rancour, and extinguishes all the seeds of good-nature, compassion and humanity. . . .

If this party-spirit has so ill an effect on our morals, it has likewise a very great one upon our judgments. We often hear a poor insipid paper or pamphlet cryed up, and sometimes a noble piece depreciated, by those who are of a different principle from the author. One who is actuated by this spirit is almost under an incapacity of discerning either real blemishes or beauties. . . .

There is one piece of sophistry practised by both sides, and that is the taking any scandalous story that has been ever whispered or invented of a private man, for a known undoubted truth, and raising suitable speculations upon it. . . . It is the restless ambition of artful men that thus breaks a people into factions, and draws several well-meaning persons to their interest by a specious concern for their country. How many honest minds are filled with uncharitable and barbarous notions, out of their zeal for the publick good? What cruelties and outrages would they not commit against men of an adverse party, whom they would honour and esteem, if instead of considering them as they are represented, they knew them as they are? Thus are persons of the greatest probity seduced into shameful errors and prejudices, and made bad men even by that noblest of principles, the love of their country. I cannot here forbear mentioning the famous Spanish proverb, *If there were neither fools nor knaves in the world, all people would be of one mind.*

For my part, I could heartily wish that all honest men would enter into an association, for the support of one another against the endeavours of those whom they ought to look upon as their common enemies, whatsoever side they may belong to. Were there such an honest body of neutral forces, we should never see the worst of men in great figures of life, because they are useful to a party; nor the best unregarded, because they are above practising those methods which would be grateful to their faction. We should then single every criminal out of the herd, and hunt him down, however formidable and over-grown he might appear: on the contrary, we should shelter distressed innocence, and defend virtue, however beset with contempt or ridicule, envy or defamation. In short, we should not any longer regard our fellow-subjects as Whigs or Tories, but should make the man of merit our friend, and the villain our enemy.

7 Joseph Addison: The Spectator (1712)

[No. 287.   29 January 1712]

I look upon it as a peculiar happiness, that were I to chuse of what religion I would be, and under what government I would live, I should most certainly give the preference to that form of religion and government which is established in my own country. In this point I think I am determined by reason and conviction; but if I shall be told that I am acted by prejudice, I am sure it is an honest prejudice, it is a prejudice that arises from the love of my country, and therefore such an one as I will always indulge. . . .

The form of government appears to me the most reasonable, which is most conformable to the equality that we find in humane nature, provided it be consistent with publick peace and tranquillity. This is what may properly be called liberty, which exempts one man from subjection to another, so far as the order and œconomy of government will permit.

Liberty should reach every individual of a people, as they all share one common nature; if it only spreads among particular branches, there had better be none at all, since such a liberty only aggravates the misfortune of those who are deprived of it, by setting before them a disagreeable subject of comparison.

This liberty is best preserved, where the legislative power is lodged in several persons, especially if those persons are of different ranks and interests; for where they are of the same rank, and consequently have an interest to manage peculiar to that rank, it differs but little from a despotical government in a single person. But the greatest security a people can have for their liberty, is when the legislative power is in the hands of persons so happily distinguished, that by providing for the particular interest of their several ranks, they are providing for the whole body of the people; or in other words, when there is no part of the people that has a common interest with at least one part of the legislators.

If there be but one body of legislators, it is no better than a tyranny; if there are only two, there will want a casting voice, and one of them must at length be swallowed up by disputes and contentions that will necessarily arise between them. Four would have the same inconveniences as two, and a greater number would cause too much confusion. I could never read a passage in Polybius, and another in Cicero, to this purpose, without a secret pleasure in applying it to the English Constitution, which it suits much better than the Roman. Both these great authors give the pre-eminence to a mixt government, consisting of three branches, the regal, the noble, and the popular. They had doubtless in their thoughts the constitution of the Roman common-wealth, in which the consul represented the king, the senate the nobles, and the tribunes the people. This division of the three powers in the Roman constitution, was by no means so distinct and natural, as it is in the English form of government. Among several objections that might be made to it, I think the chief are those that affect the consular power, which had only the ornaments without the force of regal authority. Their number had not a casting vote in it; for which reason, if one did not chance to be employed abroad, while the other sat at home, the publick business was sometimes at a stand, while the consuls pulled two different ways in it. Besides, I do not find that the consuls had ever a negative voice in the passing of a law, or decree of senate, so that indeed they were rather the chief body of the nobility, or the first ministers of state, than a distinct branch of the sovereignty, in which none can be looked upon as a part, who are not a part of the legislature. Had the consuls been invested with the regal authority to as great a degree as our monarchs, there would never have been any occasions for a dictatorship, which had in it the power of all the three orders, and ended in the subversion of the whole constitution.

Such an History as that of Suetonius, which gives us a succession of absolute princes, is to me an unanswerable argument against despotick power. Where the prince is a man of wisdom and virtue, it is indeed happy for his people that he is absolute; but since in the common run of mankind, for one that is wise and good you find ten of a contrary character, it is very dangerous for a nation to stand to its chance, or to have its publick happiness or misery depend on the virtues or vices of a single person. Look into the historian I have mentioned, or into any series of absolute princes, how many tyrants must you read through, before you come to an emperor that is supportable. But this is not all; an honest private man often grows cruel and abandoned, when converted into an absolute prince. Give a man power of doing what he pleases with impunity, you extinguish his fear, and consequently overturn in him one of the great pillars of morality. This too we find confirmed by matter of fact. How many hopeful heirs apparent to great empires, when in possession of them have become such monsters of lust and cruelty as are a reproach to humane nature?

Some tell us we ought to make our governments on earth like that in heaven, which, say they, is altogether monarchical and unlimited. Was man like his Creator in goodness and justice, I should be for following this great model; but where goodness and justice are not essential to the ruler, I would by no means put myself into his hands to be disposed of according to his particular will and pleasure.

It is odd to consider the connection between despotick government and barbarity, and how the making of one person more than man, makes the rest less. About nine parts of the world in ten are in the lowest state of slavery, and consequently sunk into the most gross and brutal ignorance. European slavery is indeed a state of liberty, if compared with that which prevails in the other three divisions of the world; and therefore it is no wonder that those who grovel under it, have many tracks of light among them, of which the others are wholly destitute.

Riches and plenty are the natural fruits of liberty, and where these abound, learning and all the liberal arts will immediately lift up their heads and flourish. As a man must have no slavish fears and apprehensions hanging upon his mind, who will indulge the flights of fancy or speculation, and push his researches into all the abstruse corners of truth, so it is necessary for him to have about him a competency of all the conveniences of life. . . . In Europe, indeed, notwithstanding several of its princes are absolute, there are men famous for knowledge and learning, but the reason is, because the subjects are many of them rich and wealthy, the prince not thinking fit to exert himself in his full tyranny like the princes of the eastern nations, lest his subjects should be invited to newmould their constitution, having so many prospects of liberty within their view. But in all despotick governments, tho' a particular prince may favour arts and letters, there is a natural degeneracy of mankind, as you observe from Augustus's reign, how the Romans lost themselves by degrees, till they fell to an equality with the most barbarous nations that surrounded them. . . . Besides poverty and want, there are other reasons that debase the minds of men, who live under slavery, though I look on this as the principal. This natural tendency of despotick power to ignorance and barbarity, tho' not insisted upon by others, is, I think, an unanswerable argument against that form of government, as it shows how repugnant it is to the good of mankind and the perfection of humane nature, which ought to be the great ends of all civil institutions.

8 Francis Atterbury, Bishop of Rochester: English Advice to the Freeholders of England (1714)

[From *Lord Somers' Tracts*, ed. Sir Walter Scott (1815), xiii, 522–41. This pamphlet, published anonymously, was much resented by the Whig government. In 1723 Atterbury was exiled for his part in a Jacobite conspiracy.]

1791614

I am firmly persuaded that there is not in their way a better set of men, generally speaking, than the freeholders of England. They are a brave, open, plain, and direct people, and when fairly left to themselves to chuse their representatives, always chuse such as are, or appear to be, true friends to their country. I could instance several elections formerly, and one or two of late, where the temper of the people, without any assistance or countenance from court or treasury, carried it for honest men under great temptations to the contrary; and I cannot recollect one bad parliament, but may be easily accounted for from the electors being bribed, and notoriously tampered with, from false returns made by sheriffs and other officers, or, lastly, from some extravagant prejudices scattered and cultivated among the people, who, wanting proper means of information, are obliged to take things at second-hand, and are therefore liable to gross mistakes.

As the case now stands, the honest part of the nation is to wrestle with each of these disadvantages in a higher degree than perhaps was ever known; and we can scarce expect things will take a happy turn, unless one side abates considerably of their zeal, and the other recovers new spirit: neither of which seems very promising as yet; since nothing is omitted on the one hand to poison the country, and on the other scarce any thing is attempted by way of antidote. Not that there is wanting a good disposition in the people: in many places several of the ordinary sort have the heroic virtue to refuse thirty, forty, a hundred pounds a man for their votes; and indeed throughout the whole kingdom they seem fully alarmed at the present posture of affairs: but I don't know how, there is a defect somewhere, the whigs outdo us in industry as much as in money: neither are we as active and bold in publishing the truth, as they in inventing falsehoods.

They go on securely, without fear or remorse, to tell you there was formed and settled a scheme by the late ministry, and the chief of the church party, with the queen at the head of them, to set the protestant succession aside, and introduce the Pretender [James Edward Stuart]: this they say loudly in their clubs, coffee-houses, addresses, and, by what appears, have thereby made an impression on the minds of those, who might be better informed if they would please to hear more than one side. The press swarms with these and the like monstrous forgeries; but not one single proof is attempted, only a parcel of invectives and libels against those who have no crimes to answer for, but too great lenity when in power, and too supine a neglect of themselves; faults indeed that could never be justly imputed to their antagonists. The sheriffs and other officers through the several boroughs and counties, are most of them men for the purpose, who know their business and are to be confided in. Bank bills, places, lies, threats, promises, entertainments, are every where employed to corrupt men's affections, and mislead their judgments. Boroughs are rated on the Royal Exchange like stocks and tallies; the price of a vote is as well known as an acre of land; and it is no secret who are the monied men, and consequently the best customers.

The country gentlemen who have stood the heat of the day for five or six-and-twenty years, are now almost quite worn out and harassed by taxes and elections: each election hath been a kind of campaign, where men are to fight *pro aris et focis* at the expence of the landed interest, which I take to be the political blood of the nation. Their enemy was a real hydra, a thriving enemy, that daily gained new recruits, and improved upon contest. The wars abroad, the support whereof weakened the country gentlemen, furnished the whigs with forces to carry on the war with advantage at home; and now that by their misrepresentation of things and persons they have got a vast acquisition of strength, they will, it is to be feared, be enabled to compass their schemes so long projected, for the destruction of the church and landed interest. They have, as they boast themselves, the game in their hands; and, to do them justice, they act like men in earnest, who are resolved to play it to purpose.

This then being our case at present, I shall examine into our circumstances, and speak my mind, as to facts, with great freedom and impartiality . . . Nor is this an affair of small importance; our all, under God, depends upon the next elections; our religion, our rights, our liberties, our present laws, and our future security are at stake: if we make a wrong step at this juncture, all the comfort we can have, is, that probably it will be our last fault of the kind, because we shall never have it in our power to be guilty of another. For if now there should happen a fatal conjunction of a corrupt parliament and a corrupt ministry, a thing not altogether inconsistent nor unprecedented; if the one should be as ready to give up the constitution, as the other demand it, we can have no resource, but must be bought and sold beyond a possibility of redemption: For I have too good an opinion of the understanding of the whigs, to think they will ever put it in our power hereafter to make reprisals or retrieve past miscarriages. If they succeed, according to all human views and probability, the next will be our last parliament that can be called free, and even that, I fear, can only be called so.

I must own, I cannot without great indignation, observe the lukewarm, indolent, cowardly, lazy, desponding, and narrow tempers of some among us: to their shame be it said, they profess honest principles, nay, and are really honest in their inclinations, but yet relinquish the cause, and think they deserve commendation, because they do not concur in the iniquity of the times. . . . But not to exert one's utmost, in a case of this nature, is almost as blameable as an overt act against one's country: although the crime be not so unnatural, it is to all intents as prejudicial. . . .

Far be it from me, and every true Briton, to insinuate we have any thing to fear from a prince of such virtues and abilities as our present gracious sovereign. On the contrary, I labour to extricate him out of difficulties I foresee the whigs design to bring him under; if they can pack a House of Commons to their mind, they will leave him no power to act but as they direct and prescribe: they will subject him to the arbitrary government of a junto, who cannot bear to be controlled even by the regal power, which, as they say, is of their own creation: according to custom, they will pronounce every thing to be arbitrary and tyrannical, which they have not leave to dictate. Thus it was they treated the late queen, until the kingdom unanimously took fire, and resolved to deliver their sovereign out of the hands of such managers. . . .

The late House of Commons, wherein the church party had a vast majority, expressed an early and affectionate concern for the illustrious house of Hanover: they omitted nothing to shew their fidelity, which certainly the king is too grateful to forget so soon. Beside, if we consider his firm resolution to maintain the church of England, his disposition to govern according to our laws, his great discernment in penetrating into men, and his tender love for his people, we cannot imagine he will desire a parliament of a complexion different from the two last, however the whigs may attempt or suggest the contrary. . . .

When one considers the conduct of the church party; how they were the men made and confirmed the act of settlement; how they were the men recognized the king's title and proclaimed him with all possible marks of duty; one is confounded to think, what colours the whigs could use to represent them as disaffected, and what could provoke the court to single them out as objects of displeasure; and much more, what can bias the country to reject these men they so lately chose. . . . All, who lay under the imputation of having been esteemed by the late queen, were treated as enemies to the king; excepting two or three at most, who, if I mistake not, will never go the lengths that are expected, and for that very suspicion are already but cloudily received. None, bating a few trimmers, who can turn with every wind, are in favour with the present court, but such as was in eminent disfavour with the last. Every one's merit is rated in proportion to that standard. You shall not see a scoundrel, that was either turned out of employment, or had none under the late administration, but expects to come in

now upon the foot of a sufferer for the succession. . . . It is vain
to look back. What behoves every honest man is, to examine
into the merits, the views, the interests of each side, and thence
to form his conduct: upon this foot we are now to proceed.
If, upon a fair disquisition of the matter, we find the whigs
are generally men of more honour and religion, truer to the
interest of their country, and less addicted to strangers than
their competitors; if their views and designs square better
with the establishment in church and state than those of their
rivals; in the name of God let all the persons in England that
have votes to give, declare for a whig parliament. But if the
reverse of all this be true, or if the whigs are at best but men,
liable to mistakes, and open to bribery; if their avowed
designs tend to the overthrow of the constitution, and at the
same time it be their interest to pursue those designs, whilst
the only reasonable prospect, the only safety the churchmen
can propose to themselves, consists in the preservation of our
religion and laws as now settled; if this, I say, be the case, then
I presume it will follow, that it is the interest of both the church
and people of England to chuse churchmen for the ensuing
parliament.

. . . First, we take it for granted, that the whigs are resolved
upon an immediate war. . . .

Again, we say the whigs resolve, if they can procure a House
of Commons to their mind, to destroy the church of England:
whereby I do not mean that they have set up gibbets in their
minds, and design to hang, draw, and quarter every member
of the church, nor that all the whigs will come into the scheme;
but we are peruaded that the generality of the whigs are averse
to the present hierarchy and government of the church; that
they neither like our doctrines nor our clergy, but would
abolish bishops, priests and deacons, assume the church lands
to themselves, appoint a small allowance to the parsons, and
prescribe them what doctrines to teach from the pulpit; that
they would introduce a general comprehension, and blend up
an ecclesiastical Babel of all the sects and heresies upon the
face of the earth; and, lastly, deprive the b shops of their vote
in the House of Lords. . . .

Another point with which we accuse the whigs is, that they

design to repeal or explain away the chief limitations of the
Act of Settlement. . . . that which is of the greatest moment to
the kingdom, and most for the safety of the king, is that part
of the act which excludes all foreigners from any employments, or grants of lands, &c. in these nations; which takes
off from the king the odium of giving up the rights of Englishmen to outlandish, craving cormorants, and also may satisfy
the people, that his majesty's affections are not settled upon
aliens and strangers. But this happens to have the fate of all
other provisions for the good of England, to be disagreeable
to the interest and inclinations of the whigs. . . . The king's
crown is to sit easy upon his head, his countrymen are to partake of his sunshine, foreigners are to be admitted as new
additional forces to the whigs, and under the name of the
the king, a corrupt, detestable junto is to govern: we are to be
made slaves, by virtue of a combination between our new
friends and old enemies, and whilst we bear a heavy German
burthen, the whigs, who have bridled their country, will shew
the sovereign use of the prerogative, when lodged in good
hands.

But these are not all the articles wherewith we tax the whigs.
These indeed should be enough to influence the country not
to trust their safety in the power of men of such designs and
principles; but over and above all these, we say, that the
whigs intend to repeal the act of triennial parliaments: and
when that is done, we may bid adieu to liberty. . . .

But compleatly to rivet our destruction, it must come upon
us like an armed man; or, which is the same, must be imposed
upon us by a standing army; and this, we say, the whigs are
bent upon. . . .

Another particular which we impute to the whigs, is a
design to take away the liberty of the press. . . .

Lastly, we impute to the whigs the outrages offered to the
memory of the late queen; . . .

Upon the whole, I am far from arrogating to our own party
all the good sense and virtue of the nation; but, compare the
bulk of each side together, and you will find the whigs posi-
tively bad, the churchmen negatively good. According to
which computation I have cast up the account, for the benefit

of those who may be at too great a distance from the fountain of affairs, to know the true state of them. The following bill of their several deserts is, I think, very exact.

The Merits of the Church-Party.	*The Merits of the Whigs.*
I. No new war, no new taxes.	**I.** A new war, six shillings in the pound, a general excise, and a poll-tax.
II. No attempt against the church.	**II.** A general and unlimited comprehension, without common-prayer book or bishops.
III. No repeal of the conditions upon which the crown was settled upon the king.	**III.** The repeal of the act of limitation of the crown, &c.
IV. No foreigners in employment.	**IV.** An equal distribution of places between Turks, Germans, and infidels.
V. No standing army.	**V.** An augmentation of troops for the better suppressing of mobs and riots.
VI. No long parliament.	**VI.** The repeal of the triennial act.
VII. No restraint on the liberty of the press.	**VII.** An act to prohibit all libels in favour of the church or churchmen, and to enable free-thinkers to write against God and the Christian religion.

VIII.	VIII.
No insulting the memory of the queen.	An encouragement to all men to speak ill of the queen and her friends.

Total.	*Total.*
No alteration of the constitution in Church and state.	An entire and thorough revolution.

Chuse which you please.

9 Joseph Addison:
The Freeholder (1716)

[No. 22. 5 March 1716]

For the honour of his Majesty, and the safety of his government, we cannot but observe, that those, who have appeared
the greatest enemies to both, are of that rank of men, who are
commonly distinguished by the title of *Fox-hunters*. As several
of these have had no part of their education in cities, camps,
or courts, it is doubtful whether they are of greater ornament
or use to the nation in which they live. It would be an everlasting reproach to politics, should such men be able to overturn an establishment which has been formed by the wisest
laws, and is supported by the ablest heads. The wrong notions
and prejudices which cleave to many of these country-
gentlemen, who have always lived out of the way of being
better informed, are not easy to be conceived by a person who
has never conversed with them.

That I may give my readers an image of these rural statesmen, I shall, without further preface, set down an account of a
discourse I chanced to have with one of them some time ago.
I was travelling towards one of the remotest parts of England,
when about three o'clock in the afternoon, seeing a country-
gentleman trotting before me with a spaniel by his horse's
side, I made up to him. Our conversation opened, as usual,
upon the weather; in which we were very unanimous; having
both agreed that it was too dry for the season of the year. My
fellow-traveller, upon this, observed to me, that there had
been no good weather since the Revolution. I was a little
startled at so extraordinary a remark, but would not interrupt
him until he proceeded to tell me of the fine weather they used

to have in King Charles the Second's reign. I only answered that I did not see how the badness of the weather could be the king's fault; and, without waiting for his reply, asked him whose house it was we saw upon a rising ground at a little distance from us. He told me it belonged to an old fanatical cur, Mr. Such-a-one. 'You must have heard of him', says he, 'he's one of the Rump.' [1] I knew the gentleman's character upon hearing his name, but assured him that to my knowledge he was a good churchman. 'Ay!' says he with a kind of surprise. 'We were told in the country, that he spoke twice in the queen's time against taking off the duties upon French claret.' This naturally led us into the proceedings of late parliaments, upon which occasion he affirmed roundly, that there had not been one good law passed since King William's accession to the throne, except the act for preserving the game [1707]. I had a mind to see him out, and therefore did not care for contradicting him. 'Is it not hard', says he, 'that honest gentlemen should be taken into custody of messengers to prevent them from acting according to their consciences? But', says he, 'what can we expect when a parcel of factious sons of — —.' He was going on in great passion, but chanced to miss his dog, who was amusing himself about a bush that grew at some distance behind us. We stood still till he had whistled him up; when he fell into a long panegyric upon his spaniel, who seemed indeed excellent in his kind: but I found the most remarkable adventure of his life was, that he had once like to have worried a dissenting-teacher. The master could hardly sit on his horse for laughing all the while he was giving me the particulars of this story, which I found had mightily endeared his dog to him, and, as he himself told me, had made him a great favourite among all the honest gentlemen of the country. We were at length diverted from this piece of mirth by a post-boy, who winding his horn at us, my companion gave him two or three curses, and left the way clear for him. 'I fancy', said I, 'that post brings news from Scotland. I shall long to see the next Gazette.' 'Sir', says he, 'I make it a

[1] The members of the Rump Parliament (1649–53) executed Charles I and were staunch opponents of an episcopalian church.

rule never to believe any of your printed news. We never see, sir, how things go, except now and then in "Dyer's Letter", and I read that more for the style than the news. The man has a clever pen, it must be owned. But is it not strange that we should be making war upon Church-of-England men, with Dutch and Swiss soldiers, men of antimonarchical principles? These foreigners will never be loved in England, sir; they have not that wit and good-breeding that we have.' I must confess I did not expect to hear my new acquaintance value himself upon these qualifications; but finding him such a critic upon foreigners, I asked him if he had ever travelled? He told me, he did not know what travelling was good for, but to teach a man to ride the great horse, to jabber French, and to talk against passive-obedience: To which he added, that he scarce ever knew a traveller in his life who had not forsook his principles, and lost his hunting-seat. 'For my part', says he, 'I and my father before me have always been for passive-obedience, and shall be always for opposing a prince who makes use of ministers that are of another opinion. But where do you intend to inn to-night? (for we were now come in sight of the next town;) I can help you to a very good land-lord if you will go along with me. He is a lusty, jolly fellow, that lives well, at least three yards in the girth, and the best Church-of-England man upon the road.' I had the curiosity to see this high-church inn-keeper, as well as to enjoy more of the conversation of my fellow-traveller, and therefore readily consented to set our horses together for that night. As we rode side by side through the town, I was let into the characters of all the principal inhabitants whom we met in our way. One was a dog, another a whelp, and another a cur, under which several denominations were comprehended all that voted on the Whig side in the last election of burgesses. As for those of his own party, he distinguished them by a nod of his head, and asking them how they did by their Christian names. Upon our arrival at the inn, my companion fetched out the jolly landlord, who knew him by his whistle. Many endearments and private whispers passed between them; though it was easy to see by the landlord's scratching his head that things did not go to their wishes. The landlord had swelled his body to a prodigious size, and worked up his complexion to a standing crimson by his zeal for the prosperity of the Church, which he expressed every hour of the day, as his customers dropt in, by repeated bumpers. He had not time to go to church himself, but, as my friend told me in my ear, had headed a mob at the pulling down of two or three meeting-houses. While supper was preparing, he enlarged upon the happiness of the neighbouring shire; 'For,' says he, 'there is a scarce a Presbyterian in the whole county, except the bishop.' In short, I found by his discourse that he had learned a great deal of politics, but not one word of religion, from the parson of his parish; and indeed, that he had scarce any other notion of religion, but that it consisted in hating Presbyterians. I had a remarkable instance of his notions in this particular. Upon seeing a poor decrepit old woman pass under the window where he sat, he desired me to take notice of her; and afterwards informed me, that she was generally reputed a witch by the country people, but that, for his part, he was apt to believe she was a Presbyterian.

Supper was no sooner served in, than he took occasion, from a shoulder of mutton that lay before us, to cry up the plenty of England, which would be the happiest country in the world, provided we would live within ourselves. Upon which, he expatiated on the inconveniences of trade, that carried from us the commodities of our country, and made a parcel of upstarts as rich as men of the most ancient families of England. He then declared frankly, that he had always been against all treaties and alliances with foreigners: 'Our wooden walls,' says he, 'are our security, and we may bid defiance to the whole world, especially if they should attack us when the militia is out.' I ventured to reply, that I had as great an opinion of the English fleet as he had; but I could not see how they could be paid, and manned, and fitted out, unless we encouraged trade and navigation. He with some vehemence, that he would undertake to prove trade would be the ruin of the English nation. I would fain have put him upon it; but he contented himself with affirming it more eagerly, to which he added two or three curses upon the London merchants, not forgetting the directors of the Bank. After supper he asked me

if I was an admirer of punch; and immediately called for a
sneaker. I took this occasion to insinuate the advantages of
trade, by observing to him, that water was the only native of
England that could be made use of on this occasion: but that
the lemons, the brandy, the sugar, and the nutmeg, were all
foreigners. This put him into some confusion: but the landlord who overheard me, brought him off, by affirming, that
for constant use there was no liquor like a cup of English
water, provided it had malt enough in it. My squire laughed
heartily at the conceit, and made the landlord sit down with
us. We sat pretty late over our punch; and amidst a great deal
of improving discourse, drank the healths of several persons
in the country, whom I had never heard of, that, they both
assured me, were the ablest statesmen in the nation; and of
some Londoners, whom they extolled to the skies for their wit,
and who, I knew, passed in town for silly fellows. It being now
midnight, and my friend perceiving by his almanack that the
moon was up, he called for his horse, and took a sudden resolution to go to his house, which was at three miles' distance from
the town, after having bethought himself that he never slept
well out of his own bed. He shook me very heartily by the
hand at parting, and discovered a great air of satisfaction in
his looks, that he had met with an opportunity of showing his
parts, and left me a much wiser man than he found me.

10 Benjamin Hoadly, Bishop of Bangor: The Nature of the Kingdom, or Church, of Christ (1717)

[A Sermon preached before the King at St James's on Sunday, 31 March 1717. This sermon provoked a large number of indignant replies and Convocation had to be suspended because of this 'Bangorian' controversy.]

I. . . . As the Church of Christ is the Kingdom of Christ, He himself is King: and in this it is implied that He is himself the sole law-giver to his subjects, and himself the sole judge of their behaviour, in the affairs of conscience and eternal salvation. And in this sense therefore, His kingdom is not of this world; that He hath, in those points, left behind him, no visible, humane authority; no vicegerents, who can be said properly to supply his place; no interpreters, upon whom his subjects are absolutely to depend; no judges over the consciences or religion of his people. For if this were so, that any such absolute vicegerent authority, either for the making new laws, or interpreting old ones, or judging his subjects, in religious matters, were lodged in any men upon earth; the consequences would be, that what still retains the name of the Church of Christ, would not be the Kingdom of Christ, but the kingdom of those men, vested with such authority. For, whoever hath such an authority of making laws, is so far a king: and whoever can add new laws to those of Christ, equally obligatory, is as truly a king, as Christ himself is: Nay, whoever hath an absolute authority to interpret any written, or spoken laws; it is he, who is truly the law-giver, to all intents and purposes; and not the person who first wrote or spoke them.

In humane society, the interpretation of laws may, of necessity, be lodged, in some cases, in the hands of those who were not originally the legislators. But this is not absolute; nor of bad consequence to society: because the legislators can resume

48

the interpretation into their own hands, as they are witnesses to what passes in the world; and as they can, and will, sensibly interpose in all those cases, in which their interposition becomes necessary. And therefore, they are still properly the legislators. But it is otherwise in religion, or the Kingdom of Christ. He himself never interposeth, since his first promulgation of his law, either to convey infallibility to such as pretend to handle it over again; or to assert the true interpretation of it, amidst the various and contradictory opinions of men about it. If He did certainly thus interpose, He himself would still be the legislator. But, as He doth not; if such an absolute authority be once lodged with men, under the notion of interpreters, they then become the legislators, and not Christ; and they rule in their own kingdom, and not in His.

It is the same thing, as to rewards and punishments, to carry forward the great end of His kingdom. If any men upon earth have a right to add to the sanction of his laws; that is, to increase the number, or alter the nature, of the rewards and punishments of his subjects, in matters of conscience, or salvation: they are so far kings in his stead; and reign in their own kingdom, and not in His. So it is, whenever they erect tribunals, and exercise a judgment over the consciences of men; and assume to themselves the determination of such points, as cannot be determined, but by One who knows the hearts; or, when they make any of their own declarations, or decisions, to concern and affect the state of Christ's subjects, with regard to the favour of God: this is so far, the taking Christ's Kingdom out of His hands, and placing it in their own. . . .

If therefore, the Church of Christ be the Kingdom of Christ; it is essential to it, that Christ himself be the sole lawgiver, and the sole judge of his subjects, in all points relating to the favour or displeasure of Almighty God; and that all his subjects, in what station soever they may be, are equally subjects to him; and that no one of them, any more than another, hath authority, either to make new laws for Christ's subjects; or to impose a sense upon the old ones, which is the same thing; or to judge, censure, or punish, the servants of another master, in matters relating purely to conscience, or salvation. . . . This enquiry will bring us back to the first, which is the only true, account of the Church of Christ, or the Kingdom of Christ, in the mouth of a Christian: that it is the number of men, whether small or great, whether dispersed or united, who truly and sincerely are subjects to Jesus Christ alone, as their law-giver and judge, in matters relating to the favour of God, and their eternal salvation. . . .

II. . . . The laws of this kingdom, therefore, as Christ left them, have nothing of this world in their view; no tendency, either to the exaltation of some, in worldly pomp and dignity; or to their absolute dominion over the faith and religious conduct of others of his subjects; or to the erecting of any sort of temporal kingdom, under the covert and name of a spiritual one.

The sanctions of Christ's law are rewards and punishments. But of what sort? Not the rewards of this world; not the offices, or glories, of this state; not the pains of prisons, banishments, fines, or any lesser and more moderate penalties; nay, not the much lesser negative discouragements that belong to humane society. He was far from thinking that these could be the instruments of such a perswasion, as He thought acceptable to God. But, as the great end of his kingdom, was to guide men to happiness, after the short images of it were over here below; so, He took his motives from that place, where his kingdom first began, and where it was at last to end; from those rewards and punishments in a future state, which had no relation to this world: And, to shew that his kingdom was not of this world, all the sanctions which He thought fit to give to his laws, were not of this world at all. . . . From what hath been said it appears that the Kingdom of Christ, which is the Church of Christ, is the number of persons who are sincerely, and willingly, subjects to him, as law-giver and judge, in all matters truly relating to conscience, or eternal salvation. And the more close and immediate this regard to him is, the more certainly and the more evidently true it is, that they are of his kingdom. . . . it evidently destroys the rule and authority of Jesus Christ, as King, to set up any other authority in his kingdom, to which his subjects are indispensably and absolutely obliged to submit their consciences, or their conduct, in what is properly called religion. There are some professed

Christians, who contend openly for such an authority, as indispensably obliges all around them to unity of profession; that is, to profess even what they do not, what they cannot, believe to be true. This sounds so grossly, that others, who think they act a glorious part in opposing such an enormity, are very willing, for their own sakes, to retain such an authority as shall oblige men, whatever they themselves think, though not to profess what they do not believe, yet, to forbear the profession and publication of what they do believe, let them believe it of never so great importance. . . . The peace of Christ's Kingdom is a manly and reasonable peace; built upon charity, and love, and mutual forbearance, and receiving one another, as God receives us. As for any other peace; founded upon a submission of our honesty, as well as our understandings; it is falsely so called. It is not the peace of the Kingdom of Christ; but the lethargy of it: and a sleep unto death, when his subjects shall throw off their relation to him; fix their subjection to others; and even in cases, and where they have a right to see, and where they think they see, his will otherwise, shall shut their eyes and go blindfold at the command of others; because those others are not pleas'd with their enquiries into the will of their great lord and judge. . . .

PART TWO

The Debate on the Working of the 'Whig' Constitution

After the Hanoverian succession the Tory party disintegrated as an effective political force, largely because it had alienated the new dynasty by failing to denounce the claims of the Pretender. The success of the Whigs guaranteed the Protestant succession, a limited measure of religious toleration and a more stable relationship between crown and parliament. Tory attitudes did not disappear overnight, however, and the Whigs were careful not to provoke a Tory backlash by pressing their political advantage too far. Walpole taught the Whigs to prefer political stability, with themselves enjoying the fruits of power, rather than to provoke the backbench squires and the parish clergy who had, in the past, rallied so strongly to the Tory party. He judiciously defused the emotive political issues which had once divided Whigs and Tories. The friction between landed and monied men was reduced by cutting both the land tax and the rate of interest on the national debt and by avoiding expensive military adventures in Europe. Walpole also refused to countenance any serious attack on the privileges of the Church of England such as the Dissenters' plan to repeal the Test and Corporation Acts. As the former disputes between Whig and Tory gradually disappeared and the political nation ceased to be organized into effective parties pursuing clearly differentiated policies, the parliamentary battle was transformed. Very often the debates in parliament revealed a simple contest between ambitious politicians for place and power; a struggle merely of 'ins' and 'outs'. This transformation was aided by the Septennial Act of 1716 which meant that general elections were less frequent and fewer constituencies were actually contested at the polls. Most M.P.s no longer appealed to the electorate on a Whig or Tory platform, but relied solely on their own local influence or that of the king or a great aristocratic patron. These developments did not mean that national issues or questions of principle had ceased to have any place in the contest for power. The larger constituencies were still frequently contested and candidates had to have more than a local interest; while in the smaller constituencies many of those elected in their own interest could remain 'independent' in the House of Commons. Unless they were ambitious for office, they refused to commit themselves to the battle of 'ins' and 'outs', but voted as they saw fit after hearing the arguments of both sides. Therefore both 'ins' and 'outs' produced political literature and propaganda in an effort to convert the uncommitted voter and the independent backbencher.

Often this material reflected the personal aspect of the battle for power, with writers commending or denigrating the character, abilities and motives of the leading 'ins' and 'outs'. In ballads and plays, in newspaper polemics from *The Craftsman* to *The North Briton* and the *Letters of Junius*, successive governments were subjected to vicious character assassination [see Nos. 15, 18, 28, 30, 33]. The battle was by no means one-sided. The ministers not only harassed opposition writers and printers, and censored the London theatre, but replied in kind. Lord Hervey's *The Conduct of the Opposition* (1734), William Arnall's *Opposition no Proof of Patriotism* (1735) [No. 20], Lord Egmont's *Faction Detected* (1743) and Dr. Johnson's *The Patriot* (1774) were among the more effective replies. More important than this kind of mud-slinging was the continuous debate over the financial and foreign policies pursued by those in power. Too often this controversy has been seen simply as a debate on day-to-day matters and devoid of any issue of principle. The opposition, in fact, made every effort in pamphlets and periodicals to convince the electorate and the independent backbenchers of the full political implications of these policies. Financial proposals, such as the abortive Excise scheme of 1733, raised questions about corruption in politics, infringement of personal liberty, the growth of the executive and the distribution of the tax burden. The conduct of foreign policy inspired debates on Britain's role in Europe, the danger of a standing army in time of peace, and the sacrificing of the country's interests to those of Hanover.

In general, the ministers concentrated their efforts on defending the wisdom of their specific policies, while their opponents used these issues as a means of attacking the government's *political methods*. The opposition spokesmen maintained that knaves or fools, such as Walpole and Bute, were in office not because of their personal merits, but because, once having ingratiated themselves at court, they were able to use corrupt practices to defeat all the arguments of their honest opponents. By exploiting the crown's patronage and the government's close links with the monied interest, the ministers could offer titles, honours, places, pensions, sinecures and downright bribes in order to secure a majority in both houses of parliament. In doing so, they were encouraging a lamentable decline in moral standards and threatening the nation's liberties by undermining the constitution.

It was a constant opposition theme throughout much of the eighteenth century that the court and the ministers were responsible for the contemporary vices of worshipping idle luxury and pursuing inordinate wealth by any possible means, while presiding over a general decline in the traditional virtues of industry, simplicity, honesty and patriotism. The court, and even London itself, was identified as the source and centre of corruption. It appeared that virtue could only be retained by those who retreated to the country where gold did not rule all. Swift, Pope, Gay, Fielding, Thomson and the young Samuel Johnson were among the many writers who wrote in this contest between Court and Country in terms of public morality [Nos. 14, 15, 16, 17, 19, 21 and 22]. Oliver Goldsmith even feared that rural virtues were being destroyed by the introduction of materialistic city values into the country-side [No. 32]. The more overtly political writers, such as Trenchard, Bolingbroke, Wilkes and Junius, emphasized the threat which political immorality posed to the nation's liberties and the constitution [Nos. 11, 18, 28, 33]. They maintained that the constitution, so carefully safeguarded by the Revolu-

tion Settlement, was only able to guarantee stability and
liberty because it combined the virtues of monarchy, aristocracy and democracy by balancing the powers of Crown,
Lords and Commons. Each of the three retained its special
rights and privileges, while also working in harmony with the
others. If any one part lost its independence, this balance
would be destroyed and the consequence would be an absolute
monarchy, a narrow oligarchy or an anarchic democracy. To
these writers the only serious threat to the balanced constitution came from the abuse of royal power. By its undue and
unwarranted influence over the electorate and both houses
of parliament, the power of the crown was endangering the
independence of the Lords and Commons and undermining
the liberties of the people.

Such fears, which may have been exaggerated for reasons
of political advantage and which modern historians might
regard as unwarranted, were nevertheless genuine expressions
of widely-held beliefs. They certainly inspired men to devise
ways and means of safeguarding the constitution. One approach was to advocate a diminution of royal influence by
reducing the size of the standing army and the departments
of state, and by preventing the corruption of either voters or
members of parliament. Another approach was to demand
more frequent general elections, an extension of the franchise
and greater liberty of the press. The most radical reforms were
suggested by the Country Whigs or Commonwealthsmen,
notably John Trenchard, Joseph Priestley and the anony-
mous author of *Liberty and Right* (1747) [Nos. 11, 31, 26], but
these policies stopped short of advocating a democratic system
of government. Trenchard, for example, was a great champion
of liberty, but he was afraid of giving any real political power
to the propertyless masses [No. 13].

Devising policies which could safeguard the constitution
was not difficult. The real problem was how to combat the
political advantages of the court and the government so that
these policies could be implemented. The ministers had control
of the levers of power and the wealth of crown patronage. They
could even claim to be the only true defenders of the 'Whig'
constitution, since their opponents were often former Tories.

They could also take advantage of the popular belief in the virtues of the British constitution and the widespread notion that parties and formed oppositions were factious [Nos. 20 and 27]. David Hume was one of the few to realise that the nature of the British constitution implied political divisions, at least into Court and Country parties, but only Edward Spelman, before Burke, was convinced of the merits of party and formed opposition in preserving the balance of the constitution [Nos. 24 and 25].

In the face of these difficulties the opposition spokesmen could only appeal for support if they assumed the role of patriots defending the interests of the nation as a whole. They tried to persuade the electorate and the independent back benchers to abandon the old, sterile divisions of Whig and Tory and to support a patriotic Country party dedicated to saving the constitution. Such appeals, made by Trenchard and Bolingbroke in particular, and to a lesser extent by Wilkes and Junius [Nos. 12, 18, 28, and 33] failed to unite the opposition into an effective national party. [See Pope's disillusionment with the patriots in his poem, *One Thousand Seven Hundred and Forty*. No. 23.] The 'patriots' therefore had recourse to another tactic, an appeal to the heir to the throne. From the later 1730s the opposition writers sought to flatter Frederick, Prince of Wales, by maintaining that the constitution could only be saved by a patriot king. This was the theme of poems, such as Richard Glover's *Leonidas*, and of numerous plays, including James Thomson's *Edward and Eleonora* and David Mallet's *Mustapha* and *The Masque of Alfred*. Probably the most famous and important contribution was Bolingbroke's treatise *The Idea of a Patriot King* (c. 1738). The death of Prince Frederick in 1751 temporarily dashed all such hopes, but they were revived for a time when George III came to the throne mouthing 'patriotic' platitudes. The new king did succeed in ditching the Whig oligarchs who had served George II for so many years, but he failed to satisfy those critics, like Wilkes and Junius, who believed that the constitution could not be saved except by a reduction of the royal influence itself.

11 John Trenchard and Thomas Gordon: Cato's Letters (1720)

[Published in *The London Journal*, 21 January 1720. Letter no. 13 by John Trenchard]

. . . Let mankind therefore learn experience from so many misfortunes, and bear no longer to hear the worst things called by the best names; nor suffer hereafter the brightest and most conspicuous virtues of the wisest and most beneficent princes, to be sullied by actions which they do not countenance, nor even know of. Let them not permit the vices of the worst of servants to be laid at the door of the best of masters.

We, in this land, are very sure that we are blessed with the best king in the world, who desires of his people nothing but their own greatness and felicity: a prince, ready to prevent their wishes, and to give them more than their duty ought to suffer them to ask. Let us shew our duty to this our great and benevolent sovereign; let us endeavour to alleviate his cares, and ease him of all ungrateful burthens; let us take upon ourselves the heavy labour of cleansing the *Augean* stables, and of cutting off all the *Hydra*'s heads at once.

The law tells us, that the King can do no wrong: and, I thank God, we have a King that would not, if he could. But the greatest servants to princes may do wrong, and often have done it; and the representatives of the people have an undoubted right to call them to an account for it.

In truth, every private subject has a right to watch the steps of those who would betray their country; nor is he to take their word about the motives of their designs, but to judge of their designs by the event.

This is the principle of a *Whig*, this is the doctrine of liberty; and 'tis as much knavery to deny this doctrine, as it is folly to ridicule it. Some will tell us, that this is setting up the mob for statesmen, and for the censurers of states. The word *Mob* does not at all move me, on this occasion, nor weaken the grounds which I go upon. It is certain, that the whole people, who are the publick, are the best judges, whether things go ill or well with the publick. It is true, that they cannot all of them see distant dangers, nor watch the motions, and guess the designs, of neighbouring states; but every cobler can judge, as well as a statesman, whether he can sit peaceably in his stall; whether he is paid for his work; whether the market, where he buys his victuals, be well provided; and whether a dragoon, or a parish-officer, comes to him for his taxes, if he pay any.

Every man too, even the meanest, can see, in a publick and sudden transition from plenty to poverty, from happiness to distress, whether the calamity comes from war, and famine, and the hand of God; or from oppression, and mismanagement, and the villainies of men. In short, the people often judge better than their superiors, and have not so many biasses to judge wrong; and politicians often rail at the people, chiefly because they have given the people occasion to rail: those ministers who cannot make the people their friends, it is to be shrewdly suspected, do not deserve their friendship; it is certain, that much honesty, and small management, rarely miss to gain it. As temporal felicity is the whole end of government; so people will always be pleased or provoked, as that increases or abates. This rule will always hold. You may judge of their affection, or disaffection, by the burthens which they bear, and the advantages which they enjoy. Here then is a sure standard for the government to judge of the people, and for the people to judge of the government. . . .

12 John Trenchard and Thomas Gordon: Cato's Letters (1722)

[*The London Journal*, 29 September 1722. Letter no. 96 by Thomas Gordon]

Of Parties in England; how they vary, and interchange characters, just as they are in power, or out of it, yet still keep their former names.

Sir,

The *English* climate, famous for variable weather, is not less famous for variable parties; which fall insensibly into an exchange of principles, and yet go on to hate and curse one another for these principles. A *Tory* under oppression, or out of place, is a *Whig;* a *Whig* with power to oppress, is a *Tory*. The *Tory* damns the *Whig*, for maintaining a resistance, which he himself never fails to practise; and the *Whig* reproaches the *Tory* with slavish principles, yet calls him rebel if he do not practise them. The truth is, all men dread the power of oppression out of their own hands, and almost all men wish it irresistible when it is there.

We change sides every day, yet keep the same names for ever. I have known a man a staunch *Whig* for a year together, yet thought and called a *Tory* by all the *Whigs*, and by the *Tories* themselves. I have known him afterwards fall in with the *Whigs*, and act another year like a *Tory*; that is, do blindly what he was bid, and serve the interest of power, right or wrong: and then all the *Tories* have agreed to call him a *Whig*; whereas all the while he was called a *Tory*, he was a *Whig*: Afterwards, by joining with the *Whigs*, he became an apostate from *Whiggism*, and turned *Tory*.

So wildly do men run on to confound names and things: we call men opprobriously *Tories*, for practising the best part of *Whiggism*; and honourably christen ourselves *Whigs*, when we are openly acting the vilest parts of *Toryism*, such parts as the *Tories* never attempted to act.

To know fully the signification of words, we must go to their source. The original principle of a *Tory* was, to let the crown do what it pleased; yet no people opposed and restrained the crown more, when they themselves did not serve and direct the crown. The original principle of a *Whig* was, to be no farther for the interest of the crown, than the crown was for the interest of the people.—A principle founded upon everlasting reason, and which the *Tories* have come into as often as temptations were taken out of their way; and a principle which the *Whigs*, whenever they have had temptations, have as vilely renounced in practice. No men upon earth have been more servile, crouching, and abandoned creatures of power, than the *Whigs* sometimes have been; I mean some former *Whigs*.

The *Tories* therefore are often *Whigs* without knowing it; and the *Whigs* are *Tories* without owning it. To prove this, it is enough to reflect upon times and instances, when the asserting of liberty, the legal and undoubted liberties of *England*, has been called *libelling* by those professed patrons of liberty, the *Whigs*; and they have taken extravagant, arbitrary and violent methods to suppress the very sound of it; whilst the *Tories* have maintained and defended it, and put checks upon those, who, though they had risen by its name, were eager to suppress the spirit, and had appointed for that worthy end an inquisition, new to the constitution, and threatening its overthrow: an inquisition, where men were used as criminals without a crime, charged with crimes without a name, and treated in some respects as if they had been guilty of the highest.

Parties like or dislike our constitution, just as they are out of power, or in it: those who are out of power like it, because it gives them the best protection against those who are in power; and those who have been in power have blamed it, for not giving them power enough to oppress all whom they would oppress. No power cares to be restrained, or to have its hands tied up, though it would tie up all hands but its own....

The very name of *France* used to be an abomination to the *Whigs*: they hated the country for the sake of its government; and were eternally upbraiding the *Tories* with a fondness for that government. Who would have expected, after all this, that ever the *Whigs*, or any of them, could have spoken with patience, much less with approbation, of the *French* government? Any the least hint of this kind was shameful and unpardonable in a *Whig*. But there are *Whigs*, who, not content to shew their dislike and resentment of every thing said or done in behalf of liberty, and the *English* constitution, have boldly told people how such things would be rewarded in *France*: that is to say, the government of *France* is defended by galleys, wheels, racks, and dragoons, and we want the same methods here; for, if they dislike such methods, how come they to mention them? If men commit crimes against the *English* government, there are *English* laws to punish them; but if they be guilty of no crime against the laws of *England*, why are they thought worthy of the arbitrary punishments of *France*, unless those who think that they are, thirst after the arbitrary power of *France*? Or, if they mean not thus, why do they talk thus; and, in shewing rage without provocation, scatter words without a meaning? I know no sort of *Englishmen* worthy of *French* chains, and *French* cruelty, but such apostate *Englishmen* as wish for the power and opportunity of inflicting them upon their countrymen, and of governing those by terrors and tortures, who despise weak capacities, and detest vile measures.

And have *Whigs* at last the face to tell us how they rule in *France*? Here is an instance of *Toryism* which every modern *Tory*, of any sense, disclaims and abhors; and which some modern *Whigs* have modestly avowed, and are therefore become old *Tories*. Thus do parties chop and change. One party, by railing with great justice at another, gets into its place; and loses it as justly, by doing the very things against which it railed.

By these means, and by thus acting every one of them contrary to their professions, all parties play the game into one another's hands, though far from intending it; and no party has ever yet found their account in it, whatever their leaders may have done: for the most part, a revolution of five or six years subjects them to oppressions of their own inventing. Others get into their seat, and turn their own hard measures upon them; nor can they complain, with a good grace, that they suffer those evils which they have made others to suffer; and their own conduct having been as bad as that of which they complain, they have not sufficient reputation to oppose the progress of publick mischief and miscarriages, which perhaps they began.

It is therefore high time for all parties to consider what is best for the whole; and to establish such rules of commutative justice and indulgence, as may prevent oppression from any party. And this can only be done by restraining the hands of power, and fixing it within certain bounds as to its limits and expence. Under every power that is exorbitant, millions must suffer to aggrandize a few; and men must be strangely partial to themselves and their own expectations, if, in the almost eternal changes and revolutions of ministries, they can hope to continue long to be any part of those few.

13 John Trenchard and Thomas Gordon: Cato's Letters (1723)

[*The London Journal*, 15 June 1723.   Letter no. 133 by John Trenchard]

Of charity, and charity-schools

. . . . to apply myself more directly to the Charity-Schools, I shall endeavour to show, that under the false pretence and affectation of charity, they destroy real charity, take away the usual support and provision from the children of lesser tradesmen, and often from those of decayed and unfortunate merchants and gentlemen, and pervert the benevolence, which would be otherwise bestowed upon helpless widows, and poor house-keepers, who cannot by reason of their poverty, maintain their families.

Every country can maintain but a certain number of shopkeepers, or retailers of commodities, which are raised or manufactured by others; and the fewer they are, the better; because they add nothing to the publick wealth; but only disperse and accommodate it to the convenience of artificers, manufacturers and husbandmen, or such who live upon their estates and professions; and serve the publick only by directing and governing the rest; but as there must be many retailers of other men's industry, and the greatest part of them will be but just able to support themselves, and with great pains, frugality, and difficulty, breed up their families, and be able to spare small sums out of their little substance to teach their children to write and cast accompt, and to put them out apprentices to those of their own degree; so those employments ought to fall to the share of such only; but now are mostly anticipated, and engrossed by the managers of the Charity-Schools; who, out of other people's pockets, give greater sums than the other can afford, only to take the lowest dregs of the people from the plough and labour, to make them tradesmen, and by consequence drive the children of tradesmen to the plough, to beg, to rob, or to starve.

The same may be said of servants, who are generally the children of the lesser shop-keepers, though sometimes of decayed merchants and gentlemen, who have given them an education above the lower rank of people, which has qualified them to earn a comfortable subsistence this way, without much labour, to which they have never been used. Now, I have often heard, that one advantage proposed by these charity-schools, is to breed up children to reading and writing, and a sober behaviour, that they may be qualified to be servants: a sort of idle and rioting vermin, by which the kingdom is already almost devoured, who are become every where a publick nuisance, and multitudes of them daily, for want of employment, betake themselves to the highway and housebreaking, others robbing and sharping, or to the stews; and must do so, if we study new methods to encrease their numbers. . . .

Oh! but say some pious, and many more impious and hypocritical people, What would you hinder poor boys and girls from being well cloathed, from serving God, and being bred scholars? I answer, that there are few instances in which the publick has suffered more, than in breeding up beggars to be what are called scholars, from the grave pedant and the solemn doctor, down to the humble writer and caster of accompts; to attain which characters, does not require the pains and acuteness that are necessary to make a good cobler; yet they immediately fancy themselves to be another rank of mankind, think that they are to be maintained in idleness, and out of the substance of others, for their fancied accomplishments; are above day-labour, and by an idle education, require a listlessness to it; and when they cannot find the sort of subsistence which they aspire to, are always perplexing the world, and disturbing other people. So that no education ought to be more discountenanced by a state, than putting chimera's and airy notions into the heads of those who ought to have pickaxes in their hands; than teaching people to read, write, and cast accompt, who, if they were employed as they ought to be, can have no occasion to make use of these requirements, unless it be now and then to read the Bible, which they seldom or never do: besides, they are told by their spiritual guides, that they must not understand it.

What benefit can accrue to the publick by taking the dregs of the people out of the kennels, and throwing their betters into them? By lessening the numbers of day-labourers, by whose industry alone, nations are supported, and the publick wealth encreased? By multiplying the number of such who add nothing to it, but must live out of the property of the rest? By taking boys and girls from the low and necessary employments of life, making them impatient of the condition which they were born to, and in which they would have thought themselves happy, to be sempstresses, footmen, and servant maids, and to teach them to read ballads? How much more useful a charity would it be, to give the same sums to their parents to help them to raise their families, and breed up their children to spinning or hard-labour; to help them to maintain themselves, and to depend for the future upon their own hands for subsistence? Whereas, this sort of charity is of no use, benefit, or ease to their parents, who must find them meat, drink, washing, and some clothes, during the whole time which they spend at school, and lose, at the same time, the little that they can otherwise earn, or what they would earn themselves, whilst they employed their children in going on errands, and doing little offices, which they can do as well: and all this for the pleasure of seeing them a little better cloathed, hearing them sing psalms, and repeating by rote a catechism made for that purpose. . . .

14 Jonathan Swift:
Gulliver's Travels (1726)

Part II. A Voyage to Brobdingnag   Chapter 6

... I began my discourse by informing his Majesty that our dominions consisted of two islands, which composed three mighty kingdoms under one sovereign, besides our plantations in America. I dwelt long upon the fertility of our soil, and the temperature of our climate. I then spoke at large upon the constitution of an English Parliament, partly made up of an illustrious body called the House of Peers, persons of the noblest blood, and of the most ancient and ample patrimonies. I described that extraordinary care always taken of their education in arts and arms, to qualify them for being counsellors born to the King and kingdom, to have a share in the legislature, to be members of the highest court of judicature from whence there could be no appeal; and to be champions always ready for the defence of their prince and country by their valour, conduct and fidelity. That these were the ornament and bulwark of the kingdom, worthy followers of their most renowned ancestors whose honour had been the reward of their virtue, from which their posterity were never once known to degenerate. To these were joined several holy persons, as part of that assembly, under the title of Bishops, whose peculiar business it is, to take care of religion, and of those who instruct the people therein. These were searched and sought out through the whole nation, by the Prince and his wisest counsellors, among such of the priesthood, as were most deservedly distinguished by the sanctity of their lives, and the depth of their erudition; who were indeed the spiritual fathers of the clergy and the people.

That the other part of the Parliament consisted of an assembly called the House of Commons, who were all principal gentlemen, *freely* picked and culled out by the people themselves, for their great abilities, and love of their country, to represent the wisdom of the whole nation. And these two bodies make up the most august assembly in Europe, to whom, in conjunction with the Prince, the whole legislature is committed.

I then descended to the Courts of Justice, over which the Judges, those venerable sages and interpreters of the law, presided, for determining the disputed rights and properties of men, as well as for the punishment of vice, and protection of innocence. I mentioned the prudent management of our Treasury, the valour and achievements of our forces by sea and land. I computed the number of our people, by reckoning how many millions there might be of each religious sect, or political party among us. I did not omit even our sports and pastimes, or any other particular which I thought might redound to the honour of my country. And, I finished all with a brief historical account of affairs and events in England for about an hundred years past.

This conversation was not ended under five audiences, each of several hours, and the King heard the whole with great attention, frequently taking notes of what I spoke, as well as memorandums of what questions he intended to ask me.

When I had put an end to these long discourses, his Majesty in a sixth audience, consulting his notes, proposed many doubts, queries, and objections, upon every article. He asked, what methods were used to cultivate the minds and bodies of our young nobility, and in what kind of business they commonly spent the first and teachable part of their lives. What course was taken to supply that assembly when any noble family became extinct. What qualifications were necessary in those who are to be created new Lords: whether the humour of the Prince, a sum of money to a Court lady, or a Prime Minister, or a design of strengthening a party opposite to the public interest, ever happened to be motives in those advancements. What share of knowledge these Lords had in the laws of their country, and how they came by it, so as to enable them to decide the properties of their fellow-subjects in the last resort. Whether they were always so free from avarice, partialities, or want, that a bribe, or some other sinister view, could have no place among them. Whether those holy Lords I spoke of were constantly promoted to that rank upon account of their knowledge in religious matters, and the sanctity of their lives; had never been compliers with the times while they were common priests or slavish prostitute chaplains to some nobleman, whose opinions they continued servilely to follow after they were admitted into that assembly.

He then desired to know what arts were practised in electing those whom I called Commoners. Whether, a stranger with a strong purse might not influence the vulgar voters to choose him before their own landlord, or the most considerable gentleman in the neighbourhood. How it came to pass, that people were so violently bent upon getting into this assembly, which I allowed to be a great trouble and expense, often to the ruin of their families, without any salary or pension: because this appeared such an exalted strain of virtue and public spirit, that his Majesty seemed to doubt it might possibly not be always sincere: and he desired to know whether such zealous gentlemen could have any views of refunding themselves for the charges and trouble they were at, by sacrificing the public good to the designs of a weak and vicious prince in conjunction with a corrupted ministry. He multiplied his questions, and sifted me thoroughly upon every part of this head, proposing numberless enquiries and objections, which I think it not prudent or convenient to repeat. . . .

He fell next upon the management of our Treasury; and said, he thought my memory had failed me, because I computed our taxes at about five or six millions a year, and when I came to mention the issues, he found they sometimes amounted to more than double; for, the notes he had taken were very particular in this point, because he hoped, as he told me, that the knowledge of our conduct might be useful to him, and he could not be deceived in his calculations. But, if what I told him were true, he was still at a loss how a king-

dom could run out of its estates like a private person. He asked
me, who were our creditors? and, where we found money to
pay them? He wondered to hear me talk of such chargeable
and extensive wars; that, certainly we must be a quarrelsome
people, or live among very bad neighbours, and that our
generals must needs be richer than our kings. He asked what
business we had out of our own islands, unless upon the score
of trade or treaty, or to defend the coasts with our fleet. Above
all, he was amazed to hear me talk of a mercenary standing
army in the midst of peace, and among a free people. He said,
if we were governed by our own consent in the persons of our
representatives, he could not imagine of whom we were afraid,
or against whom we were to fight, and would hear my opinion,
whether a private man's house not better be defended by himself, his children, and family, than by half-a-dozen rascals
picked up at a venture in the streets, for small wages, who
might get an hundred times more by cutting their throats. . . .

His Majesty in another audience was at the pains to recapi-
tulate the sum of all I had spoken, compared the questions he
made with the answers I had given; then taking me into his
hands, and stroking me gently, delivered himself in these words,
which I shall never forget, nor the manner he spoke them in.
My little friend Grildig; you have made a most admirable
panegyric upon your country. You have clearly proved that
ignorance, idleness, and vice are the proper ingredients for
qualifying a legislator. That laws are best explained, inter-
preted, and applied by those whose interest and abilities lie
in perverting, confounding, and eluding them. I observe
among you some lines of an institution, which in its original
might have been tolerable, but these half erased, and the rest
wholly blurred and blotted by corruptions. It doth not appear
from all you have said, how any one perfection is required towards the procurement of any one station among you, much
less that men are ennobled on account of their virtue, that
priests are advanced for their piety or learning, soldiers for
their conduct or valour, judges for their integrity, senators for
the love of their country, or counsellors for their wisdom. As
for yourself (continued the King) who have spent the greatest
part of your life in travelling, I am well disposed to hope you

may hitherto have escaped many vices of your country. But, by what I have gathered from your own relation, and the answers I have with much pains wringed and extorted from you, I cannot but conclude the bulk of your natures, to be the most pernicious race of little odious vermin that Nature ever suffered to crawl upon the surface of the earth.

15 Robin will be out at last (1727)
(Anonymous)

[A street ballad from *Political Ballads illustrating the Administration of Sir Robert Walpole*, ed. Milton Percival (Oxford 1916), pp. 15–16. One of the many attacks on the corrupt practices of Robert 'Robin' Walpole. His opponents hoped Walpole would be dismissed on the death of George I, but George II confirmed him in all his places.]

Good People draw near
And a Tale you shall hear,
A Story concerning one *Robin*,
Who, from not worth a Groat,
A vast Fortune has got,
By Politicks, Bubbles, and Jobbing.
     Fa, la.

But a few Years ago,
As we very well know,
He scarce had a Guinea his Fob in;
But by bribing of Friends,
To serve his dark Ends,
Now worth a full Million is *Robin*.

That his Bags he might fill,
He brought in a Bill,
Intitled, *An Act against Mobbing*;
But 'twas only a Law
To keep us in Awe,
From rising in Arms against *Robin*.

Each Post he hath fill'd
With Wretches unskill'd,
In all other Arts except Fobbing;

72

For no Man of Sense
Would ever commence
Such prostitute Creatures of *Robin*.

By the same worthy Means
We have B[ishop]s and D[ean]s
As dull as blind *Bayard* or *Dobbing*,
That both Church and State
Draw near to their Date
By the excellent Measures of *Robin*.

What a Stir hath he made
About Commerce and Trade,
About *China*-ware, Lace and Bobbing,
But it's very well known,
That all this was done,
To skreen other Projects of *Robin*.

How oft hath he swore,
That he'd save *Gibraltore*,
With a Face full as grave as Judge *Probyn*,
Yet still, like the Church,
It is left in the Lurch
By the Treaties and Juggles of *Robin*.

As oft hath he said,
That our Debts should be paid,
And the Nation be eas'd of her Throbbing;
Yet on tick we still run,
For the true Sinking Fund
Is the bottomless Pocket of *Robin*.

Then at length would you be
From such foul Usage free,
From Armies, hard Taxes and Jobbing,
You must join Heart and Hand,
And by each other stand,
To pull down the Plunderer *Robin*.

Come then let a full Glass
Round to King and Queen pass,
Who will ease our disconsolate Sobbing,
For if rightly I ween,
Such a good King and Queen,
Will give no Protection to *Robin*.

16 John Gay:
The Squire and his Cur (1732)
To a Country Gentleman

[From Gay's *Fables*, 2nd Series, Fable VI. Written about 1732, but published posthumously in 1738]

The man of pure and simple heart
Through life disdains a double part.
He never needs the screen of lies
His inward bosom to disguise.
In vain malicious tongues assail;
Let envy snarl, let slander rail,
From virtue's shield (secure from wound)
Their blunted, venomed shafts rebound.
So shines his light before mankind,
His actions prove his honest mind.
If in his country's cause he rise,
Debating senates to advise,
Unbribed, unawed, he dares impart
The honest dictates of his heart.
No ministerial frown he fears,
But in his virtue perseveres.

    But would you play the politician,
Whose heart's averse to intuition,
Your lips at all times, nay, your reason
Must be controlled by place and season.
What statesman could his power support
Were lying tongues forbid the court?
Did princely ears to truth attend,
What ministers could gain his end?
How could he raise his tools to place,
And how his honest foes disgrace?

That politician tops his part,
Who readily can lie with art:
The man's proficient in his trade;
His power is strong, his fortune's made.
By that the interest of the throne
Is made subservient to his own:
By that have kings of old, deluded,
All their own friends for his excluded.
By that, his selfish schemes pursuing,
He thrives upon the public ruin.

. . . .

17 Alexander Pope:
Epistle to Bathurst (1733)
Of the Use of Riches

[Lines 65–78, 135–52, 203–18, 375–402]

. . .
    Once, we confess, beneath the Patriot's cloak,
From the crack'd bag the dropping Guinea spoke,
And gingling down the back-stairs, told the crew,
'Old Cato is as great a Rogue as you.'
Blest paper-credit! last and best supply!
That lends Corruption lighter wings to fly!
Gold imp'd by thee, can compass hardest things,
Can pocket States, can fetch or carry Kings;
A single leaf shall waft an Army o'er,
Or ship off Senates to a distant Shore;
A leaf, like Sibyl's, scatter to and fro
Our fates and fortunes, as the wind shall blow:
Pregnant with thousands flits the Scrap unseen,
And silent sells a King, or buys a Queen.
. . .
    Much injur'd Blunt! why bears he Britain's hate?
A wizard told him in these words our fate:
'At length Corruption, like a gen'ral flood,
(So long by watchful Ministers withstood)
Shall deluge all; and Av'rice creeping on,
Spread like a low-born mist, and blot the Sun;
Statesman and Patriot ply alike the stocks,
Peeress and Butler share alike the Box,
And Judges job, and Bishops bite the town,
And mighty Dukes pack cards for half a crown.
See Britain sunk in lucre's sordid charms,

And France reveng'd of ANNE's and EDWARD's arms!'
No mean Court-badge, great Scriv'ner! fir'd thy brain,
Nor lordly Luxury, nor City Gain:
No, 'twas thy righteous end, asham'd to see
Senates degen'rate, Patriots disagree,
And nobly wishing Party-rage to cease,
To buy both sides, and give thy Country peace.

. . .

What slaughter'd hecatombs, what floods of wine,
Fill the capacious Squire, and deep Divine!
Yet no mean motive this profusion draws,
His oxen perish in his country's cause;
'Tis GEORGE and LIBERTY that crowns the cup,
And Zeal for that great House that eats him up.
The woods recede around the naked seat,
The Sylvans groan—no matter—for the Fleet:
Next goes his Wool—to clothe our valiant bands,
Last, for his Country's love, he sells his Lands.
To town he comes, completes the nation's hope,
And heads the bold Train-bands, and burns a Pope.
And shall not Britain now reward his toils,
Britain, that pays her Patriots with her Spoils?
In vain at Court the Bankrupt pleads his cause,
His thankless Country leaves him to her Laws.

. . .

Behold Sir Balaam, now a man of spirit,
Ascribes his gettings to his parts and merit,
What late he call'd a Blessing, now was Wit,
And God's good Providence, a lucky Hit.
Things change their titles, as our manners turn:
His Compting-house employ'd the Sunday morn;
Seldom at Church ('twas such a busy life)
But duly sent his family and wife.
There (so the Dev'l ordain'd one Christmas-tide)
My good old Lady catch'd a cold, and dy'd.
A Nymph of Quality admires our Knight;
He marries, bows at Court, and grows polite:
Leaves the dull Cits, and joins (to please the fair)
The well-bred cuckolds in St. James's air:

First, for his Son a gay Commission buys,
Who drinks, whores, fights, and in a duel dies:
His daughter flaunts a Viscount's tawdry wife;
She bears a Coronet and P–x for life.
In Britain's Senate he a seat obtains,
And one more Pensioner St. Stephen gains.
My Lady falls to play; so bad her chance,
He must repair it; takes a bribe from France;
The House impeach him; Coningsby harangues;
The Court forsake him, and Sir Balaam hangs.
Wife, son, and daughter, Satan, are thy own,
His wealth, yet dearer, forfeit to the Crown:
The Devil and the King divide the prize,
And sad Sir Balaam curses God and dies.

18   Henry St John, Viscount Bolingbroke: A Dissertation upon Parties (1733–4)

[*The Works of Lord Bolingbroke* (1967 ed.), ii, 115–19, 160, 163–8]

Letter XIII

Much hath been said occasionally, in the course of these letters, concerning the beauty and excellency of the British constitution. I shall make, however, no excuse for returning to the same subject, upon an occasion which introduces it so naturally, and, indeed, so necessarily. Nothing can be more apposite to the professed design of these writings; nothing of more real, and more present use. Let me speak plainly. We have been all of us, those of every side, and of every denomination, accustomed too long to value ourselves, foolishly or knavishly, on our zeal for this or that party, or for this or that government; and to make a merit of straining the constitution different ways, in order to serve the different purposes of each. It is high time we should all learn, if that be still possible, to value ourselves in the first place on our zeal for the constitution; to make all governments, and much more all parties bow to that, and to suffer that to bow to none. But how shall this constitution be known, unless we make it the subject of careful inquiry, and of frequent and sober reflection? . . . Sure I am that they must be worse than blind, if any such there are, who do not confess at this time, and under the present settlement, that our constitution is in the strictest sense a bargain, a conditional contract between the prince and the people, as it always hath been, and still is, between the representative and collective bodies of the nation.

That this bargain may not be broken, on the part of the

80

prince with the people, (though the executive power be trusted to the prince, to be exercised according to such rules, and by the ministry of such officers as are prescribed by the laws and customs of this kingdom,) the legislative, or supreme power, is vested by our constitution in three estates, whereof the king is one. Whilst the members of the other two preserve their private independency, and those estates are consequently under no dependency, except that which is in the scheme of our constitution, this control on the first will always be sufficient; and a bad king, let him be as bold as he may please to be thought, must stand in awe of an honest parliament.

That this bargain may not be broken, on the part of the representative body, with the collective body of the nation, it is not only a principal, declared right of the people of Britain, that the election of members to sit in parliament shall be free, but it hath been a principal part of the care and attention of parliaments, for more than three hundred years, to watch over this freedom, and to secure it, by removing all influence of the crown, and all other corrupt influence, from these elections. This care and this attention have gone still farther. They have provided, as far as they have been suffered to provide hitherto, by the constitutional dependency of one house on the other, and of both on the crown, that all such influence should be removed from the members after they are chosen. Even here the providence of our constitution hath not stopped. Lest all other provisions should be ineffectual to keep the members of the house of commons out of this unconstitutional dependency, which some men presume, with a silly dogmatical air of triumph, to suppose necessary to support the constitutional independency of the crown, the wisdom of our constitution hath thought fit that the representatives of the people should not have time to forget that they are such; that they are empowered to act for the people, not against them. In a word, our constitution means, that the members of this body should be kept, as it were, to their good behavior, by the frequent returns of new elections. It does all that a constitution can do, all that can be done by legal provisions, to secure the interests of the people, by maintaining the integrity of their trustees: and lest all this should fail, it gives frequent opportunities to the people to secure their interests themselves, by mending their choice of their trustees; so that as a bad king must stand in awe of an honest parliament, a corrupt house of commons must stand in awe of an honest people.

Between these two estates, or branches of the legislative power, there stands a third, the house of peers; which may seem in theory, perhaps, too much under the influence of the crown, to be a proper control upon it, because the sole right of creating peers resides in the crown; whereas the crown hath no right to intermeddle in the electing commoners. This would be the case, and an intolerable one indeed, if the crown should exercise this right often, as it hath been exercised sometimes with universal and most just disapprobation. It is possible too, that this may come to be the case, in some future age, by the method of electing peers to sit in parliament, for one part of the same kingdom, by the frequent translations of bishops, and by other means, if the wisdom and virtue of the present age, and the favorable opportunity of the present auspicious and indulgent reign do not prevent it. But in all other respects, the persons who are once created peers, and their posterity, according to the scheme of the constitution, having a right to sit and debate, and vote in the house of peers, which cannot be taken from them, except by forfeiture; all influence of the kind I have mentioned seems to be again removed, and their share in the government depending neither on the king nor the people, they constitute a middle order, and are properly mediators between the other two, in the eyes of our constitution.

It is by this mixture of monarchical, aristocratical and democratical power, blended together in one system, and by these three estates balancing one another, that our free constitution of government hath been preserved so long inviolate, or hath been brought back, after having suffered violations, to its original principles, and been renewed, and improved too, by frequent and salutary revolutions. It is by this that weak and wicked princes have been opposed, restrained, reformed, and punished by parliaments; that the real, and perhaps the doubtful, exorbitances of parliaments have been reduced by the crown, and that the heat of one house hath been moderated, or the spirit raised, by the proceedings of the other. Parliaments have had a good effect on the people, by keeping them quiet; and the people on parliaments, by keeping them within bounds, which they were tempted to transgress. A just confidence in the safe, regular, parliamentary methods of redressing grievances hath often made the freest, and not the most patient people on earth, bear the greatest grievances much longer than people held under stronger restraints, and more used to oppression, who had not the same confidence, nor the same expectation, have borne even less. The cries of the people, and the terror of approaching elections, have defeated the most dangerous projects for beggaring and enslaving the nation; and the majority without doors hath obliged the majority within doors, to truckle to the minority. In a word two things may be said with truth of our constitution, which I think neither can, nor ever could be said of any other. It secures society against the miseries which are inseparable from simple forms of government, and is liable as little as possible to the inconveniences that arise in mixed forms. It cannot become uneasy to the prince, or people, unless the former be egregiously weak or wicked; nor be destroyed, unless the latter be excessively and universally corrupt. . . .

Letter XIX

As the means then of influencing by prerogative, and of governing by force, were considered to be increased formerly [before 1688], upon every increase of power to the crown, so are the means of influencing by money, and of governing by corruption, to be considered as increased now, upon that increase of power which hath accrued to the crown by the new constitution of the revenue since the revolution. Nay farther. Not only the means of corruption are increased, on the part of the crown, but the facility of employing these means with success is increased, on the part of the people, on the part of the electors, and of the elected. Nay, farther still. These means and this facility are not only increased, but the power of the crown to corrupt, as I have hinted already, and the proneness of the people to be corrupted, must continue to increase on the same principles, unless a stop be put to the growing wealth and power of one, and the growing depravity of the other. We are, to be sure, in no danger from any advantage his majesty will take of this situation; but if advantage be not taken in favor of our constitution, of the present most happy reign, of the mild and beneficent temper of our heroical monarch, of the generous principle, instilled by nature, and improved by philosophy, of his royal consort, it may be supposed, for we speak hypothetically all along, as the reader will please to remember, even where the precaution is not used; it may be supposed, I say, that pretended friends to the government, and real enemies to this constitution, no matter whether they are such by principle, or become such by their crimes, will get into superior power, in some future time, and under some weak or wicked prince: and whenever this happens, the subversion of our constitution, and of our liberty by consequence, will be the most easy enterprise imaginable; because nothing can be more easy than the creation of an anti-constitutional dependency of the two houses of parliament on the crown will be in that case; and because such a dependency of the two houses is as real a subversion of our constitution as an absolute abolishment of parliaments would be. . . .

The increase and continuance of taxes acquire to the crown, by multiplying officers of the revenue, and by arming them with formidable powers against the rest of their fellow-subjects, a degree of power, the weight of which the inferior ranks of our people have long felt, and they most, who are most useful to the commonwealth, and which even the superior ranks may feel one time or other; for I presume it would not be difficult to show how a full exercise of the powers that are in being, with, or even without some little additions to them, for the improvement of the revenue, that stale pretence for oppression, might oblige the greatest lord of the land to bow as low to a commissioner of customs, or excise, or to some subaltern harpy, as any nobleman or gentleman in France can be obliged to bow to the intendant of his province. But the establishment of public funds, on the credit of these taxes, hath been productive of more and greater mischiefs than the taxes themselves, not only by increasing the means of corruption, and the power of the crown, but by the effect it hath had on the spirit of the nation, on our manners, and our morals. It is impossible to look back, without grief, on the necessary and unavoidable consequences of this establishment; or without indignation on that mystery of iniquity, to which this establishment gave occasion, which hath been raised upon it, and carried on, for almost half a century, by means of it. It is impossible to look forward, without horror, on the consequences that may still follow. The ordinary expenses of our government are defrayed, in great measure, by anticipations and mortgages. In times of peace, in days of prosperity, as we boast them to be, we contract new debts, and we create new funds.—What must we do in war, and in national distress? What will happen, when we have mortgaged and funded all we have to mortgage and to fund; when we have mortgaged to new creditors that sinking fund which was mortgaged to other creditors not yet paid off; when we have mortgaged all the product of our land, and even our land itself? Who can answer, that when we come to such extremities, or have them more nearly in prospect, ten millions of people will bear any longer to be hewers of wood, and drawers of water, to maintain the two hundredth part of that number at ease, and in plenty? Who can answer, that the whole body of the people will suffer themselves to be treated, in favor of a handful of men, (for they who monopolise the whole power, and may in time monopolise the whole property of the funds, are indeed but a handful,) who can answer, that the whole body of the people will suffer themselves to be treated, in favour of such a handful . . . [and] to toil and starve for the proprietors of the several funds? Who can answer, that a scheme, which oppresses the farmer, ruins the manufacturer, breaks the merchant, discourages industry, and reduces fraud into a system; which beggars so often the fair adventurer and innocent proprietor; which drains continually a portion of our national wealth away to foreigners, and draws most perniciously the rest of that immense property that was diffused among thousands, into the pockets of a few; who can answer, that such a scheme will be always endured? . . .

Now this, I suppose, hath need of no proof, and of little

explanation; for, first, the whole art of stockjobbing, the whole mystery of iniquity mentioned above, arises from this establishment, and is employed about the funds; and, secondly, the main springs that turn, or may turn, the artificial wheel of credit, and make the paper estates that are fastened to it, rise or fall, lurk behind the veil of the treasury. From hence it follows, that if this office should be ever unrighteously administered, if there should ever be at the head of it one of those veteran sharpers, who hath learned by experience how to improve the folly, and aggravate the misfortunes of his fellow subjects, of the innocent, of the poor, of the widow, and of the orphan, to his own, or any other private advantage, it follows, I say, that he must have it in his power, and there can be no doubt of his will, to employ two methods of corruption, without any incumbrance to the civil list. Such a ministerial jobber may employ the opportunities of gaining on the funds, that he can frequently create, by a thousand various artifices, (notwithstanding the excellent provisions that have been lately made against the infamous practice of stockjobbing, by the wisdom of the legislature,[1] and which we promise ourselves will be still improved,) and he may apply the gains that are thus made, to corruption, in aid of the civil list. He may corrupt men with their own spoils, and bribe even those whom he reduced by his clandestine practices to that penury which could alone make them capable of being bribed; or, when he hath to do with men of another character, (for no rank alone will be sufficient to raise them, in such an age, above the most direct and prostitute corruption,) he may bribe them by a whisper, initiate them into his mystery to gain them, and then secure them by a participation of the same fraud and the same profit. . . .

If then a spirit of rapine and venality, of fraud and corruption, continue to diffuse themselves, not only luxury and avarice, but every kind of immorality will follow; . . . Britain will then be in that very condition in which, and in which alone, her constitution, and her liberty by consequence, may

[1] Sir John Barnard, an Opposition spokesman, tried to prevent 'the infamous practice of stockjobbing'. His bill was rejected in 1733, but passed in 1734.

be destroyed; because the people may, in a state of universal corruption, and will in no other, either suffer others to betray them, or betray themselves. How near a progress we have made towards this state, I determine not. This I say; it is time for every man, who is desirous to preserve the British constitution, and to preserve it secure, to contribute all he can to prevent the ill effects of that new influence and power which have gained strength in every reign since the revolution; of those means of corruption that may be employed, one time or other, on the part of the crown, and of that proneness to corruption on the part of the people, that hath been long growing, and still grows. . . . The friends of our constitution, therefore, are in the right to join issue upon this point with the enemies of it, and to fix upon this principal and real distinction and difference, the present division of parties; since parties we must have; and since those which subsisted formerly are quite extinguished, notwithstanding all the wicked endeavors of some men, who can have no merit but party-merit, nor safety but in faction, to revive them. If there was merit, and surely there was great merit, in opposing the asserters of prerogative formerly, when it rose so high as to endanger our liberty, there is great merit in opposing the asserters of corruption now, and in exposing the means by which this expedient may be improved to the ruin of our constitution, and therefore of our liberty. Nay, the merit is greater in some respects, if corruption be in itself, in its own nature, and in the present circumstances of the nation, and dispositions of the people, more dangerous than prerogative ever was; and if the means of establishing a government of arbitrary will, by corruption, be more likely to prove effectual than those of doing it by prerogative ever were. That it should ever become harder to save our country from the effects of corruption, than it was to defeat the efforts of prerogative, God forbid. On the whole matter, a dissertation upon parties could not wind itself up more properly, we think, than by showing that the British constitution of government deserves, above all others, the constant attention, and care to maintain it, of the people who are so happy as to live under it; that it may be weakened for want of attention, which is a degree of danger; but that it cannot be destroyed, unless the peers and the commons, that is, the whole body of the people, unite to destroy it, which is a degree of madness, and such a monstrous iniquity, as nothing but confirmed and universal corruption can produce; that since the time, when all our dangers from prerogative ceased, new dangers to this constitution, more silent and less observed, are arisen; and, finally, that as nothing can be more ridiculous than to preserve the nominal division of whig and tory parties, which subsisted before the revolution, when the difference of principles, that could alone make the distinction real, exists no longer; so nothing can be more reasonable than to admit the nominal division of constitutionists and anti-constitutionists, or of a court and country-party, at this time, when an avowed difference of principles makes this distinction real. That this distinction is real cannot be denied, as long as there are men amongst us, who argue for, and who promote even a corrupt dependency of the members of the two houses of parliament on the crown; and others who maintain that such a dependency of the members takes away the constitutional independency of the two houses, and that this independency lost, our constitution is a dead letter, and we shall be only in a worse condition by preserving the forms of it.

To reduce therefore our present parties to this single division, our present disputes to this single contest, and to fix our principal attention on this object of danger, too long and too much neglected, hath been and is the sole design of these discourses. . . .

19 Henry Fielding: Don Quixote in England (1734)

[In the early 1730s Fielding wrote several plays criticising the corruption of the times. Walpole's response was to censor the London stage by the Theatre Licensing Act of 1737.]

Act I. Scene VIII
Mr. Mayor and a Voter

Mayor Well, neighbour, what's your opinion of this strange man that is come to town, Don Quixote, as he calls himself?

Voter Think! why, that he's a madman. What shou'd I think?

Mayor 'Ecod! it runs in my head that he is come to stand for parliament-man.

Voter How can that be, neighbour, they tell me he's a Spaniard?

Mayor What's that to us! let him look to his qualifications when we have chose him. If he can't sit in the house that's his fault.

Voter Nay, nay, he can't be chose if he should stand; for, to my certain knowledge, the corporation have promis'd Sir Thomas Loveland and Mr. Bouncer.

Mayor Pugh! all promises are conditional; and let me tell you, Mr. Retail, I begin to smoke a plot. I begin to apprehend no opposition, and then we're sold, neighbour.

Voter No, no, neighbour; then we shall not be sold, and that's worse: but rather than it should come to that, I would ride all over the kingdom for a candidate; and if I thought Sir Thomas intended to steal us in this manner, he should have no vote of mine, I assure you. I shall vote for no man who holds the corporation cheap.

Mayor Then suppose we were to go in a body, and solicit Sir Don Quixote to stand? as for his being mad, while he's out of Bedlam it does not signify.

Voter But there is another objection, neighbour, which I am afraid the corporation will never get over.

Mayor What's that, prithee?

Voter They say he has brought no money with him.

Mayor Ay, that indeed: but tho' he hath no money with him here, I am assur'd by his servant that he hath a very large estate: and so, if the other party come down handsomly with the ready, we may trust him; for you know, at last, we have nothing to do but to choose him, and then we may recover all he owes us.

Voter I do not care to be sold, neighbour.

Mayor Nor I neither, neighbour, by any but myself. I think that is the privilege of a free Briton.

Scene IX
Guzzle, Mayor, Retail

Guzzle Mr. Mayor, a good morrow to you, Sir; are you for a whet, this morning?

Mayor With all my heart; but what's become of the gentleman, the traveller?

Guzzle He's laid down to sleep, I believe pretty well tired with work. What the devil to do with him, I can't tell.

Mayor My neighbour and I have a strange thought come into our heads; you know Mr. Guzzle, we are like to have no opposition, and that I believe you will feel the want of, as much as any man. Now d'ye see, we have taken it into consideration, whether we should not ask this Sir Don to represent us.

Guzzle With all my heart; if either of you will hang out a sign and entertain him; but he is far enough in my books already.

Mayor You are too cautious, master Guzzle; I make no doubt but he is some very rich man, who pretends to be poor in order to get his election the cheaper; he can have no other design in staying among us. For my part, I make no doubt but that he is come to stand on the court interest.

Guzzle Nay, nay, if he stands at all, it is on the court side, no doubt; for he talks of nothing but kings, and princes, and princesses, and emperors, and empresses.

Mayor Ay, ay, an officer in the army too, I warrant him, if we knew but the bottom.

Guzzle He seems indeed to be damnably fond of free-quarter.

Retail But if you think he intends to offer himself, would it not be wiser to let him; for then, you know, if he spends never so much, we shall not be oblig'd to choose him.

Mayor Brother alderman, I have reproved you already for that way of reasoning; it savours too much of bribery. I like an opposition, because otherwise a man may be oblig'd to vote against his party; therefore when we invite a gentleman to stand, we invite him to spend his money for the honour of his party; and when both parties have spent as much as they are able, every honest man will vote according to his conscience.

Guzzle Mr. Mayor talks like a man of sense and honour, and it does me good to hear him.

Mayor Ay, ay, Mr. Guzzle, I never gave a vote contrary to my conscience. I have very earnestly recommended the country-interest to all my brethren: but before that, I recommended the town-interest, that is, the interest of this corporation; and first of all I recommended to every particular man to take a particular care of himself. And it is with a certain way of reasoning, that he that serves me best, will serve the town best; and he that serves the town best, will serve the country best.

Guzzle See what it is for to have been at Oxford, the parson in the parish himself can't out-talk him.

Mayor Come, landlord, we'll drink one bottle and drink success to the corporation: these times come but seldom, therefore we ought to make the best of them. Come along.

[Exeunt.]

20 William Arnall:
Opposition no Proof of Patriotism (1735)

[pp. 3–6, 11, 17–18, 20–4]

We have been long alarmed (I hope we are now tired) with terrible representations of men in power, their evil designs and mistakes, their corruptions at home, their blunders abroad; and publick liberty, which is now stronger than ever it was in any country or age, has been lamented as almost expiring. The ministers have been abused for every good action which they did or attempted, and even for bad actions which they neither attempted nor intended. . . .

It could not but raise our indignation to be told, that we were slaves, whilst we could not feel ourselves in possession of the highest liberty that ever people enjoyed. It could not but raise our laughter, to hear those ministers represented as fools and blunderers, who were continually defeating all the efforts of such as so represent them. It could not but move our contempt, to see the government decried as impotent and hobling by some, who, tho' very able men, could not in one instance shake or change that same weak government, which according to them was tumbling of itself. . . .

If the possession of place influences men, does not want of place influence them as much? But this truth, so glaringly evident, is never owned by those in whom it most evidently appears. Places, all places, as soon as they go out of them, become presently, in their style, dangerous, infectious, and even criminal. Yet the moment before, whilst they themselves were in place, they never once mentioned places in that style; nor do they ever confess, that when they were in place, their places had any undue influence upon *them*, tho' it is what they boldly charge upon all that remain in place, or come into *their* places. . . .

What follows then? Is all opposition to be discouraged and abolished? God forbid. Let oppression and oppressors, and every unjust administration be for ever opposed. But where the laws rule, where liberty flourishes, and where a legal administration prevails, *general opposition* ought to be out of countenance and cease. When under such a situation, the opposition continues constant and furious, all good, all calm and disinterested men will condemn it; even the vulgar will at last cease to mind it, and they who are the authors of it will make but an ill figure with posterity. . . .

Nothing is more commonly said, than that all parties are now united, and that there are no *Jacobites* amongst us. I doubt this is as little as the rest a proof of patriotism. If I were a *Jacobite* I should certainly promote this opinion, and labour to have it believed by those who are no *Jacobites*; since there cannot be a more artful or more certain expedient to make *Jacobitism* triumph, than to extinguish the fears of *Jacobitism*; for where there is no fear, there will be no precaution. . . .

Was liberty ever so largely and so equally diffused amongst all orders of men, in any country as 'tis here, and now? Was it ever so powerfully felt and prevailing in former reigns, or in any commonwealth past or present? Whence then can come its danger, if it has been continually increasing? . . . Such danger cannot arise from the nature of our constitution, the best framed of any upon earth to create and preserve liberty, unless it can be shown, that the balance of the legislature is broken, and one part master of the other; as when the parliament set aside the king, or when the king laid aside parliaments. These parts are now in perfect unison, the king in possession of the prerogative without stretching or abusing it, and every member free to vote as he pleases. It is not pretended that the parliament is too powerful for the crown; and I cannot see that the crown is too powerful for the parliament. . . .

Can government exist without places, and men to fill them? Or do men ever reason thus but in their anger? And do they ever once reason thus, when they and their friends are in place? . . .

Whoever is trusted with the publick protection, must be trusted with the power of protecting; and whatever hath power to govern and protect the whole; that is, whoever hath both the legislature and executive power, may certainly turn it to evil as well as to good, to oppress as well as to protect. Yet it doth not from hence follow, that it will always be so abused and perverted, otherwise all governments, everywhere, even the freest that exist or can be framed, would be as bad as the worst and most violent; since all governments have equal power, that is power unlimited, else they could not be called governments, which in order to subsist and answer the ends of society, must be absolute over the governed. But the security, or the want of security, liberty or slavery, arises from the manner of placing this power, equally supreme in all perfect governments. Our monarchy, and every part of the legislature, is limited; but the legislature entire is unlimited, and its power as ample and extensive as that of the Great *Turk*, over the lives, persons, and properties of men. The great difference is, that we have numerous representatives and legislators, who are themselves parties and sharers in whatever they wisely or weakly establish and ordain for the whole. This is the best and only caution men can have that their governors do not abuse and oppress them. . . .

21 James Thomson: Liberty (1734–6)

[Published in 1736. Lines 86–123, 304–25, 352–66]

Part V, The Prospect: The author addresses the Goddess of Liberty

. . . .
   'But how shall this thy mighty kingdom stand?
On what unyielding base? how finish'd shine?'
   At this her eye, collecting all its fire,
Beam'd more than human; and her awful voice,
Majestic thus she raised: 'To Britons bear
This closing strain, and with tenser note
Loud let it sound in their awaken'd ear:
   'On virtue can alone my kingdom stand,
On public virtue, every virtue join'd.
For, lost this social cement of mankind,
The greatest empires, by scarce-felt degrees,
Will moulder soft away; till, tottering loose,
They, prone at last, to total ruin rush.
Unbless'd by virtue, government a league
Becomes, a circling junto of the great,
To rob by law; religion mild, a yoke
To tame the stooping soul, a trick of state
To mask their rapine, and to share the prey.
What are, without it, senates; save a face
Of consultation deep and reason free,
While the determin'd voice and heart are sold?
What boasted freedom, save a sounding name?
And what election, but a market vile
Of slaves self-barter'd? Virtue! without thee,
There is no ruling eye, no nerve, in states;
War has no vigour, and no safety peace;

95

E'en justice warps to party, laws oppress,
Wide through the land their weak protection fails,
First broke the balance, and then scorn'd the sword.
Thus nations sink, society dissolves;
Rapine and guile and violence break loose,
Everting life, and turning love to gall;
Man hates the face of man, and Indian woods
And Libya's hissing sands to him are tame.

By those three virtues be the frame sustain'd
Of British freedom: independent life;
Integrity in office; and, o'er all
Supreme, a passion for the commonweal.

. . . .

'Should then the time arrive (which Heaven avert!)
That Britons bend unnerved, not by the force
Of arms, more generous and more manly, quell'd,
But by corruption's soul-dejecting arts,
Arts impudent! and gross! by their own gold,
In part bestow'd, to bribe them to give all.
With party raging, or immersed in sloth,
Should they Britannia's well-fought laurels yield
To slily conquering Gaul; e'en from her brow
Let her own naval oak be basely torn,
By such as tremble at the stiffening gale,
And nerveless sink while others sing rejoiced;
Or (darker prospect! scarce one gleam behind
Disclosing) should the broad corruptive plague
Breathe from the city to the furthest hut,
That sits serene within the forest shade;
The fever'd people fire, inflame their wants,
And their luxurious thirst, so gathering rage,
That, were a buyer found, they stand prepared
To sell their birthright for a cooling draught;
Should shameless pens for plain corruption plead,
The hired assassins of the commonweal!

. . .

'I paint the worst. But should these times arrive,
If any nobler passion yet remain,
Let all my sons all parties fling aside,

Despise their nonsense, and together join;
Let worth and virtue, scorning low despair,
Exerted full, from every quarter shine,
Commix'd in heighten'd blaze. Light flash'd to light,
Moral, or intellectual, more intense
By giving glows. As on pure winter's eve,
Gradual, the stars effulge; fainter, at first,
They, straggling, rise; but when the radiant host,
In thick profusion pour'd, shine out immense,
Each casting vivid influence on each,
From pole to pole a glittering deluge plays,
And worlds above rejoice, and men below.'

22 Samuel Johnson:
London: A Poem (1738)

[Lines 1–82, 91–8, 117–22, 132–51, 242–63]

Tho' Grief and Fondness in my Breast rebel,
When injur'd Thales bids the Town farewell,
Yet still my calmer Thoughts his Choice commend,
I praise the Hermit, but regret the Friend,
Resolv'd at length, from Vice and London far,
To breathe in distant Fields a purer Air,
And, fix'd on Cambria's solitary Shore,
Give to St David one *true Briton* more.

For who would leave, unbrib'd, *Hibernia*'s Land,
Or change the rocks of *Scotland* for the *Strand*?
There none are swept by sudden Fate away,
But all whom Hunger spares, with Age decay:
Here Malice, Rapine, Accident, conspire,
And now a Rabble rages, now a Fire;
Their Ambush here relentless Ruffians lay,
And here the fell Attorney prowls for Prey;
Here falling Houses thunder on your Head,
And here a female Atheist talks you dead.

While Thales waits the Wherry that contains
Of dissipated Wealth the small Remains,
On *Thames*'s Banks, in silent Thought we stood,
Where Greenwich smiles upon the silver Flood:
Struck with the Seat that gave Eliza birth,
We kneel, and kiss the consecrated Earth;

                 new,
   Pride shall hold?   view;
   ow'r and Gold?   Main,
   wn,   Dread of *Spain*,
   es your own.   e oppress'd,
   giv'n,   g Jest.
   h of Heav'n:
   ns for me,   nes bestow,
   ?   se of Woe.
   he sing,   mptuous Frown,
   ar,   ighb'ring Town.

               ese degen'rate Days
              ard of empty Praise;
              ote to Vice and Gain,
              e toils in vain;
              o double my Distress,
              es my Little less;
              teps no Staff sustains,
ngue   revels in my Veins;
g,   en, to find some happier Place,
              Sense are no Disgrace;
              k where verdant Osiers play,
              e with Nature's Paintings gay;
              arrass'd Briton found Repose,
              rty defy'd his Foes;
!   l, ye Pow'rs, indulgent give.
           e here, for — has learn'd to live.
         those reign, whom Pensions can incite
         a Patriot black, a Courtier white;
         n their Country's dear-bought Rights away.
         plead for Pirates in the Face of Day;
         slavish Tenets taint our poison'd Youth,
         lend a Lye the Confidence of Truth.

      et such raise Palaces, and Manors buy,
      Collect a Tax, or farm a Lottery,
      With warbling Eunuchs fill a licens'd Stage,
      And lull to Servitude a thoughtless Age.

Heroes, proceed! What Bounds your
What Check restrain your Thirst for
Behold rebellious Virtue quite o'erthro
Behold our Fame, our Wealth, our Liv
To such, a groaning Nation's spoils are
When publick Crimes inflame the Wrat
But what, my Friend, what Hope remai
Who start at Theft, and blush at Perjury
Who scarce forbear, tho' Britain's Court
To pluck a titled Poet's borrow'd Wing;
A Statesman's Logic, unconvinc'd can he
And dare to slumber o'er the *Gazetteer*;
Despise a Fool in half his Pension drest,
And strive in vain to laugh at Clodio's Jest

Others with softer Smile, and subtler Art,
Can sap the Principles, or taint the Heart;
With more Address a Lover's Note convey,
Or bribe a Virgin's Innocence away.
Well may they rise, while I, whose Rustic To
Ne'er knew to puzzle Right, or varnish Wron
Spurn'd as a Beggar, dreaded as a Spy,
Live unregarded, unlamented die.

. . .

The cheated Nation's happy Fav'rites, see!
Mark whom the Great caress, who frown on me
London! the needy Villain's gen'ral Home,
The Common Sewer of *Paris* and of *Rome*;
With eager Thirst, by Folly or by Fate,
Sucks in the Dregs of each corrupted State.
Forgive my Transports on a Theme like this,
I cannot bear a *French* Metropolis.

. . .

Ah! what avails it, that, from Slav'ry far,
I drew the Breath of Life in *English* Air;
Was early taught a *Briton*'s Right to prize,
And lisp the Tale of Henry's Victories;

If the gull'd Conqueror receives the Chain,
And Flattery prevails when Arms are vain?

. . .

Besides, with Justice, this discerning Age
Admires their wond'rous Talents for the Stage:
Well may they venture on the Mimic's Art,
Who play from Morn to Night a borrow'd Part;
Practis'd their Master's Notions to embrace,
Repeat his Maxims, and reflect his Face;
With ev'ry wild Absurdity comply,
And view each Object with another's Eye;
To shake with Laughter ere the Jest they hear,
To pour at Will the counterfeited Tear;
And as their Patron hints the Cold or Heat,
To shake in Dog-days, in *December* sweat.

How, when Competitors like these contend,
Can surly Virtue hope to fix a Friend?
Slaves that with serious Impudence beguile,
And lye without a Blush, without a Smile;
Exalt each Trifle, ev'ry Vice adore,
Your Taste in Snuff, your Judgment in a Whore;
Can *Balbo*'s Eloquence applaud, and swear
He gropes his Breeches with a Monarch's Air.

. . .

Scarce can our Fields, such Crowds at *Tyburn* die,
With Hemp the Gallows and the Fleet supply.
Propose your Schemes, ye Senatorian Band,
Whose *Ways and Means* support the sinking Land;
Lest Ropes be wanting in the tempting Spring,
To rig another Convoy for the K—g.

A single Jail, in Alfred's golden Reign,
Could half the Nation's Criminals contain;
Fair Justice then, without Constraint ador'd
Held high the steady Scale, but sheath'd the sword;

No Spies were paid, no *Special Juries* known,
Blest Age! but ah! how diff'rent from our own!
Much could I add,—but see the Boat at hand,
The Tide retiring, calls me from the Land:
Farewel!—When Youth, and Health, and Fortune spent,
Thou fly'st for Refuge to the Wilds of *Kent*
And tir'd like me with Follies and with Crimes,
In angry Numbers warn'st succeeding Times;
Then shall thy Friend, nor thou refuse his Aid,
Still Foe to Vice forsake his *Cambrian* Shade;
In Virtue's Cause once more exert his Rage,
Thy Satire point, and animate thy Page.

23 Alexander Pope: One Thousand Seven Hundred and Forty (1740)

[An uncompleted poem which was not published in Pope's lifetime. By 1740 he had become disenchanted with the factious and selfish tactics of the 'Patriot' opposition to Walpole.]

O WRETCHED B[ritain]! jealous now of all,
What God, what mortal, shall prevent thy fall?
Turn, turn thy eyes from wicked men in place,
And see what succour from the patriot race.
C[arteret], his own proud dupe, thinks monarchs things
Made just for him, as others fools for kings;
Controls, decides, insults thee every hour,
And antedates the hatred due to power.
     Through clouds of passion P[ulteney]'s views are clear,
He foams a patriot to subside a peer;
Impatient sees his country bought and sold,
And damns the market where he takes no gold.
     Grave, righteous S[andys] jogs on till, past belief,
He finds himself companion with a thief.
     To purge and let thee blood, with fire and sword,
Is all the help stern S[hippen] would afford.
     That those who bind and rob thee, would not kill,
Good C[ornbury] hopes and candidly sits still.
     Of Ch—s W—[1] who speaks at all,
No more than of Sir Harry or Sir P[aul]?
Whose names once up, they thought it was not wrong
To lie in bed, but sure they lay too long.
     G[owe]r, C[obha]m, B[athurs]t, pay thee due regards,
Unless the ladies bid them mind their cards.

---

[1] Impossible to identify with certainty. Scholars have suggested 'Charles Hanbury Williams' or 'Chandos, Winchilsea'.

And C[hesterfiel]d, who speaks so well and writes,
Whom (saving W.) every S. harper bites.
Whose wit and . . . equally provoke one,
Finds thee, at best, the butt to crack his joke on.
  As for the rest, each winter up they run,
And all are clear that something must be done.
Then, urged by C[artere]t, or by C[artere]t stopp'd,
Inflamed by P[ulteney], and by P[ulteney] dropp'd;
They follow reverently each wondrous wight,
Amazed that one can read, that one can write:
So geese to gander prone obedience keep,
Hiss, if he hiss, and if he slumber, sleep
Till having done whate'er was fit or fine,
Utter'd a speech, and ask'd their friends to dine;
Each hurries back to his paternal ground,
Content but for five shillings in the pound;
Yearly defeated, yearly hopes they give,
And all agree Sir Robert cannot live.

. . .

24 David Hume:
Of the Parties of Great Britain (1741)

[From Hume's *Essays, Moral and Political* (Edinburgh, 1741), essay XI, pp. 119–31, 134, 136–8]

Were the British government proposed as a subject of speculation to a studious man, he would immediately perceive in
it a source of division and party, which it would be almost
impossible for it, in any administration, to avoid. The just
balance betwixt the republican and monarchical part of our
constitution is really, in itself, so extreme delicate and uncertain, that when joined to men's passions and prejudices, 'tis
impossible but different opinions must arise concerning it,
even among persons of the best understanding. Those of mild
tempers, who love peace and order, and detest sedition and
civil wars, will always entertain more favourable sentiments
of monarchy, than men of bold spirits, who are passionate
lovers of liberty, and think no evil comparable to subjection
and slavery. And though all reasonable men agree in general
to preserve our mixt government; yet when they come to
particulars, some will incline to trust larger powers to the
crown, to bestow on it more influence, and to guard against
its encroachments with less caution, than others who are
terrified at the most distant approaches of tyranny and despotic
power. Thus there are parties of PRINCIPLE involved in the
very nature of our constitution, which may properly enough
be denominated COURT and COUNTRY parties. The strength
and violence of each of these parties will much depend upon
the particular administration. An administration may be so
bad as to throw a great majority into the Country party;
as a good administration will reconcile to the Court many
of the most passionate lovers of liberty. But, however the

nation may fluctuate betwixt these two parties, the parties will always subsist, as long as we are governed by a limited monarchy.

But, besides this difference of *principle*, those parties are very much fomented by a difference of *interest*, without which they could scarce ever be dangerous or violent. The crown will naturally bestow all its trust and power upon those, whose principles, real or pretended, are most favourable to monarchical government; and this temptation will naturally engage them to go greater lengths than their principles would otherwise carry them. Their antagonists, who are disappointed in their ambitious aims, throw themselves into the party whose principles incline them to be most jealous of royal power, and naturally carry those principles to a greater length than sound politics will justify. Thus, the Court and Country parties, which are the genuine factions of the British government, are a kind of mixt parties, and are influenced partly by principle, partly by interest. The heads of the parties are commonly most governed by the latter motive; the inferior members of them by the former. I must be understood to mean this of persons who have any motive for taking party on any side. For, to tell the truth, the greatest part are commonly men who associate themselves they know not why; from example, from passion, from idleness. . . .

As to ecclesiastical parties; we may observe, that, in all ages of the world, priests have been enemies to liberty; and 'tis certain, that this steady conduct of theirs must have been founded on fixt reasons of interest and ambition. Liberty of thinking, and of expressing our thoughts, is always fatal to priestly power, and to those pious frauds, on which it is commonly founded; and by an infallible connexion, which is found among every species of liberty, this privilege can never be enjoyed, at least, has never yet been enjoyed, but in a free government. Hence it must happen, in such a government as Britain, that the established clergy will always be of the Court party; as, on the contrary, Dissenters of all kinds will be of the Country party; since they can never hope for that toleration which they stand in need of, but by means of our free government. All princes, that have aimed at despotic power, have known this important interest of gaining the established clergy: as the clergy, on their side, have shown a great facility in entering into the views of such princes. . . .

If we consider the first rise of parties in England, during the civil wars, we shall find, that they were exactly conformable to this general theory, and that the species of the government gave birth to them, by a regular and infallible operation. The English constitution, before that time, had lain in a kind of confusion; yet so, as that the subjects possessed many noble privileges, which, though not, perhaps, exactly bounded and secured by law, were universally deemed, from long possession, to belong to them as their birthright. An ambitious, or rather an ignorant, prince arose, who esteemed all these privileges to be concessions of his predecessors, revocable at pleasure; and, in prosecution of this principle, he openly acted in violation of liberty, during the course of several years. Necessity, at last, constrained him to call a Parliament: the spirit of liberty arose: the prince, being without any support, was obliged to grant everything required of him: and his enemies, jealous and implacable, set no bounds to their pretensions. Here then begun those contests, in which it was no wonder, that men of that age were divided into different parties; since, even at this day, the impartial are at a loss to decide concerning the justice of the quarrel. The pretensions of the Parliament, if yielded to, broke the balance of our constitution, by rendering the government almost entirely republican. If not yielded to, we were, perhaps, still in danger of despotic power, from the settled principles and inveterate habits of the king, which had plainly appeared in every concession, that he had been constrained to make to his people. In this question, so delicate and uncertain, men naturally fell to the side which was most conformable to their usual principles; and those who were the most passionate favourers of monarchy, declared for the king; as the zealous friends of liberty sided with the Parliament. The hopes of success being nearly equal on both sides, *interest* had little influence in this contest: so that *Roundhead* and *Cavalier* were merely parties of principle; neither of which disowned either monarchy or liberty; but the former party inclined most to the republican part of our government, and the latter to the monarchical. In which respect they may be considered as Court and Country party enflamed into a civil war, by an unhappy concurrence of circumstances, and by the turbulent spirit of the age. The commonwealth's men, and the partizans of despotic power, lay concealed in both parties, and formed but an inconsiderable part of them.

The clergy had concurred, in a shameless manner, with the king's arbitrary designs, according to their usual maxims in such causes: and, in return, were allowed to persecute their adversaries, whom they called heretics and schismatics. The established clergy was Episcopal; the nonconformists Presbyterians: so that all things concurred to throw the former, without reserve, into the king's party; and the latter into that of the Parliament. . . .

Everyone knows the event of this quarrel; fatal to the king first, and to the Parliament afterwards. After many confusions and revolutions, the royal family was at last restored, and the government established on the same footing as before. Charles II was not made wiser by the dreadful example of his father; but prosecuted the same measures, tho' with more secrecy and caution. New parties arose, under the appellation of WHIG and TORY, which have continued ever since to confound and distract our government. What the nature is of these parties, is, perhaps, one of the most difficult problems that can be met with, and is a proof, that history may contain problems, as uncertain as any that are to be found in the most abstract sciences. We have seen the conduct of the two parties, during the course of seventy years, in a vast variety of circumstances, possessed of power, and deprived of it, during peace and during war: we meet with persons, who profess themselves of one side or t'other, every hour, in company, in our pleasures, in our serious occupations: we ourselves are constrained, in a manner, to take party; and living in a country of the highest liberty, every one may openly declare all his sentiments and opinions: and yet we are at a loss to tell the nature, pretensions, and principles of the two parties. . . .

When we compare the parties of *Whig* and *Tory*, to those of *Roundhead* and *Cavalier*, the most obvious difference, that appears betwixt them, consists in the doctrines of *passive obedience* and *indefeasible right*, which were but little heard of among the Cavaliers, but became the universal doctrine, and was the true characteristic, of a *Tory*. Were these principles pushed into their most obvious consequences, they imply a formal renunciation of all our liberties, and an avowal of absolute monarchy; since nothing can be a greater absurdity than a limited power, which must not be resisted, even when it exceeds its limitations. But as the most rational principles are often but a weak counterpoise to passion; 'tis no wonder, that these absurd principles . . . were found too weak for that effect. The *Tories*, as men, were enemies to oppression; and also, as Englishmen, they were enemies to despotick power. Their zeal for liberty, was, perhaps, less fervent than that of their antagonists; but was sufficient to make them forget all their general principles, when they saw themselves openly threatened with a subversion of the antient government. From these sentiments arose the *Revolution*; an event of mighty consequence, and the firmest foundation of British liberty. The conduct of the *Tories* during that event, and after it, will afford us a true insight into the nature of that party.

In the *first* place, they appear to have had the sentiments of true Britons in their affection to liberty, and their determined resolution not to sacrifice it to any abstract principle whatsoever, or to any imaginary rights of princes. This part of their character might justly have been doubted of before the Revolution, from the obvious tendency of their avowed principles, and from their almost unbounded compliances with a court, that made little secret of its arbitrary designs. The Revolution showed them to have been, in this respect, nothing but a genuine Court party, such as might be expected in a British government: that is, *lovers of liberty, but greater lovers of monarchy.* It must, however, be confest, that they carried their monarchical principles further, even in practice, but more so in theory, than was, in any degree, consistent with a limited government.

Secondly. Neither their principles nor affections concurred with the settlement made at the Revolution, or with that which has since taken place. This part of their character may seem contradictory to the former; since any other settlement, in those circumstances of the nation, must have been dangerous, if not fatal to liberty. But the heart of man is made to reconcile the most glaring contradictions; and this contradiction above-mentioned is not greater than that betwixt *passive obedience* and the *resistance* employed at the Revolution. A *Tory*, therefore, since the Revolution, may be defined in a few words to be *a lover of monarchy, tho' without abandoning liberty; and a partizan of the family of Stuart.* As a *Whig* may be defined to be *a lover of liberty, tho' without renouncing monarchy; and a friend to the settlement in the Protestant line.* . . .

. . . These different views, with regard to the settlement of the crown, are accidental, but natural additions to the principles of the *Court* and *Country* parties, which are the genuine parties of the British government. A passionate lover of monarchy is apt to be displeased at any change of this succession; as favouring too much of a commonwealth: a passionate lover of liberty is apt to think that every part of the government ought to be subordinate to the interests of liberty. . . .

Some, who will not venture to assert, that the *real* difference betwixt *Whig* and *Tory* was lost at the *Revolution*, seem inclined to think, that the difference is now abolished, and that affairs are so far returned to their natural state, that there are at present no other parties among us but Court and Country; that is, men, who by interest or principle are attached either to monarchy or to liberty. It must, indeed, be confest, that the Tory party has, of late, decayed much in their numbers; still more in their zeal; and I may venture to say, still more in their credit and authority. There is no man of knowledge or learning, who would not be ashamed to be thought of that party; and in almost all companies the name of OLD WHIG is mentioned as an uncontestable appellation of honour and dignity. Accordingly, the enemies of the ministry, as a reproach, call the courtiers, the true *Tories*; and as an honour, denominate the gentlemen in the *Opposition* the true *Whigs*. The Tories have been so long obliged to talk in the republican stile, that they seem to have made converts of themselves by their hypocrisy, and to have embraced the sentiments, as well as language of their adversaries. There are, however, very considerable remains of that party in England, with all their old prejudices; and a demonstrative proof, that *Court* and *Country* are not our only parties, is, that almost all the Dissenters side with the court, and the lower clergy, at least of the Church of England, with the Opposition. . . .

25   Edward Spelman:
The Preface to 'A Fragment out of the
Sixth Book of Polybius' (1743)

[Spelman translated passages from Polybius's history of Rome and added a preface 'wherein the system of Polybius is applied to the government of England'. pp. v–ix]

. . . In all free governments there ever were, and ever will be parties: we find that Sparta, Rome, Athens, and all the Greek colonies in Asia Minor had their aristocratical, and democratical parties; while the only contest among the subjects of the Kings of Persia was, who should be the greatest slaves. The truth is, different understandings, different educations, and different attachments must necessarily produce different ways of thinking every where; but these will shew themselves in free governments only, because there only they can shew themselves with impunity. However, it was not the existence of the two parties I have mentioned, that destroyed the liberties of any of those cities, but the occasional extinction of one of them, by the superiority the other had gained over it: And, if ever we should be so unhappy as to have the ballance between the three orders [Crown, Lords and Commons] destroyed; and that any one of the three should utterly extinguish the other two, the name of a party would, from that moment, be unknown in England, and we should unanimously agree in being slaves to the conqueror.

Parties, therefore, are not only the effect, but the support of liberty: I do not at all wonder that they are perpetually exclaimed at by those in power: they may have, sometimes, reason to be dissatisfied with the parties themselves, but have much more to be so with the heads of them; for these are properly their rivals: the bulk of the party aims, generally, at no more than a reformation of what they think an abuse of power; the others, at the power it self, without considering

112

the abuse, unless it be to continue it: the party quarrels with things, and the leaders with persons; consequently, a change of measures may appease the first; but nothing less than a change of ministers can satisfy the last. However, in one respect, these leaders often give some ease to ministers without designing it; for, as they generally attack them upon personal, rather than national points, their followers are unconcerned in the contest; and, considering themselves as spectators, rather than parties, do not think it incumbent on them to go great lengths for the choice of ministers; especially, since by the indifference their leaders shew for national points, when they are aiming at power (which is the season for giving hopes, as the gaining it is for disappointing them) their followers have but little reason to expect they will shew a greater warmth for them, when they have attained the possession of it.

But, whatever may be the success of the opposers, the publick reaps great benefit from the opposition; since this keeps ministers upon their guard, and, often, prevents them from pursuing bold measures, which an uncontrolled power might, otherwise, tempt them to engage in: they must act with caution, as well as fidelity, when they consider the whole nation is attentive to every step they take, and that the errors, they may commit, will not only be exposed, but aggravated: in the mean time, a thirst of power, irritated by disappointment, animates the application of the opposers to publick affairs, infinitely more than the languid impulse of national considerations: by this means, they grow able statesmen, and, when they come to be ministers, are not only capable of defending bad schemes, but, when they please, of forming good ones.

Another great advantage, that accrues to the people from this opposition, is, that each party, by appealing to them upon all occasions, constitutes them judges of every contest; and, indeed, to whom should they appeal, but to those, whose welfare is the design, or pretence, of every measure? and for whose happiness the majesty of kings, the dignity of peers, and the power of the Commons, were finally instituted. This is, undoubtedly, the end of their institution, and this end it is their glory, as well as duty, to accomplish; for, what greater honour can be done to the three orders, of which our government is so happily composed, than to look upon them as they really are, that is, as the channels, through which ease, plenty, and security are derived to millions of people? . . .

26 Liberty and Right, or an Essay Historical and Political on the Constitution and Administration of Great Britain (1747) (Anonymous)

[Possibly written by John Campbell. Despite its novel features this pamphlet attracted little comment at the time of its publication. It advocated the abolition of primogeniture and attacked standing armies, but this extract deals with the most interesting suggestions for more frequent elections, secret ballot, payment of M.P.s, etc. pp. 43–51.]

. . . Have we not seen how the crown, and the ministers of the crown, by virtue of royal prerogative and privilege, oppos'd their own private interest to the publick interest of the community; and, by posts, and places, and titles of honour, affected to raise their own power and dignity above the rights and liberties of the people? Have we not seen how, things being brought to the last extremity, that tyranny was dissolv'd, that family excluded, and a new race of princes fix'd upon the throne? Have we not seen how these very Revolution princes, one after another, by exceeding in power, and multiplying the annual revenue, have put it in the power of their ministers to introduce a national depravity of manners, to seduce or over-awe the native freedom of popular elections, and to subvert and destroy the honour and integrity of the popular representation? Have we not seen how, by this unequal and deprav'd influence of the crown, the people have been inflam'd and divided, faction promoted, and treasons and rebellions excited and multiply'd? 'Tis from the inequality of our orders, 'tis from the iniquitous and private influence of the crown, that all our present internal calamities flow, and will and must flow; for, while that influence continues, our morality will every day decay, our people will turn worse and worse, one year after another will produce greater demands from the crown and greater compliances by the people. Ministers may be chang'd one after another, popular clamour may be rais'd against particular persons in power; but unless the people and the representatives of the people, the electors and the elected, be secur'd by their orders against the influence of all ministers whatever, and against bribery and corruption of every kind, the nation never can be out of trouble, never free from danger: and, to secure them effectually, we need neither raise the power of the people beyond what it is, nor depress in any degree the legal authority of the prince; let us only preserve the just rights and independency of all parts of the legislature by the following orders.

First, concerning the manner of taking the votes of the electors of Great Britain, and of both Houses of Parliament.

That the electors of all the counties, cities, and boroughs of Great Britain chuse their representatives, or Members of Parliament, as follows, namely; that the whole freeholders or electors of every county, city, and borough, being assembled at their respective places upon the day of election, begin by drawing lots for three several proposers; that the persons, upon whom the said lots shall fall, take the oath of allegiance, as also another, to be likewise administered by the sheriff, importing, that the persons whom they shall propose as candidates, for representing the county, city, or borough to which they belong, shall be, to the best of their knowledge, such as are able and fit to serve their country in parliament; and that they have neither got any reward from these persons, nor from any person or persons in their name, nor stand in expectation by promise or otherways from them or any on their behalf, of any future favour or reward, for proposing them as candidates; which oaths being taken, the said proposers shall retire apart by themselves, to consider of the persons proper to be nominated as candidates; and, each of them having fix'd upon one, they shall set down their names in writing; he, upon whom the first lot fell, setting down the name of his candidate first, and so on in order; which nomination of candidates, being thus made out, the three proposers shall return, and deliver their list to the sheriff, who, having read the same to the electors, shall call upon each of the candidates, in the order set down in the list, who shall make oath one by one, in presence of all the freeholders and electors, that they are each of them, after all debts and incumbrances paid and clear'd, worth 600 l. per annum, if for a county; or 300 l. per annum, if for a city, or borough: Which oath, if refus'd, the person so refusing shall thereby become uncapable of standing candidate, and the proposer, who nam'd him, shall directly proceed and nominate another; and when the candidates, nam'd by the proposers, have taken the last mention'd oath, they shall retire, while the electors, beginning with the person first propos'd, and ending with the last propos'd, shall ballot, whether these persons shall be sustained as candidates or not; and he, who shall have above one half of the suffrages for him, shall be mark'd as a candidate; but he, who shall have only the one half or under, shall be rejected; and the proposer, who nominated him, shall proceed, as before, and nominate another, until three persons, thus nominated by the proposers, shall be sustain'd as candidates by the electors. Then shall the electors again ballot, which of the three candidates shall be their representative in parliament; and he of the three, who upon the whole shall have the majority of suffrages, shall be return'd by the sheriff as duly elected; the sheriff, or his depute, being always oblig'd to number the suffrages, in presence and under the inspection of all the electors; and the person, thus elected, shall immediately, and in presence of his constituents, make oath, that, in all his future conduct in parliament, he will, to the utmost of his power, study and act for the happiness and good of his country, and punctually observe and obey all such directions and instructions, as he shall from time to time receive from his county, city, or borough, concerning publick and national affairs. When the whole representation of the people are thus chose and assembled in parliament, the Lords, as well as the Commons shall, in deciding on all affairs to be brought before them, give their opinions on the same, not by voting, but by balloting; and the suffrages of the Lords, so to be given, shall be publickly examin'd and number'd by the Lord Chancellor, in presence and under the inspection of the whole house; and, in the House of Commons, the same shall be done by Mr. Speaker, in presence and under inspection of their house.

Secondly, concerning the qualification of Members of Parliament.

That every person, representing a county, have at least 600 l. per annum free estate; and every person, representing a city or borough, 300 l. per annum. That no person, having any post or pension under his Majesty, be capable of being elected a Member of Parliament; or being a member, and accepting of such post or pension, be capable of being re-elected, while he continues under such presumptive influence. That no person, having serv'd in one parliament, be capable of being elected to serve in the next ensuing; but that, next parliament being expir'd, he may lawfully stand candidate, and be elected into the next following.

Thirdly, concerning the duration and succession of parliaments.

That the parliament continue for the space of three years compleat, yet in that time be diversify'd as follows; namely, one third part of the House of Commons shall move off at the end of the first year, and be supply'd by a new third part, sent up from the several counties, cities, and boroughs, but elected to serve three years; and one third part shall move off at the end of the second year, and be supply'd as before; and the last third part, which compleats the first parliament, shall move off at the end of the third year, and be succeeded as above. Whence it is evident that the parliament, at the beginning of the fourth year, will consist entirely of new, tho' not of un-experienc'd members; as also that the first quota sent up of this new parliament, having already sat two years in the house, their time of service will be expir'd at the end of the fourth year, and a new succession take place; and the second quota, having already serv'd one year, their time will expire at the end of the fifth year, and a new succession arise; and the third quota, having not yet serv'd at all, their time won't expire till the end of the sixth year, and then will others succeed them: and thus shall the parliament be for ever renew'd, and for ever in being. And for the better effecting of the said orderly succession in parliament, be it enacted, that every county, city, and borough, send each of them up to the first parliament three members, (to be chose in the manner above set forth in the first order) electing one to be their representative for one year, a second for two, and the third for the full term of three years compleat; observing, ever after, to send up annually each of them one, for the term of three years, to succeed to the member annually out of the House of Commons.

Fourthly, concerning the period of elections.

That a time be fix'd by parliament for making these annual elections, at which time it shall be lawful for the freeholders and electors of the several counties, and cities, and boroughs, of Great Britain, to meet yearly; and, with, or without the King's Writ, elect their members and representatives in parliament.

Fifthly, concerning the expence of Members of Parliament.

That every member for a county, in parliament, receive from the said county, annually, the sum of 600 l. and that every member for a city or borough, in parliament, receive from his respective city or borough, annually, 300 l. to defray the necessary expence, attending the service of their country in parliament.

27　Robert Wallace:
　　　Characteristics of the Present Political
　　　State of Great Britain (1758)

Part II, Section II: Of the Source of the National Debt of England
[pp. 53–4, 61, 63–8]

When we consider the vast debts, that have been contracted
in England; in one view, it seems impossible intirely to justify
the conduct, which has been the cause of them; in another,
such high debts are not a bad symptom of the times, and mark
a peculiar distinction betwixt the temper of the nation before
and since the Revolution.

When a free government is able to contract great debts by
borrowing from its own subjects, this is a certain sign, that it
has gained *the confidence* of the people. . . . 'Tis by this firm
credit, among other things, that the government ever since
the Revolution has been remarkably distinguished from the
government during the four preceding reigns.

How often have we been told, with a particular emphasis,
that all our debts have been contracted since the Revolution?
To such, as know the history of former times, the mention of
this is unnecessary. None of the four preceding reigns had *any*
credit with the people. Before the Revolution the nation could
place no confidence in the administration; for they were continually giving them ground of jealousy, and were secretly
undermining, or openly invading, their constitution. . . .

. . . Since the Revolution, our princes have avoided those
rocks on which their predecessors ran with precipitation.The
British have enjoyed greater liberty and security than were
enjoyed in the preceding reigns. The great body of the people
find themselves easy and safe. The administration is equitable
and mild. The sovereign summons the parliament regularly,
according to law. The king and his parliament meet and part

amicably. They enact such laws as are thought proper. Sometimes the landed, sometimes the trading interest, is more immediately considered. Great regard is paid to the general opinion of merchants and of the people. . . .

But have there been *no* mismanagements under the government since the Revolution? Has this government fallen into *no* errors? Has it been guilty of *no* abuses? Whatever may be said by fawning parasites, the best friends of the Revoluton will not say so. They do not doubt, that men without virtue, or without ability, have too often been employed; that such men have mismanaged public affairs, and embezzled the public money; that frauds have been committed; that services have been paid for, which were never performed; that others have been purchased at an extravagant price; that many deceitful arts have been employed in the management of the stocks; and that such abuses have too seldom been punished. Though they are far from believing that the balance of power in Europe is an idea *entirely imaginary*, they will not assert, that we have not burdened ourselves *too much* in preserving it. . . . All human governments are subject to abuses. The government, since the Revolution, has not been exempted from them. Generous friends of liberty will not deny it. They will not prostitute their honour. They will not defend what is wrong. When they celebrate the government since the Revolution, they do not celebrate it on account of *the frugality* of the administration, or the watchfulness of men in power, either in preventing or punishing abuses. What they celebrate is of a different nature. By the Revolution the constitution has been rendered more perfect. That admirable and singular mixture of a hereditary limited monarchy and splendid aristocracy, without the power of oppressing, and of an equal democracy without its unsteadiness and confusion, shines with superior lustre. By means of the Revolution, the protestant religion, which seemed continually to be in danger from the influence of popish kings or popish queens, is perfectly secured. By means of the Revolution, we enjoy an entire security from all kinds of persecution, liberty of worshipping God according to our consciences, safety to our persons against arbitrary imprisonments, security of our lives and properties from arbitrary judgments, freedom from all taxes, penalties or punishments, without consent of parliament, liberty of speech and debate, of writing and printing, in the most ample manner we can desire. . . .

Tho the true friends of liberty will never deny weaknesses in the administration, they cannot but see, at the same time, that many of the abuses which they confess and lament, naturally arise from the freedom of our government, and are evils nearly connected with the blessings we enjoy above most other nations. There can be no unmixed happiness in this world. A nation cannot have *just enough* of any thing, and no more. If it enjoys a sufficient measure of liberty, it must be content to take along with it a certain portion of licentiousness. If it will have the *most perfect* security against illegal imprisonments or arbitrary judgments, it must lay its account to suffer many criminals to escape. If it would preserve the influence, dignity, and independence of the rich, and not break the spirit of the commons, it cannot expect to be without parties and factions. Wherever there are struggles and contests for power and authority, *dishonourable* as well as *honourable* methods of acquiring them will too often come into vogue. Where power is divided among many different persons and bodies of men, the distribution is the great mean of preserving freedom, and of preventing those enormous acts of tyranny, which are exercised under absolute monarchies. But it often embarrasses the administration, and makes the springs of government move more slowly. A king of Britain, as he cannot do the thousandth part of the mischief which may easily be done by an absolute monarch, sometimes cannot do so much good. His best intentions may be frustrated by contending parties. Where there are parties and factions, it is no wonder that persons, whose greatest merit consists in their powerful connexions, are sometimes chosen into offices. No form of government can have all advantages. The best is that which has the most and the greatest. If a nation will have moneyed men and rich merchants, who shall be able both to carry on a great trade, and to advance money for the urgent occasions of the government, it must admit stock-jobbing. If it will preserve a due balance of power abroad, and baffle the unjust attempts of an ambitious monarch, who disturbs the peace of mankind, encroaches on his neighbours, and would enslave the world, it must sometimes put itself to the expence of maintaining armies for its defence. If it is more rich and opulent, the administration *must* be more expensive, and must pay all its officers and servants at a much greater rate, than other nations. Thus we may easily see the original source of many abuses, that are justly complained of. . . .

28 John Wilkes:
The North Briton (1763)

[No. 45. 23 April 1763. This celebrated attack on the Bute ministry and the Treaty of Paris gained Wilkes great notoriety and launched him on his political career.]

The North Briton makes his appeal to the good sense, and to the candour of the English nation. In the present unsettled and fluctuating state of the *administration*, he is really fearful of falling into involuntary errors, and he does not wish to mislead. All his reasonings have been built on the strong foundation of *facts*; and he is not yet informed of the whole interiour state of government with such *minute precision*, as now to venture the submitting his crude ideas of the present political crisis to the discerning and impartial public. The Scottish minister [the Earl of Bute] has indeed *retired*. Is his influence at an end? or does he still govern by the *three* wretched tools of his power [Egremont, Halifax, and George Grenville], who, to their indelible infamy, have supported the most odious of his measures, the late ignominious *peace*, and the wicked extension of the arbitrary mode of *excise*? The North Briton has been steady in his opposition to a *single*, insolent, incapable, despotic minister; and is equally ready, in the service of his country, to combat the *triple-headed, Cerberean* administration, if the Scot is to assume that motley form. By him every arrangement *to this hour* has been made, and the notification has been as regularly sent by letter under his hand. *It therefore* seems clear to a demonstration, that he intends only to retire into that situation, which he held before he first took the seals; I mean the dictating to every part of the king's administration. The North Briton desires to be understood, as having pledged himself a firm and intrepid assertor of the rights of his fellow-subjects, and of the liberties of Whigs and Englishmen. . . .

This week has given the public the most abandoned instance of ministerial effrontery ever attempted to be imposed on mankind. The *minister's speech* of last Tuesday, is not to be paralleled in the annals of this country. I am in doubt, whether the imposition is greater on the sovereign or on the nation. Every friend of his country must lament that a prince of so many great and amiable qualities, whom England truly reveres, can be brought to give the sanction of his sacred name to the most odious measures, and to the most unjustifiable, public declarations, from a throne ever renowned for truth, honour, and unsullied virtue. I am sure, all foreigners, especially the king of Prussia, will hold the minister in contempt and abhorrence. He has made our sovereign declare, 'My expectations have been fully answered by the happy effects which the several allies of my crown have derived from this salutary measure of the definitive treaty. The powers at war with my good brother, the King of Prussia, have been induced to agree to such terms of accommodation, as that great prince has approved; and the success which has attended my negociation, has necessarily and immediately diffused the blessings of peace through every part of Europe.' The infamous fallacy of this whole sentence is apparent to all mankind: for it is known, that the King of Prussia did not barely *approve*, but absolutely *dictated*, as conqueror, every article of the terms of the peace.[1] No advantage of any kind has accrued to that magnanimous prince from *our negociation*, but he was basely deserted by the *Scottish* prime-minister of England. He was known by every court in Europe to be scarcely on better terms of friendship *here*, than at *Vienna*; and he was betrayed by us in the *treaty of peace*. What a strain of insolence, therefore, is it in a minister to lay claim to what he is conscious all his efforts tended to prevent, and meanly to arrogate to himself a share in the fame and glory of one of the greatest princes the world has ever seen? . . .

[1] Britain made a separate peace with France by the Treaty of Paris on 10 Feb. 1763. Her ally, Prussia, who had been fighting France, Russia, Austria, Sweden and some South German states, had to make her own terms by the Treaty of Hubertusburg on 15 Feb. 1763. This restored the *status quo ante bellum*.

The *preliminary articles of peace* were such as have drawn the contempt of mankind on our wretched negociators. All our most valuable conquests were agreed to be restored, and the *East-India company* would have been infallibly ruined by a single article of this fallacious and baneful negociation. No hireling of the minister has been hardy enough to dispute this; yet the minister himself has made our sovereign declare, *the satisfaction which he felt at the approaching re-establishment of peace upon conditions so honourable to his crown, and so beneficial to his people.* As to the *entire approbation* of parliament, which is so vainly boasted of, the world knows how that was obtained. The large debt on the *Civil List*, already above half a year in arrear, shews pretty clearly the transactions of the winter. . . .

. . . Lord *Ligonier* is now no longer at the head of the army; but Lord *Bute* in effect is: I mean that every preferment given by the crown will be found still to be obtained by *his* enormous influence, and to be bestowed only on the creatures of the *Scottish* faction. The nation is still in the same deplorable state, while *he* governs, and can make the tools of *his* power pursue the same odious measures. Such a retreat, as he intends, can only mean that personal indemnity, which, I hope, guilt will never find from an injured nation. The negociations of the late inglorious *peace*, and the *excise*, will haunt him, wherever he goes, and the terrors of the just resentment, which he must be to meet from a brave and insulted people, and which must finally crush him, will be for ever before his eyes.

In vain will such a minister, or the foul dregs of his power, the tools of corruption and despotism, preach up in *the speech* that *spirit of concord, and that obedience to the laws, which is essential to good order.* They have sent the *spirit of discord* through the land, and I will prophecy, that it will never be extinguished, but by the extinction of their power. Is the *spirit of concord* to go hand in hand with the Peace and Excise thro' this nation? Is it to be expected between an insolent Exciseman, and a *peer*, *gentleman*, *freeholder*, or *farmer*, whose private houses are now made liable to be entered and searched at pleasure? . . .

A despotic minister will always endeavour to dazzle his prince with high-flown ideas of the *prerogative* and *honour* of the crown, which the minister will make a parade of *firmly main-*

taining. I wish as much as any man in the kingdom to see *the honour of the crown* maintained in a manner truly becoming *royalty.* I lament to see it sunk even to prostitution. . . .

The *Stuart* line has ever been intoxicated with the slavish doctrines of the *absolute, independent, unlimited* power of the crown. Some of that line were so weakly advised, as to endeavour to reduce them into practice: but the *English* nation was too spirited to suffer the least encroachment on the ancient liberties of this kingdom. The *King of England* is only the first magistrate of this country; but is invested by law with the whole executive power. He is, however, responsible to his people for the due execution of the royal functions, in the choice of ministers, &c. equally with the meanest of his subjects in this particular duty. The personal character of our present amiable sovereign makes us easy and happy that so great a power is lodged in such hands; but the *favourite* has given too just cause for him to escape the general odium. The *prerogative* of the crown is to exert the constitutional powers entrusted to it in a way, not of blind favour and partiality, but of wisdom and judgment. This is the spirit of our constitution. The people too have their *prerogative*, and, I hope, the fine words of Dryden will be engraven on our hearts.

Freedom *is the English subject's* prerogative.

29 Charles Churchill:
An Epistle to William Hogarth (1763)

[An attack on Hogarth for his unflattering drawing of Wilkes. Lines 383–418]

. . . .

WHEN WILKES, our Countryman, our common friend,
Arose, his King, his Country to defend,
When tools of pow'r he bar'd to public view,
And from their holes the sneaking cowards drew,
When Rancour found it far beyond her reach
To soil his honour, and his truth impeach,
What could induce Thee, at a time and place,
Where manly Foes had blush'd to shew their face,
To make that effort, which must damn thy name,
And sink Thee deep, deep in thy grave with shame?
Did Virtue move Thee? no, 'twas Pride, rank Pride,
And if Thou had'st not done it, Thou had'st dy'd.
MALICE (who, disappointed of her end,
Whether to work the bane of Foe or Friend,
Preys on herself, and, driven to the Stake,
Gives Virtue that revenge she scorns to take)
Had kill'd Thee, tott'ring on life's utmost verge,
Had WILKES and LIBERTY escap'd thy scourge.

WHEN that GREAT CHARTER, which our Fathers bought
With their best blood, was into question brought;
When, big with ruin, o'er each English head
Vile Slav'ry hung suspended by a thread;
When LIBERTY, all trembling and aghast,
Fear'd for the future, knowing what was past;
When ev'ry breast was chill'd with deep despair,

Till Reason pointed out that PRATT was there;
Lurking, most Ruffian-like, behind a screen,
So plac'd all things to see, himself unseen,
VIRTUE, with due contempt, saw HOGARTH stand,
The murd'rous pencil in his palsied hand.
What was the cause of Liberty to him,
Or what was Honour? let them sink or swim,
So he may gratify without controul
The mean resentments of his selfish soul.
Let Freedom perish, if, to Freedom true,
In the same ruin WILKES may perish too.

. . .

30 Charles Churchill: The Duellist (1764)

[Book One, lines 147-248. Churchill's friend, John Wilkes, had just been wounded in a duel.]

. . . .
    Dark was the Night, by fate decreed
For the contrivance of a deed
More black than common, which might make
This land from her foundations shake,
Might tear up Freedom by the root,
Destroy a WILKES, and fix a BUTE.

    Deep Horror held her wide domain;
The sky in sullen drops of rain
Forewept the morn, and thro' the air,
Which, op'ning, laid his bosom bare,
Loud Thunders roll'd, and Lightning stream'd;
The Owl at Freedom's window scream'd,
The Screech-Owl, prophet dire, whose breath
Brings sickness, and whose note is death;
The Church-Yard teem'd, and from the tomb,
All Sad and Silent, thro' the gloom,
The Ghosts of Men, in former times
Whose Public Virtues were their crimes,
Indignant stalk'd; Sorrow and Rage
Blank'd their pale cheek; in his own age
The prop of Freedom, HAMPDEN [1] there
Felt after death the gen'rous care;

[1] John Hampden, the great opponent of Charles I.

130

SIDNEY [1] by grief from Heav'n was kept,
And for his brother Patriot wept;
All Friends of LIBERTY, when Fate
Prepar'd to shorten WILKES's date,
Heav'd, deeply hurt, the heart-felt groan,
And knew that wound to be their own.

Hail, LIBERTY! a glorious word,
In other countries scarcely heard,
Or heard but as a thing of course,
Without or Energy or Force;
Here felt, enjoy'd, ador'd, she springs,
Far, far beyond the reach of Kings,
Fresh blooming from our Mother Earth;
With Pride and Joy she owns her birth
Deriv'd from us, and in return
Bids in our breast her Genius burn;
Bids us with all those blessings live
Which LIBERTY alone can give,
Or nobly with that Spirit die,
Which makes Death more than Victory.

Hail those Old Patriots, on whose tongue
Persuasion in the Senate hung,
Whilst They this sacred Cause maintain'd!
Hail those Old Chiefs, to Honour train'd,
Who spread, when other methods fail'd,
War's bloody banner, and prevail'd!
Shall Men like these unmention'd sleep
Promiscuous with the common heap,
And (Gratitude forbid the crime)
Be carried down the stream of time
In Shoals, unnotic'd and forgot,
On LETHE's stream, like flags, to rot?
No—they shall live, and each fair name,
Recorded in the book of fame,

---

[1] Algernon Sidney, the Whig martyr for liberty, who was executed after the abortive Rye House Plot in 1683.

Founded on Honour's basis, fast
As the round Earth, to ages last.
Some Virtues vanish with our breath,
Virtue like this lives after death.
Old Time himself, his scythe thrown by,
Himself lost in Eternity,
An everlasting crown shall twine
To make a WILKES and SIDNEY join.

But should some slave-got Villain dare
Chains for his Country to prepare,
And, by his birth to slav'ry broke,
Make her too feel the galling yoke,
May he be evermore accurs'd,
Amongst bad men be rank'd the worst,
May he be still Himself, and still
Go on in Vice, and perfect Ill,
May his broad crimes each day increase,
Till he can't Live, nor Die in Peace,
May he be plung'd so deep in shame
That S[andwich] may'nt endure his name,
And hear, scarce crawling on the earth,
His children curse him for their birth,
May LIBERTY, beyond the grave,
Ordain him to be still a slave,
Grant him what here he most requires,
And damn him with his own desires!

But should some Villain, in support
And zeal for a despairing Court,
Placing in Craft his confidence
And making Honour a pretence
To do a deed of deepest shame,
Whilst filthy lucre is his aim;
Should such a Wretch, with sword or knife,
Contrive to practice 'gainst the life
Of One, who, honour'd thro' the land,
For Freedom made a glorious stand,

> Whose chief, perhaps his only crime,
> Is (if plain Truth at such a time
> May dare her sentiments to tell)
> That He his Country loves too well;
> May He,—but words are all too weak
> The feelings of my heart to speak—
> May He—O for a noble curse
> Which might his very marrow pierce—
> The general contempt engage,
> And be the MARTIN [1] of his age.

[1] Samuel Martin, M.P., Secretary to the Treasury and one of Bute's creatures. He fought a duel with Wilkes in November 1763 and severely wounded him.

31 Joseph Priestley:
An Essay on the First Principles of
Government (1768)

Part I. Of Political Liberty [pp. 15–45]

In countries where every member of the society enjoys an
equal power of arriving at the supreme offices, and consequently of directing the strength and the sentiments of the
whole community, there is a state of the most perfect political
liberty. On the other hand, in countries where a man is, by his
birth or fortune, excluded from these offices, or from a power of
voting for proper persons to fill them; that man, whatever be
the form of the government, or whatever civil liberty, or power
over his own actions he may have, has no power over those of
another, has no share in the government, and therefore has
no political liberty at all. Nay his own conduct, as far as the
society does interfere, is, in all cases, directed by others. . . .
Let it be observed, in this place, that I by no means assert,
that the good of mankind requires a state of the most perfect
political liberty. This, indeed, is not possible, except in exceeding small states. . . . In general, it should seem, that [in large
states] none but persons of considerable fortune should be
capable of arriving at the highest offices in the government;
not only because, all other circumstances being equal, such
persons will generally have had the best education, and consequently be the best qualified to act for the public good; but
also, as they will necessarily have the most property at stake,
and will, therefore, be most interested in the fate of their
country.

For the same reason, it may, perhaps, be more eligible, that those who are extremely dependent should not be allowed to have votes in the nomination of the chief magistrates; because this might in some instances, be only throwing more votes into the hands of those persons on whom they depend. But if, in every state of considerable extent, we suppose a gradation of elective offices, and if we likewise suppose the lowest classes of the people to have votes in the nomination of the lowest officers, and, as they increase in wealth and importance, to have a share in the choice of persons to fill the higher posts, till they themselves be admitted candidates for places of public trust; we shall, perhaps, form an idea of as much political liberty as is consistent with the state of mankind. And I think experience shews, that the highest offices of all, equivalent to that of king, ought to be in some measure hereditary, as in England; elective monarchies having generally been the theatre of cabals, confusion, and misery. . . .

But if there be any truth in the principles above laid down, it must be a fundamental maxim in all governments, that if any man hold what is called a high rank, or enjoy privileges, and prerogatives in a state, it is because the good of the state requires that he should hold that rank, or enjoy those privileges; and such persons, whether they be called kings, senators, or nobles; or by whatever names, or titles, they be distinguished, are, to all intents and purposes, the servants of the public, and accountable to the people for the discharge of their respective offices.

If such magistrates abuse their trust, in the people, therefore, lies the right of deposing, and consequently of punishing them. And the only reason why abuses which have crept into offices have been connived at, is, that the correcting of them, by having recourse to first principles, and the people taking into their own hands their right to appoint or change their officers, and to ascertain the bounds of their authority, is far from being easy, except in small states; so that the remedy would often be worse than the disease.

But, in the largest states, if the abuses of government should, at any time, be great and manifest; if the servants of the people, forgetting their masters, and their masters' interest, should pursue a separate one of their own; if, instead of considering

that they are made for the people, they should consider the
people as made for them; if the oppressions and violations of
right should be great, flagrant, and universally resented; if the
tyrannical governors should have no friends but a few syco-
phants, who had long preyed upon the vitals of their fellow
citizens, and who might be expected to desert a government,
whenever their interests should be detached from it: if, in
consequence of these circumstances, it should become manifest,
that the risque, which would be run in attempting a revolution would be trifling, and the evils which might be apprehended from it, were far less than these which were actually
suffered, and which were daily increasing; in the name of
God, I ask, what principles are those, which ought to restrain
an injured and insulted people from asserting their natural
rights, and from changing, or even punishing their governors
that is their servants, who had abused their trust; or from
altering the whole form of their government, if it appeared to
be of a structure so liable to abuse?

To say that these forms of government have been long
established, and that these oppressions have been long suffered,
without any complaint, is to supply the strongest argument
for their abolition. . . . Nothing can more justly excite the
indignation of an honest and oppressed citizen, than to hear
a prelate, who enjoys a considerable benefice, under a corrupt
government, pleading for its support by those abominable
perversions of scripture, which have been too common on
this occasion; as by urging in its favour that passage of St.
Paul, *The powers which be are ordained of God*, and others of a
similar import. It is a sufficient answer to such an absurd
quotation as this, that, for the same reason, the powers which
will be will be ordained of God also. . . .

It will be said, that it is opening a door to rebellion, to assert
that magistrates, abusing their power, may be set aside by
the people, who are of course their own judges when that
power is abused. May not the people, it is said, abuse their
power, as well as their governors? I answer, it is very possible
they may abuse their power: it is possible they may imagine
themselves oppressed when they are not: it is possible that
their animosity may be artfully and unreasonably inflamed,

by ambitious and enterprising men, whose views are often best answered by popular tumults and insurrections; and the people may suffer in consequence of their folly and precipitancy. But what man is there, or what body of men (whose right to direct their own conduct was never called in question) but are liable to be imposed upon, and to suffer in consequence of their mistaken apprehensions and precipitate conduct? . . . English history will inform us, that the people of this country have always borne extreme oppression, for a long time before there has appeared any danger of a general insurrection against the government. . . .

The sum of what hath been advanced upon this head, is a maxim, than which nothing is more true, that *every government, whatever be the form of it, is originally, and antecedent to its present form, an equal republic*; and, consequently, that every man, when he comes to be sensible of his natural rights, and to feel his own importance, will consider himself as fully equal to any other person whatever. The consideration of riches and power, however acquired, must be entirely set aside, when we come to these first principles. The very idea of property, or right of any kind, is founded upon a regard to the general good of the society, under whose protection it is enjoyed; and nothing is properly *a man's own*, but what general rules, which have for their object the good of the whole, give to him. To whomsoever the society delegates its power, it is delegated to them for the more easy management of public affairs, and in order to make the more effectual provision for the happiness of the whole. Whoever enjoys property, or riches in the state, enjoys them for the good of the state, as well as for himself; and whenever those powers, riches, or rights of any kind, are abused, to the injury of the whole, that awful and ultimate tribunal, in which every citizen hath an equal voice, may demand the resignation of them . . . Magistrates, therefore, who consult not the good of the public, and who employ their power to oppress the people, are a public nuisance, and their power is abrogated *ipso facto*. . . .

32 Oliver Goldsmith:
The Deserted Village (1770)

[Lines 35–74, 265–336]

. . .
   Sweet smiling village, loveliest of the lawn,
Thy sports are fled, and all thy charms withdrawn;
Amidst thy bowers the tyrant's hand is seen,
And desolation saddens all thy green:
One only master grasps the whole domain,
And half a tillage stints thy smiling plain.
No more thy glassy brook reflects the day,
But, chok'd with sedges, works its weedy way;
Along thy glades, a solitary guest,
The hollow-sounding bittern guards its nest;
Amidst thy desert-walks the lapwing flies,
And tires their echoes with unvaried cries;
Sunk are thy bowers in shapeless ruin all,
And the long grass o'ertops the mouldering wall;
And trembling, shrinking from the spoiler's hand,
Far, far away thy children leave the land.
   Ill fares the land, to hastening ills a prey,
Where wealth accumulates, and men decay:
Princes and lords may flourish, or may fade;
A breath can make them, as a breath has made:
But a bold peasantry, their country's pride,
When once destroy'd, can never be supplied.
   A time there was, ere England's griefs began,
When every rood of ground maintain'd its man;
For him light labour spread her wholesome store,
Just gave what life requir'd, but gave no more:

His best companions, innocence and health;
And his best riches, ignorance of wealth.
    But times are alter'd; trade's unfeeling train
Usurp the land and dispossess the swain;
Along the lawn, where scatter'd hamlets rose,
Unwieldy wealth and cumbrous pomp repose,
And every want to opulence allied,
And every pang that folly pays to pride.
These gentle hours that plenty bade to bloom,
Those calm desires that ask'd but little room,
Those healthful sports that grac'd the peaceful scene,
Liv'd in each look, and brighten'd all the green;
These, far departing, seek a kinder shore,
And rural mirth and manners are no more.
. . .
Ye friends to truth, ye statesmen who survey
The rich man's joys increase, the poor's decay,
'Tis yours to judge how wide the limits stand
Between a splendid and an happy land.
Proud swells the tide with loads of freighted ore,
And shouting folly hails them from her shore;
Hoards even beyond the miser's wish abound,
And rich men flock from all the world around;
Yet count our gains; this wealth is but a name
That leaves our useful products still the same.
Not so the loss. The man of wealth and pride
Takes up a space that many poor supplied;
Space for his lake, his park's extended bounds,
Space for his horses, equipage, and hounds:
The robe that wraps his limbs in silken sloth
Has robbed the neighbouring fields of half their growth;
His seat, where solitary sports are seen,
Indignant spurns the cottage from the green:
Around the world each needful product flies,
For all the luxuries the world supplies;
While thus the land, adorn'd for pleasure, all
In barren splendour feebly waits the fall.
    As some fair female unadorn'd and plain,
Secure to please while youth confirms her reign,

Slights every borrow'd charm that dress supplies,
Nor shares with art the triumph of her eyes;
But when those charms are past, for charms are frail,
When time advances, and when lovers fail,
She then shines forth, solicitous to bless,
In all the glaring impotence of dress,
Thus fares the land, by luxury betray'd:
In nature's simplest charms at first array'd,
But verging to decline, its splendours rise;
Its vistas strike, its palaces surprise:
While, scourg'd by famine from the smiling land,
The mournful peasant leads his humble band,
And while he sinks, without one arm to save,
The country blooms—a garden, and a grave.

Where then, ah! where shall poverty reside,
To 'scape the pressure of contiguous pride?
If to some common's fenceless limits stray'd
He drives his flock to pick the scanty blade,
Those fenceless fields the sons of wealth divide,
And even the bare-worn common is denied.

If to the city sped—what waits him there?
To see profusion that he must not share;
To see ten thousand baneful arts combin'd
To pamper luxury and thin mankind;
To see those joys the sons of pleasure know
Extorted from his fellow-creature's woe.
Here while the courtier glitters in brocade,
There the pale artist plies the sickly trade;
Here, while the proud their long-drawn pomps display,
There, the black gibbet glooms beside the way.
The dome where pleasure holds her midnight reign
Here, richly deckt, admits the gorgeous train:
Tumultuous grandeur crowds the blazing square,
The rattling chariots clash, the torches glare.
Sure scenes like these no troubles e'er annoy!
Sure these denote one universal joy!
Are these thy serious thoughts?—Ah, turn thine eyes
Where the poor houseless shivering female lies.
She once, perhaps, in village plenty blest,

Has wept at tales of innocence distrest;
Her modest looks the cottage might adorn,
Sweet as the primrose peeps beneath the thorn:
Now lost to all,—her friends, her virtue fled,—
Near her betrayer's door she lays her head,
And, pinched with cold, and shrinking from the shower,
With heavy heart deplores that luckless hour
When idly first, ambitious of the town,
She left her wheel, and robes of country brown.

. . .

33 A Letter of Junius (1771) (Anonymous)

[Between 1769 and 1772 Junius sent to the *Public Advertiser* many letters critical of the ministers and their policies. It is still uncertain to this day who wrote them, but most experts believe that it was Sir Philip Francis.]

Letter XLIV

To the Printer of the *Public Advertiser*.   22 April 1771.
Sir,
. . . The persons who, till within these few years, have been most distinguished by their zeal for high church and prerogative, are now, it seems, the great assertors of the privileges of the House of Commons. This sudden alteration of their sentiments or language carries with it a suspicious appearance. When I hear the undefined privileges of the popular branch of the legislature exalted by Tories and Jacobites, at the expense of those strict rights, which are known to the subject, and limited by the laws, I cannot but suspect, that some mischievous scheme is in agitation, to destroy both law and privilege, by opposing them to each other. They who have uniformly denied the power of the whole legislature to alter the descent of the crown, and whose ancestors, in rebellion against his Majesty's family, have defended that doctrine at the hazard of their lives, now tell us that privilege of parliament is the only rule of right, and the chief security of the public freedom.—I fear, Sir, that, while forms remain, there has been some material change in the substance of our constitution. The opinions of these men were too absurd to be so easily renounced. Liberal minds are open to conviction.—Liberal doctrines are capable of improvement.—There are proselytes from atheism, but none from superstition.—If their present professions were sincere, I think they could not

but be highly offended at seeing a question, concerning parliamentary privilege, unnecessarily started at a season so unfavourable to the House of Commons, . . .

The state of things is much altered in this country, since it was necessary to protect our representatives against the direct power of the crown. We have nothing to apprehend from prerogative, but every thing from undue influence. Formerly it was the interest of the people, that the privileges of parliament should be left unlimited and undefined. At present it is not only their interest, but I hold it to be essentially necessary to the preservation of the constitution, that the privileges of parliament should be strictly ascertained, and confined within the narrowest bounds the nature of their institution will admit of. Upon the same principle, on which I would have resisted prerogative in the last century, I now resist privilege. It is indifferent to me, whether the crown, by its own immediate act, imposes new and dispenses with old laws, or whether the same arbitrary power produces the same effects through the medium of the House of Commons. We trusted our representatives with privileges for their own defence and ours. We cannot hinder their desertion, but we can prevent their carrying over their arms to the service of the enemy.—It will be said, that I begin with endeavouring to reduce the argument concerning privilege to a mere question of convenience;—that I deny at one moment what I would allow at another; and that to resist the power of a prostituted House of Commons may establish a precedent injurious to all future parliaments.—To this I answer generally, that human affairs are in no instance governed by strict positive right. If change of circumstances were to have no weight in directing our conduct and opinions, the mutual intercourse of mankind would be nothing more than a contention between positive and equitable right. Society would be a state of war, and law itself would be injustice. On this general ground, it is highly reasonable, that the degree of our submission to privileges, which have never been defined by any positive law, should be considered as a question of convenience, and proportioned to the confidence we repose in the integrity of our representatives. As to the injury we may do to any future and more respectable House of Commons, I own I am not now sanguine enough to expect a more plentiful harvest of parliamentary virtue in one year than another. Our political climate is severely altered; and without dwelling upon the depravity of modern times, I think no reasonable man will expect that, as human nature is constituted, the enormous influence of the crown should cease to prevail over 'the virtue of individuals. The mischief lies too deep to be cured by any remedy less than some great convulsion, which may either carry back the constitution to its original principles, or utterly destroy it. I do not doubt that, in the first session after the next election, some popular measures may be adopted. The present House of Commons have injured themselves by a too early and public profession of their principles, and if a strain of prostitution, which had no example, were within the reach of emulation, it might be imprudent to hazard the experiment too soon. But after all, Sir, it is very immaterial whether a House of Commons shall preserve their virtue for a week, a month, or a year. The influence which makes a septennial parliament dependent upon the pleasure of the crown, has a permanent operation, and cannot fail of success.—My premises, I know, will be denied in argument, but every man's conscience tells him they are true. It remains then to be considered, whether it be for the interest of the people that privilege of parliament (which, in respect to the purposes for which it has hitherto been acquiesced under, is merely nominal) should be contracted within some certain limits, or whether the subject shall be left at the mercy of a power, arbitrary upon the face of it, and notoriously under the direction of the crown. . . .

PART THREE

The Debate on Reforming the 'Whig' Constitution

During the middle decades of the eighteenth century, from the 1720s to the early 1770s, the critics of the way the constitution was working under the Whig supremacy made little headway. The influence of the crown was not diminished, the aristocratic Whig connections remained entrenched in power and a conservative interpretation of the constitution prevailed. Nevertheless, during these years there had been a great deal of serious political debate on such questions as corruption and liberty, the influence of the crown and the independence of parliament, and the structure of politics and the need for an effective opposition. These arguments were given wide currency not only in parliament, but in newspapers and pamphlets, poems and plays. While they failed to dent the ministerial majority in parliament, largely because the country was enjoying such unprecedented stability and prosperity, the 'patriots' had provided an excellent political education for an extra-parliamentary audience. Through their endeavours some of the weaknesses in the existing political system were clearly revealed in print even if they were not yet widely accepted. When, in the later eighteenth century, significant new developments began to threaten the country's stability and prosperity, the debate on the working of the constitution became far less academic and far less the preserve of frustrated politicians. Increasingly, the question that came to be debated was whether the constitution might not require fundamental changes.

The two most obvious causes for the growing dissatisfaction

145

with the prevailing political system were the successful revolutions in America and in France. The American colonists, claiming the political liberties of British subjects and borrowing many of the arguments of the British 'patriots' in their dispute with the government in London, successfully asserted their right to independence. This was Britain's greatest reverse in the whole eighteenth century. In the 1790s the French Revolution not only challenged all the established and conservative regimes of Europe, including Britain, but provoked an intense debate on such radical political notions as liberty, democracy, republicanism and the natural equality of all men. Together these two revolutions helped to divide Britain into two broad political groups: those who desired and those who opposed constitutional reforms. These political tensions were exacerbated by the rapid social and economic transformation Britain experienced in the late eighteenth century as the industrial revolution gained momentum. Most of those who already enjoyed political power were hostile to reform and became increasingly hostile as the threat from radicals at home and abroad advanced significantly in the 1790s. The reformers can be roughly divided into moderates and radicals. The former included such extra-parliamentary organisations as the Yorkshire Association of the early 1780s and the parliamentary Foxite Whigs of the 1790s. The radicals were only on the fringes of the political nation, sometimes having the vote but rarely, if ever, getting into parliament. They appeared to be a powerful force in the early 1790s, but were soon crushed by the repressive policies of a thoroughly alarmed government.

At first the demands for reform came from those who already enjoyed a measure of political power. Not surprisingly their policies echoed the demands of earlier 'patriots' but some significant advances began to be made. The Rockingham connection, one of the most powerful Whig groups, was convinced that it was being unfairly denied office by the personal prejudices of George III. The group's leading ideologue and most able spokesman, Edmund Burke, believed that he and his political friends would not gain power merely by a campaign to reduce the influence of the crown. What was needed was a united opposition party with a programme capable of gaining the support of a parliamentary majority. Whereas Bolingbroke had wanted one national Country party which would melt away once it had successfully rejected the political methods of Walpole, Burke was ready to accept the existence of permanent parties each with its own particular programme [No. 34]. In 1774 James Burgh advocated some of the traditional patriot or Country policies, including annual parliaments, the expulsion of placemen from the Commons and an independent militia; but he went on to demand a reform of parliament. He wanted greater representation for the commercial, industrial and monied interests, and also a widening of the franchise [No. 35]. The Yorkshire Association, led by Christopher Wyvill, was more moderate in its demands, but was the most important extra-parliamentary organization that had yet appeared in the eighteenth century. Its remedies for the nation's constitutional ills were a reduction of the crown's influence in parliament and an increase of county constituencies to guarantee the independence of the House of Commons [No. 36].

Christopher Wyvill created the Yorkshire Association, but his methods were soon copied by other county associations whose leaders demanded more far-reaching reforms. Major Cartwright and John Jebb, for example, proposed more extensive alterations in both parliamentary representation and the franchise itself. Jebb wanted not only to increase the county representation, but to abolish the worst pocket and rotten boroughs which were in the control of a single patron. He also pressed for a limited extension of the franchise and for annual parliaments [No. 37]. The Society for Constitutional Information, stimulated by the activities and demands of the county associations, began to argue the case for the equality of all men in the choice of parliamentary representatives [No. 38].

The political gains made by the extra-parliamentary groups of the early 1780s were limited to a measure of 'economical' reform. Revenue officers were disfranchised, government contractors were excluded from the Commons and a few sinecures were abolished, but the crown's parliamentary influence was not seriously diminished. In 1785 the Younger Pitt, the prime minister, did make an effort to abolish the worst thirty-six rotten boroughs and to re-distribute these seventy-two seats to London and the counties, but this proposal was defeated in the Commons. Despite the shock of the loss of the American colonies, a majority of the political nation was still convinced of the virtues of the British constitution. Democratic ideas were still anathema to men convinced that political power should be firmly in the hands of the men of landed property. Most of the great Whig aristocrats, who had considerable influence in both houses of parliament, were reluctant even to consider a moderate measure of reform. They were ready to reduce the influence of the crown, but they jealously protected their own. Economic reform might achieve the former, but parliamentary reform would endanger the latter. Not surprisingly, their political motives came in for scathing criticisms from some commentators, notably Josiah Tucker [No. 39].

The reform movement languished in the later 1780s until the debate on the reform of the British constitution was revived and revitalized by the shock-wave created by the dramatic events in France. A ferment of ideas and tremendous enthusiasm for political reform were stimulated by the French Revolution. Corresponding societies, which sought links with the French revolutionary leaders and echoed their demands for extensive reforms, sprang up throughout Britain, while poets such as Wordsworth, Coleridge and Southey welcomed the liberation of the human spirit [Nos. 45, 49, 50 and 51]. Richard Price, an old campaigner, and the London Corresponding Society demanded universal male suffrage [Nos. 40 and 45]. When the Bishop of Llandaff preached a sermon attacking the French Revolution, William Wordsworth prepared an eloquent defence of liberty and of the equal rights of all men. Unfortunately, he neither sent nor published his reply to the bishop [No. 49].

In many ways the demands of radicals like Thomas Hardy and Richard Price were a natural and logical extension of the ideas of earlier reformers such as Priestley, Jebb and Cartwright. Other radicals, however, made more significant advances in defending the natural rights of man and in proposing more revolutionary programmes of reform. Tom Paine wrote probably the greatest defence of the rights of man and also advocated such social reforms as old age pensions and family allowances which presaged some of the socialist demands of the next two centuries [No. 42]. In some ways William Godwin, with Paine the most influential radical political theorist of the 1790s, was a moderate democrat who was against the organization of political parties and opposed violent revolution. He maintained that steady political progress could only be made by means of advancing knowledge and improved education. Yet he was one of the greatest critics of all political authority which he regarded as unnecessary restrictions on a man's natural right to freedom [No. 46]. Paine and Godwin were the greatest radical theorists of the 1790s, but others proposed more far-reaching practical reforms. Godwin's wife, Mary Wollstonecraft, demanded that legal reforms should be made which would put women on the same footing as men [No. 44]. Thomas Spence, who had first put forward his ideas in a lecture in 1775, maintained that political equality could not be secured without economic equality. He therefore advocated an equal re-distribution of the wealth and property of the country [No. 47].

The revolutionary proposals of the 1790s, combined with the French threat to export revolution to the rest of Europe, provoked a much more spirited and vocal resistance than did the reform movement of the early 1780s. The government itself, thoroughly alarmed, initiated a whole series of repressive measures designed to destroy the radical movement in Britain. The corresponding societies were suppressed, freedom of association and expression were curtailed [No. 51], and such radicals as Paine, Spence and Hardy were subjected to political persecution. A pamphlet war was also waged against the radicals. Some of these works simply appealed to patriotism and pandered to prejudice. They asserted, but did not demonstrate, the virtues of the British constitution, while accusing the French of all manner of political excesses [No. 48]. Some, like the declaration of the Church and King Club, were convinced that the constitution was perfect and in no need of even moderate reform [No. 43]. Most of these were poor replies to the works of Paine, Godwin and others. In Edmund Burke's *Reflections on the Revolution in France*, however, there was one brilliant defence of the old Whig constitution. Burke not only criticized the excesses and follies of the French revolutionaries, but made an incisive attack on the whole doctrine of the equal natural rights of man [No. 41].

It is impossible to calculate the political influence of the great writers of the 1790s. Burke, Paine and Godwin were undoubtedly widely read and their works are of permanent value, but it is possible that they were only preaching to the converted or, at most, convincing the hesitant. Both sides certainly provided formidable arguments for those who had their own reasons for advocating or resisting the reform of the Whig constitution. The victory may have gone to Burke and the radicals may have been defeated, but this was not solely due to the intrinsic merits of their works. Those already entrenched in power did not need Burke to persuade them to defend their privileges, while the radicals never had the kind of mass support needed to challenge the political establishment. Even such friends of liberty as Coleridge, Wordsworth and Burns abandoned any desire for reform once Britain was engaged in a life or death struggle with France [Nos. 52 and 53], though Wyvill and the Foxite Whigs kept alive the hope of moderate parliamentary reform. Despite their defeat, however, the radical writers need to be studied; not only because they influenced future generations of reformers, but because their work testifies to the ferment of political ideas in the late eighteenth century. The nature and content of a political debate are as important to the historian as the immediate outcome of it.

34 Edmund Burke:
Thoughts on the Cause of the Present Discontents (1770)

[Having argued that the cause of the present discontents is the appearance of a court cabal of 'king's friends', which has destroyed the influence of the great Whig connections and has weakened the independence of parliament, Burke goes on to suggest how these developments can be arrested and the balance of the constitution restored. In seeking to justify the 'formed opposition' of the Rockingham connection Burke undoubtedly exaggerated the power of the crown and the dependence of parliament. *The Works of Edmund Burke* (Bohn edition, 1886), i, 365–81]

. . . The first ideas which generally suggest themselves, for the cure of parliamentary disorders, are, to shorten the duration of parliaments; and to disqualify all, or a great number, of placemen from a seat in the House of Commons. Whatever efficacy there may be in those remedies, I am sure in the present state of things it is impossible to apply them. A restoration of the right of free election is a preliminary indispensable to every other reformation. What alterations ought afterwards to be made in the constitution, is a matter of deep and difficult research. . . . I confess, then, that I have no sort of reliance upon either a triennial parliament, or a place-bill. With regard to the former, perhaps, it might rather serve to counteract, than to promote, the ends that are proposed by it. To say nothing of the horrible disorders among the people attending frequent elections, I should be fearful of committing, every three years, the independent gentlemen of the country into a contest with the treasury. It is easy to see which of the contending parties would be ruined first. . . . It is not easy to foresee, what the effect would be of disconnecting with parliament the greatest part of those who hold civil employments, and of such mighty and important bodies as the military and naval establishments. It were better, perhaps, that they should have a corrupt interest in the forms of the constitution, than that they should have none at all. This is a question altogether different from the disqualification of a particular description of revenue officers from seats in parliament; or, perhaps, of all the lower sorts of them from votes in elections. In the former case, only the few are affected; in the latter, only the inconsiderable. But a great official, a great professional, a great military and naval interest, all necessarily comprehending many people of the first weight, ability, wealth, and spirit, has been gradually formed in the kingdom. These new interests must be let into a share of representation, else possibly they may be inclined to destroy those institutions of which they are not permitted to partake. . . . It were better, undoubtedly, that no influence at all could affect the mind of a member of parliament. But of all modes of influence, in my opinion, a place under the government is the least disgraceful to the man who holds it, and by far the most safe to the country. I would not shut out that sort of influence which is open and visible, which is connected with the dignity and the service of the state, when it is not in my power to prevent the influence of contracts, of subscriptions, of direct bribery, and those innumerable methods of clandestine corruption, which are abundantly in the hands of the court, and which will be applied as long as these means of corruption, and the disposition to be corrupted, have existence amongst us. . . .

. . . Government may in a great measure be restored, if any considerable bodies of men have honesty and resolution enough never to accept administration, unless this garrison of *king's men*, which is stationed, as in a citadel, to control and enslave it, be entirely broken and disbanded, and every work they have thrown up be levelled with the ground. . . . This cabal [of King's Friends] has, with great success, propagated a doctrine which serves for a colour to those acts of treachery; and whilst it receives any degree of countenance, it will be utterly senseless to look for a vigorous opposition to the court party. The doctrine is this: That all political connexions are in their nature factious, and as such ought to be dissipated and destroyed; and that the rule for forming administrations is mere personal ability, rated by the judgment of this cabal upon it, and taken by draughts from every division and denomination of public men. . . . That connexion and faction are equivalent terms, is an opinion which has been carefully inculcated at all times by unconstitutional statesmen. The reason is evident. Whilst men are linked together, they easily and speedily communicate the alarm of any evil design. They are enabled to fathom it with united strength. Whereas, when they lie dispersed, without concert, order, or discipline, communication is uncertain, counsel difficult, and resistance impracticable. . . In a connexion, the most inconsiderable man, by adding to the weight of the whole, has his value, and his use; out of it, the greatest talents are wholly unserviceable to the public. No man, who is not inflamed by vain-glory into enthusiasm, can flatter himself that his single, unsupported, desultory, unsystematic endeavours, are of power to defeat the subtle designs and united cabals of ambitious citizens. When bad men combine, the good must associate; else they will fall, one by one, an unpitied sacrifice in a contemptible struggle. . . .

In one of the most fortunate periods of our history this country was governed by a *connexion*; I mean the great connexion of Whigs in the reign of Queen Anne. . . . They believed that no men could act with effect, who did not act in concert; that no men could act in concert, who did not act with confidence; that no men could act with confidence, who were not bound together by common opinions, common affections, and common interests. . . . Party is a body of men united, for promoting by their joint endeavours the national interest, upon some particular principle in which they are all agreed. For my part, I find it impossible to conceive, that any one believes in his own politics, or thinks them to be of any weight, who refuses to adopt the means of having them reduced into practice. . . . Therefore every honourable connexion will avow it is their first purpose, to pursue every just method to put the men who hold their opinions into such a condition as may enable them to carry their common plans into execution, with all the power and authority of the state. As this power is attached to certain situations, it is their duty to contend for these situations. . . . Such a generous contention for power, on such manly and honourable maxims, will easily be distinguished from the mean and interested struggle for place and emolument. . . .

Men thinking freely, will, in particular instances, think differently. But still as the greater part of the measures which arise in the course of public business are related to, or dependent on, some great *leading general principles in government*, a man must be peculiarly unfortunate in the choice of his political company if he does not agree with them at least nine times in ten. If he does not concur in these general principles upon which the party is founded, and which necessarily draw on a concurrence in their application, he ought from the beginning to have chosen some other, more conformable to his opinions. . . .

If the reader believes that there really exists such a faction as I have described; a faction ruling by the private inclinations of a court, against the general sense of the people; and that this faction, whilst it pursues a scheme for undermining all the foundations of our freedom, weakens (for the present at least) all the powers of executory government, rendering us abroad contemptible, and at home distracted; he will believe also, that nothing but a firm combination of public men against this body, and that, too, supported by the hearty concurrence of the people at large, can possibly get the better of it. . . . If other ideas should prevail, things must remain in their present confusion; until they are hurried into all the rage of civil violence; or until they sink into the dead repose of despotism.

35 James Burgh: Political Disquisitions (1774)

[From Vol. i, 28–9, 36–8, 51–4]

. . . Every government, to have a reasonable expectation of permanency, ought to be founded in truth, justice, and the reason of things. Our admirable constitution, the envy of Europe, is founded in injustice. Eight hundred individuals rule all, themselves accountable to none. Of these about 300 are born rulers, whether qualified or not. Of the others, a great many are said to be elected by a handful of beggars instead of the number and property, who have the right to be electors. And of these pretended electors, the greatest part are obliged to choose the person nominated by some lord, or by the minister. Instead of the power's returning annually into the hands of the people, or, to speak properly, of the boroughs, the lengthening of parliament to septennial has deprived them of six parts in seven of their power; and if the power returned annually, as it ought, all the people would still have reason to complain, but the handful, who vote the members into the house.

In consequence of the inadequate state of representation, the sense of the people may be grossly misapprehended, or misrepresented, and it may turn out to be of very little consequence, that members were willing to obey the instructions of their constituents; because that would not be obeying the general sense of the people. For the people are not their constituents. The people of England are the innumerable multitude which fills, like one continued city, a great part of Middlesex, Kent and Surrey; the countless inhabitants of the vast ridings of Yorkshire; the multitudes, who swarm in the cities and great towns of Bristol, Liverpool, Manchester, Birmingham, Ely, and others; some of which places have no representatives at all, and the rest are unequally represented. These places comprehend the greatest part of the people. Whereas the instructions would be sent from the hungry boroughs of Cornwal, Devonshire, &c. In short, the sense of the constituents would be, at best, only the sense of a few thousands; whereas it ought to be that of several hundreds of thousands, . . .

. . . It is commonly insisted on, that persons in servitude to others, and those who receive alms, ought not to be admitted to vote for members of parliament, because it is supposed, that their votes will be influenced by those, on whom they depend.

But the objection from influence would fall to the ground, if the state were on a right foot, and parliament free from court-influence. . . . Every man has what may be called property, and unalienable property. Every man has a life, a personal liberty, a character, a right to his earnings, a right to a religious profession and worship according to his conscience, &c. and many men, who are in a state of dependence upon others, and who receive charity, have wives and children, in whom they have a right. Thus the poor are in danger of being injured by the government in a variety of ways. But, according to the commonly received doctrine, that servants, and those who receive alms, have no right to vote for members of parliament, an immense multitude of the people are utterly deprived of all power in determining who shall be the protectors of their lives, their personal liberty, their little property (which though singly considered is of small value, yet is upon the whole a very great object) and the chastity of their wives and daughters, &c. What is particularly hard upon the poor in this case is, that though they have no share in determining who shall be the lawgivers of their country, they have a very heavy share in raising the taxes which support government. The taxes on malt, on beer, leather, soap, candles, and other articles, which are paid chiefly by the poor, who are allowed no votes for members of parliament, amount to as much as a heavy land-tax. The landed interest would complain grievously, if they had no power of electing representatives. And it is an established maxim in free states, that whoever contributes to the expences of government ought to be satisfied concerning the application of the money contributed by them; consequently ought to have a share in electing those, who have the power of applying their money. . . .

. . . Representation in the house of commons is inadequate in other respects besides those already mentioned.

In antient times, when parliaments were first established, there was no property, but that of land. Therefore all powers, and all honours, were heaped on the landed men. The consequence was, that the landed interest was too well represented, to the detriment (in our times) of the mercantile and monied. This is an occasion of various evils. For many of our country-gentlemen are but bad judges of the importance of the mercantile interest, and do not wisely consult it in their bills and acts. Of this kind are the game-act, the dog-act, and taxes on every necessary of life, which give our rivals in trade a great advantage over us. And ministers, to curry favour with the house of commons, are tempted to burden commerce with taxes for the sake of easing the landed interest. See the art of Walpole to this purpose, by proposing to ease the land of one shilling in the pound, and laying a duty on salt for three years, to make up the deficiency. It was objected to this proposal, that the salt-duty was always reckoned a grievous burden upon the manufacturing poor, and was therefore taken off; and that it was a strange paradox, that the landed gentlemen were poorer than the poor, and therefore in more need of relief from a heavy tax.

It is the overbalance of the power in the hands of the landed men, that has produced the bounty on exportation of corn (of which more fully hereafter) which increases the manufacturer's expence of living, and discourages the exportation of our manufactures. This is, in the end, hurtful to the landed interest. But short sighted and selfish men do not see it in that light; nor will seem to understand, that the land-tax, while nominally three shillings in the pound, is not really ninepence. The time was, when land in England might have been purchased for a 50th part of its present value. What has given it the 49 parts additional worth? Can any one imagine, the difference is owing to any thing, but our trade and manufactures? . . . .

Is not an aristocracy a government in the hands of a few, or of one class, or one interest, excluding the body of the people of property from their due weight in government? Is not our house of peers wholly, and our house of commons chiefly filled with men, whose property is land? Is not therefore the government of this mercantile and manufacturing country in the hands of the landed interest to the exclusion of the mercantile and manufactural? Does not then the government of this country tend too much to aristocracy?

The eldest sons of Scotch peers are declared incapable of sitting in the house of commons. But the sons of English peers may sit, so that ten individuals out of one family may be legislators. Is not this too aristocratical?

It is said, property in land is more capable of being proved, than in merchandice, manufactures, or stocks. But this is frivolous; for any man, though possessed of an ostensible land-estate, may be in debt to more than the value of his estate; and where is then his qualification?

The interest of merchants is so much the interest of the nation, that there can hardly be too many merchants in parliament. The London members almost always vote on the side of liberty. It is objected, that each merchant will probably vote in parliament for what is most for the advantage of his own particular branch. True. Therefore let a considerable number of merchants always have seats in the house, and then all different interests will be consulted. It has likewise been argued, that merchants are bad members, because they are liable to be influenced in favour of the court by government contracts. But here again comes in my observation concerning partial reformations. Correct all the other abuses, and court-influence will become impossible. Then will appear the advantage of merchants in the house of commons. . . .

As to the monied interest, if the public debts are not to be paid, or some substantial security found for them, it would be very proper, that the monied interest (as such) should have representation in parliament. Else what security have we, that a profligate court will not shut up the exchequer, as

Charles II did, and obtain, by corrupt means, the sanction of parliament for the measure? It is indeed alledged, that the mercantile, manufactural, and monied interests are represented by the members for the cities, and boroughs. But this is nothing to the purpose. Because the qualification required is always to be in land.

[From *The Annual Register*, 1780, pp. 338–9]

To the Honourable the Commons of Great Britain, in Parliament assembled:

The Petition of the Gentlemen, Clergy, and Freeholders of the County of York, sheweth that this nation hath been engaged for several years in a most expensive and unfortunate war; that many of our valuable colonies, having actually declared themselves independent, have formed a strict confederacy with France and Spain the dangerous and inveterate enemies of Great Britain, that the consequence of those combined misfortunes hath been a large addition to the nation's debt, a heavy accumulation on taxes, a rapid decline of the trade, manufactures, and land-rents of the kingdom.

Alarmed at the diminished resources and growing burthens of this country, and convinced that rigid frugality is now indispensably necessary in every department of the state, your petitioners observe with grief, that notwithstanding the calamitous and impoverished condition of the nation, much public money has been improvidently squandered, and that many individuals enjoy sinecure places, efficient places with exorbitent emoluments, and pensions unmerited by public-service, to a large and still increasing amount; whence the crown has acquired a great and unconstitutional influence, which, if not checked, may soon prove fatal to the liberties of this country.

Your petitioners conceiving that the true end of every legitimate government is not the emolument of an individual, but the welfare of the community; and considering that by the constitution of this realm the national purse is intrusted in a peculiar manner to the custody of this honourable house; beg leave further to represent, that until effectual measures be taken to redress the oppressive grievances herein stated, the grant of any additional sum of public money, beyond the produce of the present taxes, will be injurious to the rights and property of the people, and derogatory from the honour and dignity of parliament.

Your petitioners therefore, appealing to the justice of this honourable house, do most earnestly request that, before any new burthens are laid upon this country, effectual measures may be taken by this house to enquire into and correct the gross abuses in the expenditure of public money; to reduce all exorbitent emoluments, to rescind and abolish all sinecure places and unmerited pensions; and to appropriate the produce to the necessities of the state in such manner as to the wisdom of parliament shall seem meet.

And your petitioners shall ever pray, &c. &c.

The following counties presented petitions nearly in the same words:

Middlesex	Dorset
Chester	Devon
Hants.	Norfolk
Hertford	Berks.
Sussex	Bucks.
Huntingdon	Nottingham
Surrey	Kent
Cumberland	Northumberland
Bedford	Suffolk
Essex	Hereford
Gloucester	Cambridge
Somerset	Derby
Wilts.	

Also the cities of London, Westminster, York, Bristol, and the towns of Cambridge, Nottingham, Newcastle, Reading and Bridgewater. The county of Northampton agreed to instruct their members on the points of the petition.

37   John Jebb:
A Letter to Sir Robert Bernard, Chairman of the Huntingdonshire Committee (1781)

[A report after a meeting of the county associations. From *The Works of John Jebb* (1787), ii, 496–504]

. . . It seemed to be the general opinion of the delegates, that parliamentary freedom and independence might be restored by an improved arrangement of the present electors of this kingdom. I did not, therefore, controvert the idea in this stage of the business; I concurred with them in practice as far as they went; but my theory led me to more extensive conclusions.

I considered that the persons, who at present exercise the power of election, in the name of the people of England, might be distributed into three classes.

In the first class would be contained those inhabitants of this kingdom, who possess freeholds to the amount of forty shillings a year and upwards, supposed to number 130,000, and electing ninety-two members to serve for fifty-two counties.

The second class would comprehend 43,000 citizens, freemen, and others, who elect fifty-two members for the twenty-three cities and the two universities.

In the third or last class would be found 41,000 electors, who choose 369 members for 192 towns and boroughs.

It was proposed by the deputies of Yorkshire, that the members elected by the 130,000 freeholders should amount at the least to 192.

As a further barrier against undue influence, I proposed that one hundred should be subtracted from the 369 burgesses, chosen at present by the 41,000 electors, in order that the sum total of the members elected by the present freeholders, citizens, freemen, burgesses, and other electors of England, might remain the same as before.

The motion was not supported; the reasons that induced me to propose this alteration are as follows:

In the first place, it appeared to me, that the house of commons is already sufficiently numerous for all the purposes of its institution. . . .

I secondly reflected, that the persons, who elect the 369 members to serve for the towns and boroughs of the kingdom, are the most dependent part of the nation; and are acknowledged to be, in every respect, the least worthy of being intrusted with the exercise of so important a power as they at present enjoy, to the great injury of the landed and commercial interests of this country.

In the last place, I considered, that the popular sentiment seemed more favourable to the idea of diminishing the number of the borough members, than to the proposed augmentation in the counties. And although it was alledged, that in case this idea were adopted, we should have the interest of the proprietors of boroughs to contend with, it appeared to me such interest might be purchased, in many instances, by a proper compensation; and that even in case some reluctance should be manifested by any of the parties concerned, such persons would probably not continue to oppose the general wish, when they reflected, that the power they enjoyed was utterly inconsistent with the people's undoubted right to an equal representation, whenever they might think proper to assert it.

In proposing this improvement, I proceeded upon the idea, adopted by my brethren of the delegation. But, in fact, I esteem all propositions for an improved arrangement of the present voters of this kingdom, in no further degree worthy of the attention of the public, than as they are preparatory steps to that complete reformation, which I am now more than ever persuaded might be effected by the peaceful efforts of the people, acting by their committees, and uniting in a general association to support their resolves.

I am, as will afterwards more fully appear, decidedly of opinion, that an English house of commons should be a representation of persons, not of property; of men, not of things; and that there is no necessity for the delegation of the impor-

tant right of election to any portion of the community, intermediate between the representative and the great collective
body of the people. But supposing these points were to be
conceded, and supposing the sum total of the standing electors
of this kingdom, who are at present allowed to exercise this
power in derogation of the right of more than a million of their
fellow-citizens, now excluded from their franchise, were to
remain as at this day, it may reasonably be demanded, whether
the 130,000 freeholders, who now enjoy the privilege of electing
ninety-two members, are the persons, whom the landed interest
would depute for this important purpose? Whether there be
not a large proportion of them, who, notwithstanding their
legal qualification, cannot claim, from their station in life,
this great pre-eminence: and whether many copyholders are
not rejected in the present system, whose independent circumstances would render them fitter objects of this trust?

With respect to the 84,000 citizens, burgesses, and other
inhabitants of England, who elect the remaining 421 members,
can we seriously maintain, that they properly represent the
various branches of the commercial interest of this country?
And can it be imagined, that the liberties and properties of
more than five millions of people can be safe, when intrusted
in the hands of representatives, of whom it has been demon-
strated the majority may be returned by a number of electors
less than 6,000, consisting, in general, of the most dependent
and most venal part of the community?

I will dismiss the subject of representation for the present,
and proceed to the next object of parliamentary reformation
proposed by the Yorkshire committee, viz. the shortening the
duration of parliaments to a period not exceeding three
years. . . . I have always imagined the triennial bill to be
equally a violation of the constitution with the septennial. I
conceive, also, that the proper business of a representative, as
indeed is evident from the tenor of the ancient writs, is to act
as an agent for his constituents in the great assembly of the
nation, and, in their name, to assent to such measures, as he
apprehends they would approve. I would ask whether the
sense of the people can with propriety be supposed to be
expressed in that assembly, by persons delegated, as it might

happen, nearly three years before the actual issuing of the yearly proclamation for its convention?

Urged by the force of these reflections, I made the following motion, which, for want of being supported, occasioned no debate:

'Resolved,

That the people of England have an undoubted right to an annual election of members to serve in the commons' house of parliament; and that the act of the sixth of William the third, which afforded the first legal sanction to the duration of parliaments beyond a single session, was subversive of the constitution, and a violation, on the part of the representatives, of the sacred trust reposed in them by their constituents.' . . . .

38 Declaration of those Rights of the Commonalty of Great Britain, without which they cannot be Free (c. 1782)

[Printed and distributed free by the Societyf or Constitutional Information]

It is declared,

First, That the government of this realm, and the making of laws for the same, ought to be lodged in the hands of King, Lords of Parliament, and Representatives of the whole body of the freemen of this realm.

Secondly, That every man of the commonalty (excepting infants, insane persons, and criminals) is, of common right, and by the laws of God, a freeman, and entitled to the full enjoyment of liberty.

Thirdly, That liberty, or freedom, consists in having an actual share in the appointing of those who frame the laws, and who are to be the guardians of every man's life, property, and peace: for the all of one man is as dear to him as the all of another; and the poor man has an equal right, but more need, to have representatives in the legislature than the rich one.

Fourthly, That they who have no voice nor vote in the electing of representatives do not enjoy liberty, but are absolutely enslaved to those who have votes, and to their representatives: for to be enslaved, is to have governors whom other men have set over us, and to be subject to laws made by the representatives of others, without having had representatives of our own to give consent in our behalf.

Fifthly, That a very great majority of the commonalty of this realm are denied the privilege of voting for representatives in parliament, and consequently they are enslaved to a small number, who do now enjoy this privilege exclusively to themselves; but who, it may be presumed, are far from wishing to continue in the exclusive possession of a privilege, by which their fellow-subjects are deprived of common right of justice, of liberty; and which, if not communicated to all, must speedily cause the certain overthrow of our happy constitution, and enslave us all. And,

Sixthly and lastly, we also say and do assert, that it is the right of the commonalty of this realm to elect a new House of Commons once in every year, according to ancient and sacred laws of the land: because, whenever a parliament continues in being for a longer term, very great numbers of the commonalty, who have arrived at the years of manhood since the last election, and therefore have a right to be actually represented in the House of Commons, are then unjustly deprived of that right. At the same time the cause of virtue suffers through the dissipation, and extravagance of the rising generation, whom the enjoyment of the universal right of suffrage would recall from unworthy pleasures, and animate to the full exertion of every generous and patriotic principle which can ornament the mind of man.

When the above Declaration is compared with the present long parliaments, and unequal representation of the people, which have brought this kingdom to the brink of ruin; every true friend to his country is solemnly called upon to demand annual parliaments, and that right of voting which God and the constitution have given him. In the hearty exertion to obtain these civil and just rights, let every one practise that Christian rule, to do unto others as we would they should do unto us. Then will that blessed era come when every man shall be free and happy under his vine, on earth peace, and consequently glory to God in the highest.

A Real Friend to the People.

Josiah Tucker:
Four Letters on Important National
Subjects (1783)

[From Letter II, pp. 23-4, 27-31]
Addressed to the Earl of Shelburne

My Lord,
Were mankind those absolutely free, and independent beings,
which some of our republican doctors have represented them
to be, it would be impossible for them to be under any influence
at all. They would be such masters of themselves, that no
power on earth could bias their judgments, or compel their
actions. But this is such a system of metaphysical politics as none
but the worst of men would attempt to inculcate, and none,
but the weakest, could really believe. It being therefore to be
assumed, as a given point in this debate, that influence of
some sort, and in some degree or other, will ever take place
in human affairs, the next thing observable is, that such influence may be either morally good, or morally bad, or perfectly
indifferent, according to the nature and tendency of it, and
the internal persuasion of the person to be affected by it. . . .

Influence, therefore, of some sort, and in some degree or
other, there ever was, and ever will be, used in the conduct of
human affairs. Good influence ought to be encouraged; bad
influence ought to be discouraged as much as possible: . . . . .

Now, my Lord, be pleased to examine your own conduct,
and that of your (late) illustrious associates by this test. The
thing, which you have all taken for granted; and which has
been laid down as a fundamental rule, is, that the influence
of the crown is always bad. (Heretofore it was a maxim in our
common law, that the king can do no wrong: now the maxim
seems to be reversed,—the king can do no right.) Indeed I do
not say that regal influence is always rightly applied: and I

desire your lordship to take notice of this voluntary acknow-
ledgment. But I will be bold to say, that for these last fifty
years past, courtiers have been as often in the right as anti-
courtiers, and have used their influence to as good national
purposes,—if not to better. Nay, perhaps, now that your lordship has obtained your end in being the pilot of the state, with
so many others under you, even Lord Shelburne may be more
of my opinion than he professed to be a few months ago. Either
therefore all influence ought to be condemned alike; or that
of the crown ought not to be branded more than the rest, as
being peculiarly criminal, and to be held up as the only object
of public hatred, and national detestation.

Your lordship has the command of two boroughs already:
and the public shrewdly suspect, that you would have no
qualms of conscience against commanding two more,—or
even twenty-two. Mr Fox and Lord Holland's family command one: the late Marquis of Rockingham had at least two,
which he might, and did call his own: and were I to proceed
after the same manner throughout the peerage, and the great
landed interest, also the commercial, and the manufacturing
interest of the realm, perhaps I might enumerate not less than
two hundred, viz. boroughs and cities, and even counties,
whose voters chuse representatives, and return members to
parliament, more according to the good will and pleasure of
those who have the ascendency over them, than according to
their own private judgments, or personal determinations.

Therefore, my Lord, will you propose a law, that no ascendency of this sort shall be suffered to prevail for the future?
Will you bring in a bill to enact pains and penalties against
all landlords, their stewards, or agents, who shall dare to interfere directly or indirectly, with the votes of their respective
tenants, tradesmen, or dependents?—Against all magistrates,
&c. in corporations, or against all Justices of the Peace at
their county meetings, if they should insinuate to the keepers
of ale-houses, and to others, that the granting of licences, or
any the like favours, vested in them by law, will depend on
the giving of their votes for this, or that particular candidate?
—Against all masters of families, principal manufacturers,
merchants and tradesmen, who shall presume to whisper to

their journeymen, servants, or underlings, that they expect them to vote according as they shall direct,—and that a submission must be paid to their wills and pleasures, if they hope to be employed by them, or retained in their service? Much more might be added:—But oh! my Lord, lay your hand on your heart, and tell me plainly,—or rather tell your country, which hath the right to ask the question,—Was this ever any part of the plan either of yourself, or of your quondam, or present associates? Did either you, or they, when such tragical exclamations were raised against the influence of the crown, ever intend to lessen your own? Did you ever propose to set the first example by enacting a self-denying ordinance against yourselves?—No. my Lord, so far from it, that many, if not most of your illustrious band grounded all their hopes, and all their schemes, for their own exaltation, on the depression, and humiliation of the monarchy. In short, while the general liberty of the people was the pretence and cry, the particular emolument and grandeur of about a score of lords, and twice as many commoners, were the real end and aim of all these patriotic endeavours. . . .

40   Richard Price:
A Discourse on the Love of Our Country
(1790)

[A lecture given on 4 November 1789 to The Society for Commemorating the Revolution in Great Britain. Published in 1790. pp. 26–35, 40–2]

. . . . We are met to thank God for that event in this country to which the name of THE REVOLUTION has been given; and which for more than a century, it has been usual for the friends of freedom, and more especially Protestant Dissenters, under the title of the REVOLUTION SOCIETY, to celebrate with expressions of joy and exaltation. . . . We have particular reason, as Protestant Dissenters, to rejoice on this occasion. It was at this time we were rescued from persecution, and obtained the liberty of worshipping God in the manner we think most acceptable to him. It was then our meeting houses were opened, our worship was taken under the protection of the law, and the principles of toleration gained a triumph. We have, therefore, on this occasion, peculiar reasons for thanksgiving—But let us remember that we ought not to satisfy ourselves with thanksgivings. Our gratitude, if genuine, will be accompanied with endeavours to give stability to the deliverance our country has obtained, and to extend and improve the happiness with which the Revolution has blest us—Let us, in particular, take care not to forget the principles of the Revolution. This Society has, very properly, in its Reports, held out these principles, as an instruction to the public. I will only take notice of the three following:

First; The right to liberty of conscience in religious matters.
Secondly; The right to resist power when abused. And,
Thirdly; The right to chuse our own governors; to cashier them for misconduct; and to frame a government for ourselves.

On these three principles, and more especially the last, was the Revolution founded. Were it not true that liberty of conscience is a sacred right; that power abused justifies resistance; and that civil authority is a delegation from the people— Were not, I say, all this true, the Revolution would have been, not an ASSERTION, but an INVASION of rights; not a REVOLUTION, but a REBELLION. Cherish in your breasts this conviction, and act under its influence; detesting the odious doctrines of passive obedience, non-resistance, and the divine right of kings—doctrines which, had they been acted upon in this country, would have left us at this time wretched slaves— doctrines which imply, that God made mankind to be oppressed and plundered; and which are no less a blasphemy against him, than an insult on common sense.

I would farther direct you to remember, that though the Revolution was a great work, it was by no means a perfect work; and that all was not then gained which was necessary to put the kingdom in the secure and complete possession of the blessings of liberty.—In particular, you should recollect, that the toleration then obtained was imperfect. It included only those who could declare their faith in the doctrinal articles of the church of England. It has, indeed, been since extended, but not sufficiently; for there still exist penal laws on account of religious opinions, which (were they carried into execution) would shut up many of our places of worship, and silence and imprison some of our ablest and best men.— The TEST LAWS are also still in force; and deprive of eligibility to civil and military offices, all who cannot conform to the established worship. It is with great pleasure I find that the body of Protestant Dissenters, though defeated in two late attempts (in 1789 and 1790) to deliver their country from this disgrace to it, have determined to persevere. Should they at last succeed, they will have the satisfaction, not only of removing from themselves a proscription they do not deserve, but of contributing to lessen the number of our public iniquities. . . .

But the most important instance of the imperfect state in which the Revolution left our constitution, is the INEQUALITY OF OUR REPRESENTATION. I think, indeed, this defect in our constitution so gross and palpable, as to make it excellent chiefly in form and theory. You should remember that a representation in the Legislature of a kingdom is the *basis* of constitutional liberty in it, and of all legitimate government; and that, without it, a government is nothing but a usurpation. When the representation is fair and equal, and at the same time vested with such powers as our House of Commons possesses, a kingdom may be said to govern itself, and consequently to possess true liberty. When the representation is partial, a kingdom possesses liberty only partially; and if extremely partial, it only gives a *semblance* of liberty; but if not only extremely partial, but corruptly chosen, and under corrupt influence after being chosen, it becomes a *nuisance*, and produces the worst of all forms of government—a government by corruption—a government carried on and supported by spreading venality and profligacy through a kingdom. May heaven preserve this kingdom from a calamity so dreadful! It is the point of depravity to which abuses under such a government as ours naturally tend, and, the last stage of national unhappiness. We are, at present, I hope, at a great distance from it. But it cannot be pretended that there are no advances towards it, or that there is no reason for apprehension and alarm.

The inadequateness of our representation has been long a subject of complaint. This is, in truth, our fundamental grievance; and I do not think that any thing is much more our duty, as men who love their country, and are grateful for the Revolution, than to unite our zeal in endeavouring to get it redressed. At the time of the American war, associations were formed for this purpose in LONDON, and other parts of the kingdom; and our present Minister himself has, since that war, directed to it an effort which made him a favourite with many of us. But all attention to it seems now lost, and the probability is, that this inattention will continue, and that nothing will be done towards gaining for us this essential blessing, till some great calamity again alarms our fears, or till some great abuse of power again provokes our resentment; or, perhaps, till the acquisition of a pure and equal representation by other countries (while we are mocked with the shadow) kindles our shame.

Such is the conduct by which we ought to express our gratitude for the Revolution. We should always bear in mind the principles that justify it. We should contribute all we can towards supplying what it left deficient; and shew ourselves anxious about transmitting the blessings obtained by it to our posterity, unimpaired and improved. But, brethren, while we thus shew our patriotic zeal, let us take care not to disgrace the cause of patriotism by any licentious or immoral conduct. . . .

. . . I must not conclude without recalling particularly to your recollection, a consideration to which I have more than once alluded, and which, probably, your thoughts have been all along anticipating: A consideration with which my mind is impressed more than I can express. I mean the consideration of the favourableness of the present times to all exertions in the cause of public liberty.

What an eventful period is this! I am thankful that I have lived to see it . . . I have lived to see a diffusion of knowledge, which has undermined superstition and error—I have lived to see the rights of men better understood than ever: and nations panting for liberty, which seemed to have lost the idea of it. I have lived to see THIRTY MILLIONS of people, indignant and resolute, spurning at slavery, and demanding liberty, with an irresistible voice; their king led in triumph, and an arbitrary monarch surrendering himself to his subjects.—After sharing in the benefits of one Revolution, I have been spared to be a witness to two other Revolutions, both glorious.— And now, methinks, I see the ardor for liberty catching and spreading; a general amendment beginning in human affairs; the dominion of kings changed for the dominion of laws, and the dominion of priests giving way to the dominion of reason and conscience.

Be encouraged, all ye friends of freedom, and writers in its defence! The times are auspicious. Your labours have not been in vain. Behold kingdoms admonished by you, starting from sleep, breaking their fetters, and claiming justice from their oppressors! Behold the light you have struck out, after setting AMERICA free, reflected to FRANCE, and there kindled into a blaze that lays despotism in ashes, and warms and illuminates all EUROPE!

Tremble all ye oppressors of the world! Take warning all ye supporters of slavish governments, and slavish hierarchies! Call no more (absurdly and wickedly) REFORMATION, innovation. You cannot now hold the world in darkness. Struggle no longer against increasing light and liberality. Restore to mankind their rights; and consent to the correction of abuses, before they and you are destroyed together.

41 Edmund Burke:
Reflections on the Revolution in France
(1790)

[*Everyman edition* (1910), pp. 6–7, 14–15, 29–32, 55–9]

. . . I flatter myself that I love a manly, moral, regulated liberty as well as any gentleman. . . . But I cannot stand forward, and give praise or blame to anything which relates to human actions, and human concerns, on a simple view of the object, as it stands stripped of every relation, in all the nakedness and solitude of metaphysical abstraction. Circumstances (which with some gentlemen pass for nothing) give in reality to every political principle its distinguishing colour and discriminating effect. The circumstances are what render every civil and political scheme beneficial or noxious to mankind. . . . Is it because liberty in the abstract may be classed amongst the blessings of mankind, that I am seriously to felicitate a madman, who has escaped from the protecting restraint and wholesome darkness of his cell, on his restoration to the enjoyment of light and liberty? Am I to congratulate a highwayman and murderer, who broke prison, upon the recovery of his natural rights? . . . The effect of liberty to individuals is, that they may do what they please: we ought to see what it will please them to do, before we risque congratulations, which may be soon turned into complaints. Prudence would dictate this in the case of separate, insulated, private men; but liberty when men act in bodies, is *power*. Considerate people, before they declare themselves, will observe the use which is made of *power*; and particularly of so trying a thing as *new* power in *new* persons, of whose principles, tempers, and dispositions they have little or no experience, . . .

. . . If the *principles* of the Revolution of 1688 are anywhere to be found, it is in the statute called the *Declaration of Right*. In that most wise, sober, and considerate declaration, drawn up by great lawyers and great statesmen, and not by warm and inexperienced enthusiasts, not one word is said, nor one suggestion made, of a general right 'to choose our own *governors*; to cashier them for misconduct; and to *form* a government for *ourselves*.' . . . The Revolution was made to preserve our *ancient*, indisputable laws and liberties, and that *ancient* constitution of government which is our only security for law and liberty. . . . The very idea of the fabrication of a new government is enough to fill us with disgust and horror. We wished at the period of the Revolution, and do now wish, to derive all we possess as *an inheritance from our forefathers*. Upon that body and stock of inheritance we have taken care not to inoculate any scion alien to the nature of the original plant. All the reformations we have hitherto made have proceeded upon the principle of reference to antiquity; . . . The same policy pervades all the laws which have since been made for the preservation of our liberties. In the 1st of William and Mary, in the famous statute, called the Declaration of Right, the two Houses utter not a syllable of 'a right to frame a government by themselves.' You will see that their whole care was to secure the religion, laws, and liberties, that had been long possessed, and had been lately endangered. . . . You will observe, that from Magna Charta to the Declaration of Right, it has been the uniform policy of our constitution to claim and assert our liberties, as an *entailed inheritance* derived to us from our forefathers, and to be transmitted to our posterity; as an estate especially belonging to the people of this kingdom, without any reference whatever to any other more general or prior right. By this means our constitution preserves an unity in so great a diversity of its parts. We have an inheritable crown; an inheritable peerage; and a House of Commons and a people inheriting privileges, franchises, and liberties, from a long line of ancestors.

The policy appears to me to be the result of profound reflection; or rather the happy effect of following nature, which is wisdom without reflection, and above it. A spirit of innovation is generally the result of a selfish temper, and confined views. People will not look forward to posterity, who never look backward to their ancestors. Besides, the people of England well know, that the idea of inheritance furnishes a sure principle of conservation, and a sure principle of transmission; without at all excluding a principle of improvement. It leaves acquisition free; but it secures what it acquires. . . . Our political system is placed in a just correspondence and symmetry with the order of the world, and with the mode of existence decreed to a permanent body composed of transitory parts; wherein, by the disposition of a stupendous wisdom, moulding together the great mysterious incorporation of the human race, the whole, at one time, is never old, or middle-aged, or young, but, in a condition of unchangeable constancy, moves on through the varied tenor of perpetual decay, fall, renovation, and progression. Thus, by preserving the method of nature in the conduct of the state, in what we improve, we are never wholly new; in what we retain, we are never wholly obsolete. By adhering in this manner and on those principles to our forefathers, we are guided not by the superstition of antiquarians, but by the spirit of philosophic analogy. . . . .

. . . Whilst they [the members of the Revolution Society] are possessed by these notions [of the rights of man], it is vain to talk to them of the practice of their ancestors, the fundamental laws of their country, the fixed form of a constitution, whose merits are confirmed by the solid test of long experience, and an increasing public strength and national prosperity. They despise experience as the wisdom of unlettered men; and as for the rest, they have wrought under ground a mine that will blow up, at one grand explosion, all examples of antiquity, all precedents, charters, and acts of parliament. They have 'the rights of men.' Against these there can be no prescription; against these no argument is binding; these admit no temperament, and no compromise: anything withheld from their full demand is so much of fraud and injustice. Against these their rights of men let no government look for security in the length of its continuance, or in the justice and lenity of its administration. The objections of these speculatists, if its forms do not quadrate with their theories, are as valid against such an old and beneficent government, as against the most violent tyranny, or the greenest usurpation. They are always at issue with governments, not on a question of abuse, but a question of competency, and a question of title. . . .

. . . If civil society be made for the advantage of man, all the advantages for which it is made become his right. It is an institution of beneficence; and law itself is only beneficence; acting by a rule. Men have a right to live by that rule; they have a right to do justice; as between their fellows, whether their fellows are in politic function or in ordinary occupation. They have a right to the fruits of their industry; and to the means of making their industry fruitful. They have a right to the acquisitions of their parents; to the nourishment and improvement of their offspring; to instruction in life, and to consolation in death. Whatever each man can separately do, without trespassing upon others, he has a right to do for himself; and he had a right to a fair portion of all which society, with all its combinations of skill and force, can do in his favour. In this partnership all men have equal rights; but not to equal things. He that has but five shillings in the partnership, has as good a right to it as he that has five hundred pounds has to his larger proportion. But he has not a right to an equal dividend in the product of the joint stock; and as to the share of power, authority, and direction which each individual ought to have in the management of the state, that I must deny to be amongst the direct original rights of man in civil society; for I have in my contemplation the civil social man, and no other. It is a thing to be settled by convention. . . . Government is a contrivance of human wisdom to provide for human *wants*. Men have a right that these wants should be provided for by this wisdom. Among these wants is to be reckoned the want, out of civil society, of a sufficient restraint upon their passions. Society requires not only that the passions of individuals should be subjected, but that even in the mass and body, as well as in the individuals, the inclinations of men should frequently be thwarted, their will controlled, and their passions brought into subjection. This can only be done *by a power out of themselves*; and not, in the exercise of its function, subject to that will and to those passions which it is its office to bridle and subdue. In this sense the restraints on men, as well as their liberties, are to be reckoned among their rights. But as the liberties and restrictions vary with times and circumstances, and admit of infinite modifications, they cannot be settled upon any abstract rule; and nothing is so foolish as to discuss them upon that principle. . . . The science of government being therefore so practical in itself, and intended for such practical purposes, a matter which requires experience, and even more experience than any person can gain in his whole life, however sagacious and observing he may be, it is with infinite caution that any man ought to venture upon pulling down an edifice, which has answered in any tolerable degree for ages the common purposes of society, or on building it up again, without having models and patterns of approved utility before his eyes. . . .

42 Thomas Paine:
Rights of Man (1791–2)

[Paine's work had an immense and immediate impact. The government condemned his writings as seditious and he fled to France. He was declared an outlaw and never returned to England. *Everyman edition* (1915), pp. 12, 41–5, 47, 221–2, 228–9, 232, 246–8, 250, 265–6.]

Part One (1791)

. . . There never did, there never will, and there never can exist a parliament, or any description of men, or any generation of men, in any country, possessed of the right or the power of binding and controlling posterity to the '*end of time*', or of commanding for ever how the world shall be governed, or who shall govern it; and therefore, all such clauses, acts or declarations, by which the makers of them attempt to do what they have neither the right nor the power to do, nor the power to execute, are in themselves null and void.—Every age and generation must be as free to act for itself, *in all cases*, as the ages and generations which preceded it. The vanity and presumption of governing beyond the grave, is the most ridiculous and insolent of all tyrannies. Man has no property in man; neither has any generation a property in the generations which are to follow. The parliament or the people of 1688, or of any other period, has no more right to dispose of the people of the present day, or to bind or to control them *in any shape whatever*, than the parliament or the people of the present day have to dispose of, bind or control those who are to live a hundred or a thousand years hence. Every generation is, and must be, competent to all the purposes which its occasions require. It is the living, and not the dead, that are to be accommodated. . . .

The error of those who reason by precedents drawn from antiquity, respecting the rights of man, is, that they do not go far enough into antiquity. They do not go the whole way.

They stop in some of the intermediate stages of an hundred or a thousand years, and produce what was then done, as a rule for the present day. This is no authority at all. If we travel still farther into antiquity, we shall find a direct contrary opinion and practice prevailing; and if antiquity is to be authority, a thousand such authorities may be produced, successively contradicting each other. But if we proceed on, we shall at last come out right; we shall come to the time when man came from the hand of his Maker. What was he then? Man. Man was his high and only title, and a higher cannot be given him.—But of titles I shall speak hereafter.

We are now got at the origin of man, and at the origin of his rights. As to the manner in which the world has been governed from that day to this, it is no further any concern of ours than to make a proper use of the errors or the improvements which the history of it presents. Those who lived a hundred or a thousand years ago, were then moderns, as we are now. They had *their* ancients, and those ancients had others, and we also shall be ancients in our turn. If the mere name of antiquity is to govern in the affairs of life, the people who are to live an hundred or a thousand years hence, may as well take us for a precedent, as we make a precedent of those who lived an hundred or a thousand years ago. The fact is, that portions of antiquity, by proving everything, establish nothing. It is authority against authority all the way, till we come to the divine origin of the rights of man at the creation. Here our inquiries find a resting-place, and our reason finds a home. If a dispute about the rights of man had arisen at the distance of an hundred years from the creation, it is to this source of authority they must have referred, and it is to the same source of authority that we must now refer.

Though I mean not to touch upon any sectarian principle of religion, yet it may be worth observing, that the genealogy of Christ is traced to Adam. Why then not trace the rights of man to the creation of man? I will answer the question. Because there have been upstart governments, thrusting themselves between, and presumptuously working to *un-make* man.

If any generation of men ever possessed the right of dictating the mode by which the world should be governed for ever, it was the first generation that existed; and if that generation did it not, no succeeding generation can show any authority for doing it, nor can set any up. The illuminating and divine principle of the equal rights of man, (for it has its origin from the Maker of man) relates, not only to the living individuals, but to generations of men succeeding each other. Every generation is equal in rights to the generations which preceded it, by the same rule that every individual is born equal in rights with his contemporary.

Every history of the creation, and every traditional account, whether from the lettered or unlettered world, however they may vary in their opinion or belief of certain particulars, all agree in establishing one point, *the unity of man*; by which I mean, that men are all of *one degree*, and consequently that all men are born equal, and with equal natural right, in the same manner as if posterity had been continued by *creation* instead of *generation*, the latter being only the mode by which the former is carried forward; and consequently, every child born into the world must be considered as deriving its existence from God. The world is as new to him as it was to the first man that existed, and his natural right in it is of the same kind.

The Mosaic account of the creation, whether taken as divine authority, or merely historical, is full to this point, *the unity or equality of man*. The expressions admit of no controversy. 'And God said, Let us make man in our own image. In the image of God created he him; male and female created he them.' The distinction of sexes is pointed out, but no other distinction is even implied. If this be not divine authority, it is at least historical authority, and shows that the equality of man, so far from being a modern doctrine, is the oldest upon record. . . .

Hitherto we have spoken only (and that but in part) of the natural rights of man. We have now to consider the civil rights of man, and to show how the one originates from the other. Man did not enter into society to become *worse* than he was before, nor to have fewer rights than he had before, but to have those rights better secured. His natural rights are the foundation of all his civil rights. . . .

First, That every civil right grows out of a natural right; or, in other words, is a natural right exchanged.

Secondly, That civil power, properly considered as such, is made up of the aggregate of that class of the natural rights of man, which becomes defective in the individual in point of power, and answers not his purpose; but when collected to a focus, becomes competent to the purpose of every one.

Thirdly, That the power produced from the aggregate of natural rights, imperfect in power in the individual, cannot be applied to invade the natural rights which are retained in the individual, and in which the power to execute is as perfect as the right itself. . . .

It has been thought a considerable advance towards establishing the principles of Freedom, to say, that government is a compact between those who govern and those who are governed: but this cannot be true, because it is putting the effect before the cause; for as man must have existed before governments existed, there necessarily was a time when governments did not exist, and consequently there could originally exist no governors to form such a compact with. The fact therefore must be, that the *individuals themselves*, each in his own personal and sovereign right, *entered into a compact with each other* to produce a government: and this is the only mode in which governments have a right to arise, and the only principle on which they have a right to exist. . . .

Part Two (1792)   Chapter 5

. . . When, in countries that are called civilized, we see age going to the workhouse and youth to the gallows, something must be wrong in the system of government. . . .

Civil government does not exist in executions; but in making that provision for the instruction of youth, and the support of age, as to exclude, as much as possible, profligacy from the one, and despair from the other. Instead of this, the resources of a country are lavished upon kings, upon courts, upon hirelings, impostors, and prostitutes; and even the poor themselves, with all their wants upon them, are compelled to support the fraud that oppresses them.

Why is it, that scarcely any are executed but the poor? The

fact is a proof, among other things, of a wretchedness in their condition. Bred up without morals, and cast upon the world without a prospect, they are the exposed sacrifice of vice and legal barbarity. The millions that are superfluously wasted upon governments, are more than sufficient to reform those evils, and to benefit the condition of every man in a nation, not included within the purlieus of a court. . . .

What pillar of security does the landed interest require more than any other interest in the state, or what right has it to a distinct and separate representation from the general interest of a nation? The only use to be made of this power, (and which it has always made,) is to ward off taxes from itself, and throw the burden upon such articles of consumption by which itself would be least affected. . . . Before the coming of the Hanoverians, the taxes were divided in nearly equal proportions between the land and articles of consumption, the land bearing rather the largest share: but since that era, nearly thirteen millions annually of new taxes has seen a constant increase in the number and wretchedness of the poor, and in the amount of the poor-rates. . . . If a house of legislation is to be composed of men of one class, for the purpose of protecting a distinct interest, all the other interests should have the same. The inequality, as well as the burden of taxation, arises from admitting it in one case, and not in all. . . .

. . . In the present state of things, a labouring man, with a wife and two or three children does not pay less than between seven and eight pounds a year in taxes. He is not sensible of this, because it is disguised to him in the articles which he buys, and he thinks only of their dearness; but as the taxes take from him, at least, a fourth part of his yearly earnings, he is consequently disabled from providing for a family, especially, if himself, or any of them, are afflicted with sickness.

The first step, therefore, of practical relief, would be to abolish the poor rates entirely, and in lieu thereof, to make a remission of taxes to the poor of double the amount of the present poor-rates, viz. four millions annually out of the surplus taxes. Having thus ascertained the greatest number that can be supposed to need support on account of young families, I proceed to the mode of relief or distribution, which is,

To pay as a remission of taxes to every poor family, out of the surplus taxes, and in room of poor-rates, four pounds a year for every child under fourteen years of age; enjoining the parents of such children to send them to school, to learn reading, writing, and common arithmetic; the ministers of every parish, of every denomination, to certify jointly to an office, for that purpose, that this duty is performed. . . .

. . . Having thus ascertained the probable proportion of the number of aged persons, I proceed to the mode of rendering their condition comfortable, which is,

To pay to every person of the age of fifty years, and until he shall arrive at the age of sixty, the sum of six pounds *per ann.* out of the surplus taxes; and ten pounds *per ann.* during life after sixty. . . . This support, as already remarked, is not of the nature of a charity, but of a right. Every person in England, male and female, pays on an average in taxes, two pounds eight shillings and sixpence *per ann.* from the day of his (or her) birth; and, if the expense of collection be added, he pays two pounds eleven shillings and sixpence; consequently, at the end of fifty years he has paid one hundred and twenty-eight pounds fifteen shillings. Converting, therefore, his (or her) individual tax into a tontine, the money he shall receive after fifty years, is but little more than the legal interest of the net money he has paid; the rest is made up from those whose circumstances do not require them to draw such support, and the capital in both cases defrays the expenses of government. . . .

Several laws are in existence for regulating and limiting workmen's wages. Why not leave them as free to make their own bargains, as the law-makers are to let their farms and houses? Personal labour is all the property they have. Why is that little, and the little freedom they enjoy to be infringed? But the injustice will appear stronger, if we consider the operation and effect of such laws. When wages are fixed by what is called a law, the legal wages remain stationary, while everything else is in progression; and as those who make that law, still continue to lay on new taxes by other laws, they increase the expense of living by one law, and take away the means by another. . . .

43   The Church and King Club (1792)

[A society set up in Manchester in 1792 to combat the reformers and revolutionaries. From Thomas Walker, *A Review of some of the Political Events which have occurred in Manchester during the Last Five Years* (1794), pp. 17–18.]

DECLARATION

This Society beholds with infinite concern the many dangerous plots and associations that are forming in different parts of this kingdom, for the avowed purpose of disseminating discord, and for subverting the order of one of the most beautiful systems of government, that the combined efforts of human wisdom has ever yet been able to accomplish.

When we see such *deadly wounds* aimed at our glorious constitution, we consider it the duty of all good citizens, publicly to step forward, and express their abhorrence of the malevolent and most wicked intentions of those disappointed men, who are audaciously clamorous for a reform in parliament, but whose real object is to excite civil commotion in this our *happy* and well-governed state.

We are far from believing, should they ever effect their purpose, (which Heaven forbid!) that the change would be for the better, but must always regard those persons as the bane of civil society, who have given so many proofs of an innate propensity for power, and of that restless ambition which has long been their most distinguished characteristic.

PRINCIPLES OF THE CHURCH AND KING CLUB

It is a principle of this Society, to revere the Constitution and obey the King, according to the Laws of that Constitution.

It is a principle of this Society, to reprobate the wild theories and seditious doctrines respecting the Rights of Man, which have been lately promulgated by the enemies of our most excellent constitution in church and state, as they are subversive of all civil authority; and that, if they were put in practice, would tend to nothing but anarchy and confusion, which is contrary to all order.

It is a principle of this Society, that the Constitution of this country was renovated and fixed at the time of the glorious Revolution.

It is a principle of this Society, that the Constitution has not since that time been essentially departed from.

It is a principle of this Society, that the Legislature of this country ought ever to consist of King, Lords, and Commons.

It is a principle of this Society, that all other modes of legislation, than by King, Lords, and Commons, has always been found, by experience, repugnant to the genius of Englishmen.

It is a principle of this Society, that the Establishment in Church and State, is not to be altered but by the Legislature itself; consequently any other mode would be attended with extreme danger.

It is a principle of this Society that it is requisite in every good governed state, that there must exist an established Church, and that no one is to bear any office, either in church or state, but such as will conform, and be in communion with that church.

It is a principle of this Society, that the Corporation and Test Acts are the great bulwarks of our constitution in church and state, therefore ought never to be repealed.

It is a principle of this Society, that Toleration in religious matters is to be extended to Dissenters of every denomination.

Finally, it is the fixed determination of this Society, at all times and in all places, to avow and maintain the above principles to be truly constitutional.

[Manchester, 23 June 1792.]

44 Mary Wollstonecraft: A Vindication of the Rights of Woman (1792)

[Everyman edition (1929), pp. 154–5, 158–64]

Chapter IX: Of the pernicious effects which arise from the unnatural distinctions established in society.

... It is vain to expect virtue from women till they are in some degree independent of men; nay, it is vain to expect that strength of natural affection which would make them good wives and mothers. Whilst they are absolutely dependent on their husbands they will be cunning, mean, and selfish; and the men who can be gratified by the fawning fondness of spaniel-like affection have not much delicacy, for love is not to be bought; in any sense of the words, its silken wings are instantly shrivelled up when anything beside a return in kind is sought. Yet whilst wealth enervates men, and women live, as it were, by their personal charms, how can we expect them to discharge those ennobling duties which equally require exertion and self-denial? ...

The preposterous distinctions of rank, which render civilisation a curse, by dividing the world between voluptuous tyrants and cunning envious dependents, corrupt, almost equally, every class of people, because respectability is not attached to the discharge of the relative duties of life, but to the station, and when the duties are not fulfilled the affections cannot gain sufficient strength to fortify the virtue of which they are the natural reward. Still there are some loop-holes out of which a man may creep, and dare to think and act for himself; but for a woman it is an herculean task, because she has difficulties peculiar to her sex to overcome, which require almost super-human power. ...

Women are, in common with men, rendered weak and luxurious by the relaxing pleasures which wealth procures; but added to this they are made slaves to their passions, and must render them alluring that man may lend them his reason to guide their tottering steps aright. Or should they be ambitious, they must govern their tyrants by sinister tricks, for without rights there cannot be any incumbent duties. The laws respecting woman, which I mean to discuss in a future part, make an absurd unit of a man and his wife; and then, by the easy transition of only considering him as responsible, she is reduced to a mere cipher.

The being who discharges the duties of its station is independent; and, speaking of women at large, their first duty is to themselves as rational creatures, and the next, in point of importance, as citizens, is that, which includes so many, of a mother. The rank in life which dispenses with their fulfilling this duty, necessarily degrades them by making them mere dolls. Or should they turn to something more important than merely fitting drapery upon a smooth block, their minds are only occupied by some soft platonic attachment; or the actual management of an intrigue may keep their thoughts in motion; for when they neglect domestic duties, they have it not in their power to take the field and march and counter-march like soldiers, or wrangle in the senate to keep their faculties from rusting. . . .

But to render her really virtuous and useful, she must not, if she discharge her civil duties, want individually the protection of civil laws; she must not be dependent on her husband's bounty for her subsistence during his life, or support after his death; for how can a being be generous who has nothing of its own? or virtuous who is not free? The wife, in the present state of things, who is faithful to her husband, and neither suckles nor educates her children, scarcely deserves the name of a wife, and has no right to that of a citizen. But take away natural rights, and duties become null. . . .

Besides, when poverty is more disgraceful than even vice, is not morality cut to the quick? Still to avoid misconstruction, though I consider that women in the common walks of life are called to fulfil the duties of wives and mothers, by religion and reason, I cannot help lamenting that women of a superior cast have not a road open by which they can pursue more extensive plans of usefulness and independence. I may excite laughter, by dropping an hint, which I mean to pursue, some future time, for I really think that women ought to have representatives, instead of being arbitrarily governed without having any direct share allowed them in the deliberations of government.

But, as the whole system of representation is now, in this country, only a convenient handle for despotism, they need not complain, for they are as well represented as a numerous class of hard-working mechanics, who pay for the support of royalty when they can scarcely stop their children's mouths with bread. How are they represented whose very sweat supports the splendid stud of an heir-apparent, or varnishes the chariot of some female favourite who looks down on shame? Taxes on the very necessaries of life, enable an endless tribe of idle princes and princesses to pass with stupid pomp before a gaping crowd, who almost worship the very parade which costs them so dear. This is mere gothic grandeur, something like the barbarous useless parade of having sentinels on horseback at Whitehall, which I could never view without a mixture of contempt and indignation. . . .

In the superior ranks of life, every duty is done by deputies, as if duties could ever be waived, and the vain pleasures which consequent idleness forces the rich to pursue, appear so enticing to the next rank, that the numerous scramblers for wealth sacrifice everything to tread on their heels. The most sacred trusts are then considered as sinecures, because they were procured by interest, and only sought to enable a man to keep *good company*. Women, in particular, all want to be ladies. Which is simply to have nothing to do, but listlessly to go they scarcely care where, for they cannot tell what.

But what have women to do in society? I may be asked, but to loiter with easy grace; surely you would not condemn them all to suckle fools and chronicle small beer! No. Women might certainly study the art of healing, and be physicians as well as nurses. And midwifery, decency seems to allot to them, though I am afraid, the word midwife, in our dictionaries, will soon give place to *accoucheur*, and one proof of the former delicacy of the sex be effaced from the language.

They might also study politics, and settle their benevolence on the broadest basis; for the reading of history will scarcely be more useful than the perusal of romances, if read as mere biography; if the character of the times, the political improvements, arts, etc., be not observed. In short, if it be not considered as the history of man; and not of particular men, who filled a niche in the temple of fame, and dropped into the black rolling stream of time, that silently sweeps all before it into the shapeless void called—eternity.—For shape, can it be called, 'that shape hath none'?

Business of various kinds, they might likewise pursue, if they were educated in a more orderly manner, which might save many from common and legal prostitution. Women would not then marry for a support, as men accept of places under Government, and neglect the implied duties; nor would an attempt to earn their own subsistence, a most laudable one! sink them almost to the level of those poor abandoned creatures who live by prostitution. For are not milliners and mantua-makers reckoned the next class? The few employments open to women, so far, from being liberal, are menial; and when a superior education enables them to take charge of the education of children as governesses, they are not treated like the tutors of sons, though even clerical tutors are not always treated in a manner calculated to render them respectable in the eyes of their pupils, to say nothing of the private comfort of the individual. But as women educated like gentlewomen, are never designed for the humiliating situation which necessity sometimes forces them to fill; these situations are considered in the light of a degradation; and they know little of the human heart, who need to be told, that nothing so painfully sharpens sensibility as such a fall in life.

Some of these women might be restrained from marrying by a proper spirit of delicacy, and others may not have had it in their power to escape in this pitiful way from servitude; is not that Government then very defective, and very unmindful of the happiness of one-half of its members, that does not provide for honest, independent women, by encouraging them to fill respectable stations? But in order to render their private a public benefit, they must have a civil existence in the State, married or single; else we shall continually see some worthy woman, whose sensibility has been rendered painfully acute by undeserved contempt, droop like 'the lily broken down by a plowshare.'

It is a melancholy truth; yet such is the blessed effect of civilisation! the most respectable women are the most oppressed; and, unless they have understandings far superior to the common run of understandings, taking in both sexes, they must, from being treated like contemptible beings, become contemptible. How many women thus waste life away the prey of discontent, who might have practised as physicians, regulated a farm, managed a shop, and stood erect, supported by their own industry, instead of hanging their heads surcharged with the dew of sensibility, that consumes the beauty to which it at first gave lustre; nay, I doubt whether pity and love are so near akin as poets feign, for I have seldom seen much compassion excited by the helplessness of females, unless they were fair; then, perhaps, pity was the soft handmaid of love, or the harbinger of lust.

How much more respectable is the woman who earns her own bread by fulfilling any duty, than the most accomplished beauty!—beauty did I say!—so sensible am I of the beauty of moral loveliness, or the harmonious propriety that attunes the passions of a well-regulated mind, that I blush at making the comparison; yet I sigh to think how few women aim at attaining this respectability by withdrawing from the giddy whirl of pleasure, or the indolent calm that stupefies the good sort of women it sucks in. . . .

Would men but generously snap our chains, and be content with rational fellowship instead of slavish obedience, they would find us more observant daughters, more affectionate sisters, more faithful wives, more reasonable mothers—in a word, better citizens. We should then love them with true affection, because we should learn to respect ourselves; and the peace of mind of a worthy man would not be interrupted by the idle vanity of his wife, nor the babes sent to nestle in a strange bosom, having never found a home in their mother's.

45   An Address to the Nation from the
     London Corresponding Society, on the
     Subject of a Thorough Parliamentary
     Reform (1793)

[In 1794 Thomas Hardy, the Secretary of the London Corresponding
Society, was prosecuted for high treason but was acquitted. The Society
however was suppressed in 1799.]

FRIENDS AND FELLOW COUNTRYMEN,

Gloomy as is the prospect now before us, and unpleasing as is
the talk to bring forth into open day the calamitous situation
of our Country: We conceive it necessary to direct the public
eye, to the cause of our misfortunes, and to awaken the sleeping
reason of our Countrymen, to the pursuit of the only remedy
which can ever prove effectual, namely;—*A thorough Reform
in Parliament, by the adoption of an equal Representation obtained by
Annual Elections and Universal Suffrage.*—We do not address you
in the confidence of personal importance—We do not presume
upon the splendor of exalted situation; but as Members of the
same Society, as Individuals, zealously labouring for the welfare
of the Community; we think ourselves entitled to a share of
your attention. . . .

Here it is proper to remind you of the false and calumnious
aspersions, which have been so industriously circulated since
November last: At that time of general Consternation, when
the cry of danger to the Constitution was raised and extensively propagated;[1] when the alarm of *Rtois and Insurrections*, was founded by Royal Proclamations and re-echoed
by Parish Associations; Reform was branded by the name
of Innovation, and whoever dared to affirm, that the House
of Commons ought to be restored to that state of independ-

[1] The outbreak of disturbances and the growth of radical societies
inspired John Reeves to found, in November 1792, the Association for
Preserving Liberty and Property against Republicans and Levellers.

ence in which it was settled at the Revolution; and that unnecessary Places and Pensions ought to be abolished, was stigmatized as a leveller and an enemy to his King and Country. . . .

To obtain a compleat Representation is our only aim—contemning all party distinctions, we seek no advantage which every individual of the community will not enjoy equally with ourselves—We are not engaged in Speculative and Theoretical schemes; the motive of our present conduct is the actual sense of injury and oppression; We feel the weight of innumerable abuses, to which the invasion of our rights has given birth, and which their restoration can alone remove.

But sensible that our efforts, if not seconded by the Nation at large, must prove ineffectual, and only needlessly expose us to the malevolence of the public plunderers; we conjure you, by the love you bear your country, by your attachment to freedom, and by your anxious care for the welfare of your posterity, to suffer yourselves no longer to be deluded by artful speeches, and by interested men; but to sanction with your approbations, our constitutional endeavours, and pursue with union and firmness the track we have pointed out: Thus countenanced by our country, we pledge ourselves, as you will perceive by the following resolutions, never to recede or slacken, but on every occasion to redouble our zealous exertions in the cause of Constitutional Freedom.

RESOLVED UNANIMOUSLY

   I. That nothing but a fair, adequate and annually renovated Representation in Parliament, can ensure the freedom of this country.

  II. That we are fully convinced, a thorough Parliamentary Reform, would remove every grievance under which we labour.

 III. That we will never give up the pursuit of such Parliamentary Reform.

  IV. That if it be a part of the power of the king to declare war when and against whom he pleases, we are convinced that such power must have been granted to him under the condition, that it should ever be subservient to the national advantage.

V. That the present war against France, and the existing alliance with the Germanic Powers, so far as it relates to the prosecution of that war, has hitherto produced, and is likely to produce nothing but national calamity, if not utter ruin.

VI. That it appears to Us that the wars in which Great Britain has engaged, within the last hundred years, have cost her upwards of *Three hundred and Seventy Millions*! not to mention the private misery occasioned thereby, or the lives sacrificed; therefore it is a dreadful speculation for the people of this country to look up to; That the Cabinet have engaged in a treaty with a foreign Prince, to be supplied with troops for a long period of years, and for a purpose unknown to the people of England.

VII. That we are persuaded the majority, if not the whole of those wars, originated in Cabinet intrigue, rather than in absolute necessity.

VIII. That every nation has an unalienable right to chuse the mode in which it will be governed, and that it is an act of Tyranny and Oppression in any other nation to interfere with, or attempt to controul their choice.

IX. That peace being the greatest blessings, ought to be sought most diligently by every wise government, to be most joyfully accepted when reasonably proffered, and to be concluded most speedily when the object of the war is accomplished.

X. That we do exhort every well wisher to his country, not to delay in improving himself in constitutional knowledge.

XI. That those men who were the first to be seized with a panic, should be the last whom prudence would entrust with the management of a war.

XII. That Great Britain is not Hanover!

XIII. That regarding union as indispensably necessary to ensure success, we will endeavour to the utmost of our power, to unite more closely with every political Society in the nation, associated upon the same principles with ourselves.

XIV. That the next general Meeting of this Society, be held on the first Monday in September, unless the Committee of Delegates shall find it necessary to call such meeting sooner.

XV. That the foregoing Address and Resolutions be signed by the Chairman and by the Secretary, and that *Twenty Thousand Copies* of them be printed, published and distributed [gratis.]

                                      Maurice Margarot, Chairman.
[8 July, 1793.]   Thomas Hardy, Secretary.

46 William Godwin:
Enquiry Concerning Political Justice
(1793)

[3rd edn, 2 vols, 1798]

Book III, Chapter IV: Of Political Authority [Vol. i, 214–16]

. . . Government then being first supposed necessary for the
welfare of mankind, the most important principle that can be
imagined relative to its structure, seems to be this; that, as
government is a transaction in the name and for the benefit
of the whole, every member of the community ought to have
some share in the selection of its measures. The arguments in
support of this proposition are various.

First, it has already appeared that there is no satisfactory
criterion, marking out any man, or set of men, to preside over
the rest.

Secondly, all men are partakers of the common faculty,
reason; and may be supposed to have some communication
with the common instructor truth. It would be wrong in an
affair of such momentous concern, that any chance for additional wisdom should be rejected; nor can we tell, in many
cases, till after the experiment, how eminent any individual
may be found, in the business of guiding and deliberating for
his fellows.

Thirdly, government is a contrivance instituted for the
security of individuals; and it seems both reasonable, that
each man should have a share in providing for his own security; and probable, that partiality and cabal will by this means
be most effectually excluded.

Lastly, to give each man a voice in the public concerns
comes nearest to that fundamental purpose of which we should

never lose sight, the uncontrolled exercise of private judgement. Each man will thus be inspired with a consciousness of his own importance, and the slavish feelings that shrink up the soul in the presence of an imagined superior, will be unknown.

Admitting then the propriety of each man having a share in directing the affairs of the whole in the first instance, it seems necessary that he should concur in electing a house of representatives, if he be the member of a large state; or, even in a small one, that he should assist in the appointment of officers and administrators; which implies, first, a delegation of authority to these officers, and, secondly, a tacit consent, or rather an admission of the necessity, that the questions to be debated should abide the decision of a majority. . . .

Book III, Chapter VI: Of Obedience [Vol. i, 225–6, 229–32, 234–5, 238–9]

. . . The reason a man lives under any particular government is partly necessity; he cannot easily avoid living under some government, and it is often scarcely in his power to abandon the country in which he was born; it is also partly a choice of evils; no man can be said, in this case, to enjoy that freedom which is essential to the forming a contract, unless it could be shown that he had a power of instituting, somewhere, a government adapted to his own conceptions.—Government in reality, as has abundantly appeared, is a question of force, and not of consent. It is desirable, that a government should be made as agreeable as possible to the ideas and inclinations of its subjects; and that they should be consulted, as extensively as may be, respecting its construction and regulations. But, at last, the best constituted government that can be formed, particularly for a large community, will contain many provisions that, far from having obtained the consent of all its members, encounter even in their outset a strenuous, though ineffectual, opposition. . . .

The greatest mischief that can arise in the progress of obedience, is, where it shall lead us, in any degree, to depart from the independence of our understanding, a departure which general and unlimited confidence necessarily includes.

In this view, the best advice that could be given to a person in a state of subjection, is, 'Comply, where the necessity of the case demands it; but criticize while you comply. Obey the unjust mandates of your governors; for this prudence and a consideration of the common safety may require; but treat them with no false lenity, regard them with no indulgence. Obey; this may be right; but beware of reverence. Reverence nothing but wisdom and skill: government may be vested in the fittest persons; then they are entitled to reverence, because they are wise, and not because they are governors: and it may be vested in the worst. Obedience will occasionally be right in both cases: you may run south, to avoid a wild beast advancing in that direction, though you want to go north. But be upon your guard against confounding things, so totally unconnected with each other, as a purely political obedience, and respect. Government is nothing but regulated force; force is its appropriate claim upon your attention. It is the business of individuals to persuade; the tendency of concerted strength, is only to give consistency and permanence to an influence more compendious than persuasion.' . . . It is a violation of political justice to confound the authority which depends upon force, with the authority which arises from reverence and esteem. . . . These two kinds of authority may happen to vest in the same person; but they are altogether distinct and independent of each other.

The consequence which has flowed from confounding them, has been, a greater debasement of the human character, than could easily have followed upon a direct and unqualified slavery. . . . One of the lessons most assiduously inculcated upon mankind in all ages and countries, is that of reverence to our superiors. If by this maxim be intended our superiors in wisdom, it may be admitted, but with some qualification. But, if it imply our superiors in station only, nothing can be more contrary to reason and justice. Is it not enough that they have usurped certain advantages over us to which they can show no equitable claim; and must we also humble our courage, and renounce our independence, in their presence? Why reverence a man because he happens to be born to certain privileges; or because a concurrence of circumstances (for wisdom, as we have already seen, gives a claim to respect utterly distinct from power) has procured him a share in the legislative or executive government of our country? Let him content himself with the obedience which is the result of force; for to that only is he entitled. . . . The true supporters of government are the weak and uninformed, and not the wise. In proportion as weakness and ignorance shall diminish, the basis of government will also decay. This however is an event which ought not to be contemplated with alarm. . . . It may be to a certain degree doubtful, whether the human species will ever be emancipated from their present subjection and pupillage, but let it not be forgotten that this is their condition. . . .

Book III, Chapter VII: Of Forms of Government [Vol. i, 242, 244–245]

. . . Government, in particular, is founded in opinion; nor can any attempt to govern men, otherwise in conformity to their own conceptions, be expected to prove salutary. A project therefore to introduce abruptly any species of political institution, merely from a view to its absolute excellence, and without taking into account the state of the public mind, must be absurd and injurious. The best mode of political society, will, no doubt, be considered by the enlightened friend of his species, as the ultimate object of his speculations and efforts. But he will be on his guard against precipitate measures. The only mode for its secure and auspicious establishment, is through the medium of a general preference in its favour. . . . Again: if conviction of the understanding be the compass which is to direct our proceedings in the general affairs, we shall have many reforms, but no revolutions. As it is only in a gradual manner that the public can be instructed, a violent explosion in the community, is by no means the most likely to happen, as the result of instruction. . . . Incessant change, everlasting innovation, seem to be dictated by the true interests of mankind. But government is the perpetual enemy of change. What was admirably observed of a particular system of government, is in a great degree true of all: They 'lay their hand on the spring there is in society, and put a stop to its motion.' Their tendency is to perpetuate abuse. Whatever was once thought right and useful, they undertake to entail to the latest posterity. They reverse the genuine propensities of man, and, instead of suffering us to proceed, teach us to look backward for perfection. . . .

Book IV, Chapter I: Of Resistance [Vol. i, 256–7]

. . . The great cause of humanity, which is now pleading in the face of the universe, has but two enemies; those friends of antiquity, and those friends of innovation, who impatient of suspense, are inclined violently to interrupt the calm, the incessant, the rapid and auspicious progress which thought and reflection appear to be making in the world. Happy would it be for mankind, if those persons who interest themselves most zealously in these great questions, would confine their exertions, to the diffusing, in every possible mode, a spirit of enquiry, and the embracing every opportunity of increasing the stock, and generalizing the communication, of political knowledge! . . . In this case nothing can be more indefensible, than a project for introducing by violence that state of society, which our judgements may happen to approve. In the first place, no persons are ripe for the participation of a benefit, the advantage of which they do not understand. No people are competent to enjoy a state of freedom, who are not already imbued with a love of freedom. The most dreadful tragedies will infallibly result, from an attempt to goad mankind prematurely into a position, however abstractedly excellent, for which they are in no degree prepared. Secondly, to endeavour to impose our sentiments by force, is the most detestable species of persecution. Others are as much entitled to deem themselves in the right as we are. The most sacred of all privileges, is that, by which each man has a certain sphere, relative to the government of his own actions, and the exercise of his discretion, not liable to be trenched upon by the intemperate zeal or dictatorial temper of his neighbour. To dragoon men into the adoption of what we think right, is an intolerable tyranny. It leads to unlimited disorder and injustice. . . .

Book IV, Chapter II: Of Revolutions [Vol. i, 268, 270–1, 273–4]

. . . Revolution is instigated by a horror against tyranny, yet
its own tyranny is not without peculiar aggravations. There
is no period more at war with the existence of liberty. . . .
During a period of revolution, enquiry, and all those patient
speculations to which mankind are indebted for their greatest
improvements are suspended. Such speculations demand a
period of security and permanence; they can scarcely be
pursued, when men cannot foresee what shall happen to-
morrow, and the most astonishing vicissitudes are affairs of
perpetual recurrence. Such speculations demand leisure, and
a tranquil and dispassionate temper; they can scarcely be
pursued, when all the passions of men are afloat, and we are
hourly under the strongest impressions, of fear and hope,
apprehension and desire, dejection and triumph. . . .

Revolutions are a struggle between two parties, each persuaded of the justice of its cause, a struggle, not decided by
compromise or patient expostulation, but by force only. Such
a decision can scarcely be expected to put an end to the
mutual animosity and variance. . . .

The only method according to which social improvements
can be carried on, with sufficient prospect of an auspicious
event, is, when the improvement of our institutions advances,
in a just proportion to the illumination of the public understanding. . . . Under this view of the subject then it appears,
that revolutions, instead of being truly beneficial to mankind,
answer no other purpose than that of marring the salutary
and uninterrupted progress, which might be expected to attend
upon political truth and social improvement. . . .

Book IV, Chapter III: Of Political Associations [Vol. i, 286–7, 294–
295]

. . . One of the most obvious features of political association,
is its tendency to make a part stand for the whole. A number
of persons, sometimes greater and sometimes less, combine
together. The tendency of their combination, often avowed, but
always unavoidable, is to give to their opinion a weight and

operation, which the opinion of unconnected individuals cannot have. A greater number, some from the urgency of their private affairs, some from a temper averse to scenes of concourse and contention, and others from a conscientious disapprobation of the measures pursued, withhold themselves from such combinations. The acrimonious, the intemperate, and the artful, will generally be found among the most forward in matters of this kind. The prudent, the sober, the sceptical, and the contemplative, those who have no resentments to gratify, and no selfish purposes to promote, will be overborne and lost in the progress. What justification can be advanced, for a few persons who thus from mere impetuosity and incontinence of temper, occupy a post, the very principle of which is, the passing them for something greater and more important in the community than they are? Is the business of reform likely to be well and judiciously conducted in such hands? Add to this, that associations in favour of one set of political tenets, are likely to engender counter associations in favour of another. Thus we should probably be involved in all the mischiefs of resistance, and all the uproar of revolution. . . . But, though association, in the received sense of that term, must be granted to be an instrument of very dangerous nature, unreserved communication, especially among persons who are already awakened to the pursuit of truth, is of no less unquestionable advantage. . . . conversation accustoms us to hear a variety of sentiments, obliges us to exercise patience and attention, and gives freedom and elasticity to our disquisitions. . . . It follows, that the promoting the best interests of mankind, eminently depends upon the freedom of social communication. . . .

Book V, Chapter XIV: General Features of Democracy [Vol. ii, 114, 117, 119-20]

Democracy is a system of government, according to which every member of society is considered as a man, and nothing more. So far as positive regulation is concerned, if indeed that can, with any propriety, be termed regulation, which is the mere recognition of the simplest of all moral principles, every man is regarded as equal. Talents and wealth, wherever they exist, will not fail to obtain a certain degree of influence, without requiring positive institution to second their operation.

But there are certain disadvantages, that may seem the necessary result of democratical equality. In political society, it is reasonable to suppose, that the wise will be outnumbered by the unwise. . . . Supposing that we should even be obliged to take democracy with all the disadvantages that were ever annexed to it, and that no remedy could be discovered for any of its defects, it would still be preferable to the exclusive system of other forms. . . . In the estimate that is usually made of democracy, one of the sources of our erroneous judgement, lies in our taking mankind such as monarchy and aristocracy have made them, and thence judging how fit they are to manage for themselves. Monarchy and aristocracy would be no evils, if their tendency were not to undermine the virtues and the understandings of their subjects. The thing most necessary, is to remove all those restraints which prevent the human mind from attaining its genuine strength. Implicit faith, blind submission to authority, timid fear, a distrust of our powers, an inattention to our own importance and the good purposes we are able to effect, these are the chief obstacles to human improvement. Democracy restores to man a consciousness of his value, teaches him, by the removal of authority and oppression, to listen only to the suggestions of reason, gives him confidence to treat all other men with frankness and simplicity, and induces him to regard them no longer, as enemies against whom to be upon his guard, but as brethren whom it becomes him to assist. The citizen of a democratical state, when he looks upon the oppression and injustice that prevail in the countries around him, cannot but entertain an inexpressible esteem for the advantages he enjoys, and the most unalterable determination to preserve them. . . .

47 Thomas Spence:
The Real Rights of Man (1793)

[A Lecture delivered at Newcastle upon Tyne on 8 November 1775 and later published in 1793. It was re-issued in 1796 as *The Meridian Sun of Liberty* and printed in *The Pioneers of Land Reform*, ed. M. Beer (1920), pp. 5–16. Spence was continually publishing and selling radical tracts. He was imprisoned for a few months in 1794 and again in 1801.]

... That property in land and liberty among men in a state of nature ought to be equal, few, one would be fain to hope, would be foolish to deny. Therefore, taking this to be granted, the country of any people, in a native state, is properly their common, in which each of them has an equal property, with free liberty to sustain himself and family with the animals, fruits and other products thereof. . . . Well, methinks some are now ready to say, but is it lawful, reasonable and just, for this people to sell, or make a present even, of the whole of their country, or common, to whom they will, to be held by them and their heirs for ever?

To this I answer, if their posterity require no grosser materials to live and move upon than air, it would certainly be very ill-natured to dispute their right of parting, for what of their own, their posterity would never have occasion for; but if their posterity cannot live but as grossly as they do, the same gross materials must be left them to live upon. For the right to deprive anything of the means of living, supposes a right to deprive it of life; and this right ancestors are not supposed to have over their posterity. . . .

If we look back to the origin of the present nations, we shall see that the land, with all its appurtenances, was claimed by a few, and divided among themselves, in as assured a manner as if they had manufactured it and it had been the work of their own hands; and by being unquestioned, or not called to an account for such usurpations and unjust claims, they fell into a habit of thinking, or, which is the same thing to the rest of mankind, of acting as if the earth was made for or by them, and did not scruple to call it their own property, which they might dispose of without regard to any other living creature in the universe. Accordingly they did so; and no man, more than any other creature, could claim a right to so much as a blade of grass, or a nut or an acorn, a fish or a fowl, or any natural production whatever, though to save his life, without the permission of the pretended proprietor; and not a foot of land, water, rock or heath but was claimed by one or other of those lords; . . . . And any one of them still can, by laws of their own making, oblige every living creature to remove off his property (which, to the great distress of mankind, is too often put in execution); so of consequence were all the land-holders to be of one mind, and determined to take their properties into their own hands, all the rest of mankind might go to heaven if they would, for there would be no place found for them here. Thus men may not live in any part of this world, not even where they are born, but as strangers, and by the permission of the pretender to the property thereof; . . .

But lest it should be said that a system whereby they may reap more advantages consistent with the nature of society cannot be proposed, I will attempt to show the outlines of such a plan.

Let it be supposed, then, that the whole people in some country, after much reasoning and deliberation, should conclude that every man has an equal property in the land in the neighbourhood where he resides. They therefore resolve that if they live in society together, it shall only be with a view that everyone may reap all the benefits from their natural rights and privileges possible.

Therefore a day is appointed on which the inhabitants of each parish meet, in their respective parishes, to take their long-lost rights into possession, and to form themselves into corporations. So then each parish becomes a corporation, and all men who are inhabitants become members or burghers. The land, with all that appertains to it, is in every parish made the property of the corporation or parish, with as ample power to let, repair, or alter all or any part thereof as a lord of the manor enjoys over his lands, houses, etc.; but the power of alienating the least morsel, in any manner, from the parish either at this or any time hereafter is denied. . . . Thus are there no more nor other lands in the whole country than the parishes; and each of them is sovereign lord of its own territories.

Then you may behold the rent which the people have paid into the parish treasuries, employed by each parish in paying the government its share of the sum which the Parliament or National Congress at any time grants; in maintaining and relieving its own poor, and people out of work; in paying the necessary officers their salaries; in building, repairing, and adorning its houses, bridges and other structures; in making and maintaining convenient and delightful streets, highways, and passages both for foot and carriages; in making and maintaining canals and other conveniences for trade and navigation; in planting and taking in waste grounds; in providing and keeping up a magazine of ammunition, and all sorts of arms sufficient for all its inhabitants in case of danger from enemies; in premiums for the encouragement of agriculture, or anything else thought worthy of encouragement; and, in a word, in doing whatever the people think proper; and not, as formerly, to support and spread luxury, pride, and all manner of vice. As for corruption in elections, it has now no being or effect among them; all affairs to be determined by voting, either in a full meeting of a parish, its committees, or in the house of representatives, are done by balloting, so that voting or elections among them occasion no animosities, for none need to let another know for which side he votes; all that can be done, therefore, in order to gain a majority of votes for anything, is to make it appear in the best light possible by speaking or writing. Among them Government does not meddle in every trifle; but on the contrary, allows each parish the power of putting the laws in force in all cases, and does not interfere but when they act manifestly to the prejudice of society and the rights and liberties of mankind, as established in their glorious constitution and laws. . . .

A certain number of neighbouring parishes, as those in a town or county, have each an equal vote in the election of persons to represent them in Parliament, Senate, or Congress;

and each of them pays equally towards their maintenance. They are chosen thus: all the candidates are proposed in every parish on the same day, when the election by balloting immediately proceeds in all the parishes at once, to prevent too great a concourse in one place; and they who are found to have a majority, on a proper survey of the several poll-books, are acknowledged to be their representatives. . . .

All men in every parish, at times of their own choosing, repair together to a field for that purpose, with their officers, arms, banners, and all sorts of martial music, in order to learn or retain the complete art of war; there they become soldiers. Yet not to molest their neighbours unprovoked, but to be able to defend what none have a right to dispute their title to the enjoyment of; . . . There is no army kept in pay among them in times of peace; as all have property alike to defend, they are alike ready to run to arms when their country is in danger; . . . Freedom to do anything whatever cannot there be bought; a thing is either entirely prohibited, as theft or murder; or entirely free to everyone without tax or price, and the rents are still not so high, notwithstanding all that is done with them, as they were formerly for only the maintenance of a few haughty, unthankful landlords. For the government, which may be said to be the greatest mouth, having neither excise-men, custom-house men, collectors, army, pensioners, bribery, nor such like ruination vermin to maintain, is soon satisfied, and moreover there are no more persons employed in offices, either about the government or parishes, than are absolutely necessary; and their salaries are but just sufficient to maintain them suitably to their offices. . . .

But what makes this prospect yet more glowing is that after this empire of right and reason is thus established, it will stand for ever. Force and corruption attempting its downfall shall equally be baffled, and all other nations, struck with wonder and admiration at its happiness and stability, shall follow the example; and thus the whole earth shall at last be happy and live like brethren.

48 Hannah More:
Village Politics (1793)

[*The Works of Hannah More* (Bohn edition, 1854), ii, 221–36. Hannah More wrote several such 'Tracts for the Times' to prevent the dissemination of radical ideas among the labouring poor. Her tracts have been aptly described as 'Burke for Beginners'.]

Addressed to all the Mechanics, Journeymen, and Labourers in Great Britain. By Will Chap, a country carpenter

A dialogue between Jack Anvil, the Blacksmith—and Tom Hod, the Mason.

Jack . . . What is the matter?

Tom Matter? Why, I want liberty.

Jack Liberty! That's bad, indeed! What! has anyone fetched a warrant for thee? Come, man, cheer up, I'll be bound for thee. Thou art an honest fellow in the main, tho' thou dost tipple and prate a little too much at the Rose and Crown.

Tom. No, no, I want a new constitution.

Jack Indeed! Why, I thought thou hadst been a desperate healthy fellow. Send for the doctor directly.

Tom I'm not sick; I want liberty and equality, and the rights of man.

Jack Oh, now I understand thee. What! thou art a leveller and a republican, I warrant?

Tom I'm a friend of the people. I want a reform.

Jhck Then the shortest way is to mend thyself.

Tom But I want a *general* reform.

Jack Then let every one mend one.

Tom Pooh! I want freedom and happiness, the same as they have got in France.

Jack What, Tom, we imitate them! We follow the French! Why, they only began all this mischief at first, in order to

210

be just what *we* are already; and what a blessed land must this be, to be in actual possession of all they ever hoped to gain by all their hurly-burly. Imitate them, indeed! Why, I'd sooner go to the Negroes to get learning, or to the Turks to get religion, than to the French for freedom and happiness.

Tom What do you mean by that? ar'n't the French free?

Jack Free, Tom! ay, free with a witness. They are all so free, that there's nobody safe. They make free to rob whom they will, and kill whom they will. If they don't like a man's looks, they make free to hang him without judge or jury, and the next lamp-post serves for the gallows; so then they call themselves free, because you see they have no law left to condemn them, and no king to take them up and hang them for it.

Tom Ah, Jack, didn't their king formerly hang people for nothing, too? and besides, were not they all papists before the revolution?

Jack Why, true enough, they had but a poor sort of religion; but bad is better than none, Tom. And so was the government bad enough too; for they could clap an innocent man into prison, and keep him there too, as long as they would, and never say, with your leave, or by your leave, gentlemen of the jury. But what's all that to us?

Tom To us! Why, don't our governors put many of our poor folks in prison against their will? What are all the jails for? Down with the jails, I say! all men should be free.

Jack Harkee, Tom, a few rogues in prison keep the rest in order, and then honest men go about their business in safety, afraid of nobody; that's the way to be free. And let me tell thee, Tom, thou and I are tried by our peers as much as a lord is. Why, the *king* can't send me to prison, if I do no harm; and if I do, there's reason good why I should go there. I may go to law with Sir John at the great castle yonder; and he no more dares lift his little finger against me than if I were his equal. A lord is hanged for hanging matter, as thou or I should be. . . .

Tom But still I should have no one over my head.

Jack That's a mistake: I'm stronger than thou; and Standish, the exciseman, is a better scholar; so that we should not remain equal a minute. I shou'd out-*fight* thee, and he'd out-*wit* thee. And if such a sturdy fellow as I am, was to come and break down thy hedge for a little firing, or take away the crop from thy ground, I'm not so sure that these new-fangled laws wou'd see thee righted. I tell thee, Tom, we have a fine constitution already, and our forefathers thought so.

Tom They were a pack of fools, and had never read the Rights of Man.

Jack I'll tell thee a story. When sir John married, my lady, who is a little fantastical, and likes to do everything like the French, begged him to pull down yonder fine old castle, and build it up in her frippery way. No, says sir John, what! shall I pull down this noble building, raised by the wisdom of my brave ancestors; which outstood the civil wars, and only underwent a little needful repair at the Revolution; a castle which all my neighbours come to take a pattern by —shall I pull it all down, I say, only because there may be a dark closet, or an awkward passage, or an inconvenient room or two in it? Our ancestors took time for what they did. They understood foundation work; no running up your little slight lath-and-plaster buildings, which are up in a day, and down in a night. My lady mumpt and grumbled; but the castle was let stand, and a glorious building it is; tho' a few decays want stopping; so now and then they mend a little thing, and they'll go on mending, I dare say, as they have leisure, to the end of the chapter, if they are let alone. But no pull-me-down works. What is it you are crying out for, Tom?

Tom Why, for a perfect government?

Jack You might as well cry for the moon. There's nothing perfect in this world, take my word for it: tho' sir John says, we come nearer to it than any country in the world ever did. . . .

Tom But I say all men are equal. Why should one be above another?

Jack If that's thy talk, Tom, thou dost quarrel with Providence, and not with Government. For the woman is below her husband, and the children are below their mother, and the servant is below his master.

Tom But the subject is not below the king: all kings are 'crowned ruffians;' and all governments are wicked. For my part, I'm resolved I'll pay no more taxes to any of them.

Jack Tom, Tom, if thou didst go oftener to church, thou wou'dst know where it is said, 'Render unto Caesar the things that are Caesar's;' and also, 'Fear God, honour the king.' *Your* book tells you that we need obey no government but that of the people; and that we may fashion and alter the government according to our whimsies: but *mine* tells me, 'Let everyone be subject to the higher powers, for all power is of God, the powers that be are ordained of God; whosoever therefore resisteth the power, resisteth the ordinance of God.' . . .

Tom I say we shall never be happy, till we do as the French have done.

Jack The French and we contending for liberty, Tom, is just as if thou and I were to pretend to run a race; thou to set out from the starting-post when I am in already; thou to have all the ground to travel, when I have reached the end. Why, we've got it man! we've no race to run! we're there already! Our constitution is no more like what the French one was, than a mug of our Taunton beer is like a platter of their soup-maigre.

Tom I know we shall be undone, if we don't get a new *constitution*—that's all.

Jack And I know we shall be undone if we *do*. . . .

Tom Well, still, as the old saying is—I shou'd like to do as they do in France.

Jack What, shou'dst like to be murdered with as little ceremony as Hackabout, the butcher, knocks down a calf? or, shou'dst like to get rid of thy wife for every little bit of tiff? And as to liberty of conscience, which they brag so much about, why, they have driven away their parsons, (ay, and murdered many of 'em,) because they would not swear as they would have them. And then they talk of liberty of the press; why, Tom, only t'other day they hang'd a man for printing a book against this pretty government of theirs.

Tom But you said, yourself, it was sad times in France, before they pull'd down the old government.

Jack Well, and suppose the French were as much in the right as I know them to be in the wrong; what does that argue for *us*? Because my neighbour Furrow t'other day pull'd down a crazy old barn, is that a reason why I must set fire to my tight cottage? . . .

Tom What then dost thou take French *liberty* to be?

Jack To murder more men in one night, than ever their poor king did in his whole life.

Tom And what dost thou take a *Democrat* to be?

Jack One who likes to be governed by a thousand tyrants, and yet can't bear a king.

Tom What is *Equality*?

Jack For every man to pull down every one that is above him; while, instead of raising those below him to his own level, he only makes use of them as steps to raise himself to the place of those he has tumbled down.

Tom What is *the new rights of man*?

Jack Battle, murder, and sudden death.

Tom What is it to be an *enlightened people*?

Jack To put out the light of the gospel, confound right and wrong, and grope about in pitch darkness.

Tom What is *Philosophy*, that Tim Standish talks so much about?

Jack To believe that there's neither God, nor devil, nor heaven, nor hell; . . .

Tom And dost thou think our rights of man will lead to all this wickedness?

Jack As sure as eggs are eggs.

Tom I begin to think we are better off as we are.

Jack I'm sure on't. This is only a scheme to make us go back in every thing. 'Tis making ourselves poor when we are getting rich, and discontented when we are comfortable. . . .

Tom And thou art very sure we are not ruined?

Jack I'll tell thee how we are ruined. We have a king, so loving, that he wou'd not hurt the people if he cou'd; and so kept in, that he cou'd not hurt the people if he wou'd. We have as much liberty as can make us happy, and more trade and riches than allows us to be good. We have the best laws in the world, if they were more strictly enforced; and the best religion in the world, if it was but better followed. While Old England is safe, I'll glory in her, and pray for her; and when she is in danger, I'll fight for her, and die for her.

Tom And so will I too, Jack, that's what I will. (sings) 'O the roast beef of Old England!'

Jack Thou art an honest fellow, Tom. . . . Come along.

Tom No; first I'll stay to burn my book, and then I'll go and make a bonfire, and—

Jack Hold, Tom. There is but one thing worse than a bitter enemy; and that is an imprudent friend. If thou wou'dst shew thy love to thy king and country, let's have no drinking, no riot, no bonfires, but put in practice this text, which our parson preached on last Sunday, 'Study to be quiet, work with your own hands, and mind your own business.'

Tom And so I will, Jack—Come on.

49   William Wordsworth:
A Letter to the Bishop of Llandaff (1793)

[In 1793 Dr Watson, Bishop of Llandaff, published a sermon on 'The Wisdom and Goodness of God in having made both Rich and Poor', to which he added an appendix attacking the French Revolution. Wordsworth prepared a reply, but this was neither sent nor published. It can be found in *The Prose Works of William Wordsworth*, ed. Alexander B. Grosart (London, 1876), i, 3–23.]

. . . You say: 'I fly with terror and abhorrence even from the altar of Liberty, when I see it stained with the blood of the aged, of the innocent, of the defenceless sex, of the ministers of religion, and of the faithful adherents of a fallen monarch.' What! have you so little knowledge of the nature of man as to be ignorant that a time of revolution is not the season of true Liberty? Alas, the obstinacy and perversion of man is such that she is too often obliged to borrow the very arms of Despotism to overthrow him, and, in order to reign in peace, must establish herself by violence. She deplores such stern necessities, but the safety of the people, her supreme law, is her consolation. . . .

I now proceed to principles. Your Lordship very properly asserts that 'the liberty of man in a state of society consists in his being subject to no law but the law enacted by the general will of the society to which he belongs.' You approved of the object which the French had in view when, in the infancy of the Revolution, they were attempting to destroy arbitrary power, and to erect a temple to Liberty on its remains. It is with surprise, then, that I find you afterwards presuming to dictate to the world a servile adoption of the British constitution. It is with indignation I perceive you 'reprobate' a people for having imagined happiness and liberty more likely to flourish in the open field of a Republic than under the shade of Monarchy. You are therefore guilty of a most glaring contradiction. Twenty-five millions of Frenchmen have felt that they could have no security for their liberties under any modification of monarchical power. They have in consequence unanimously chosen a Republic. You cannot but observe that they have only exercised that right in which, by your own confession, liberty essentially resides. . . . Slavery is a bitter and a poisonous draught. We have but one consolation under it, that a Nation may dash the cup to the ground when she pleases. Do not imagine that by taking from its bitterness you weaken its deadly quality; no, by rendering it more palatable you contribute to its power of destruction. We submit without repining to the chastisements of Providence, aware that we are creatures, that opposition is vain and remonstrance impossible. But when redress is in our own power and resistance is rational, we suffer with the same humility from beings like ourselves, because we are taught from infancy that we were born in a state of inferiority to our oppressors, that they were sent into the world to scourge, and we to be scourged. Accordingly we see the bulk of mankind, actuated by these fatal prejudices, even more ready to lay themselves under the feet of *the great* than the great are to trample upon them. . . . As the magnitude of almost all States prevents the possibility of their enjoying a pure democracy, philosophers—from a wish, as far as it is in their power, to make the governors and the governed one— will turn their thoughts to the system of universal representa- tion, and will annex an equal importance to the suffrage of every individual. . . . Sensible that at the moment of election an interest distinct from that of the general body is created, an enlightened legislator will endeavour by every possible method to diminish the operation of such interest. The first and most natural mode that presents itself is that of shortening the regular duration of this trust, in order that the man who has betrayed it may soon be superseded by a more worthy successor. But this is not enough; aware of the possibility of imposition, and of the natural tendency of power to corrupt the heart of man, a sensible Republican will think it essential that the office of legislator be not intrusted to the same man for a succession of years. . . . But, to resume the subject of univer- sal representation, I ought to have mentioned before, that in the choice of its representatives a people will not immorally hold out wealth as a criterion of integrity, nor lay down as a fundamental rule, that to be qualified for the trying duties of legislation a citizen should be possessed of a certain fixed property. Virtues, talents, and acquirements are all that it will look for. . . . And this brings me to my grand objection to monarchy, which is drawn from THE ETERNAL NATURE OF MAN. The office of king is a trial to which human virtue is not equal. Pure and universal representation, by which alone liberty can be secured, cannot, I think, exist together with monarchy. It seems madness to expect a manifestation of the *general* will, at the same time that we allow to a *particular* will that weight which it must obtain in all governments that can with any propriety be called monarchical. They must war with each other till one of them is extinguished. . . .

. . . our legislators . . . have unjustly left unprotected that most important part of property, not less real because it has no material existence, that which ought to enable the labourer to provide food for himself and his family. I appeal to innumerable statutes, whose constant and professed object it is to lower the price of labour, to compel the workman to be *content* with arbitrary wages, evidently too small from the necessity of legal enforcement of the acceptance of them. . . . I am not an advocate for the agrarian law [to redistribute land among the people] nor for sumptuary regulations, but I contend that the people amongst whom the law of primogeniture exists, and among whom corporate bodies are encouraged, and immense salaries annexed to useless and indeed hereditary offices, is oppressed by an inequality in the distribution of wealth which does not necessarily attend men in a state of civil society. . . .

You ask with triumphant confidence, to what other law are the people of England subject than the general will of the society to which they belong? Is your Lordship to be told that acquiescence is not choice, and that obedience is not freedom? If there is a single man in Great Britain who has no suffrage in the election of a representative, the will of the society of which he is a member is not generally expressed; he is a Helot in that society. . . .

[Written in 1794, published surreptitiously in 1817 but not officially until
the edition of Southey's Poetical Works in 1837. In praising Wat Tyler and
John Ball, the leaders and heroes of the Peasants' Revolt of 1381, Southey
was expressing his sympathy with radical ideas and his fears of a policy of
repression by the government.]

Act II Scene I

. . .

John Ball addresses Wat Tyler and his friends:
   Friends, brethren! for ye are my
      brethren all;
   Englishmen, met in arms to advocate
   The cause of freedom, hear me; pause awhile
   In the career of vengeance!—It is true
   I am a priest, but, as these rags may speak,
   Not one who riots in the poor man's spoil,
   Or trades with his religion. I am one
   Who preaches the law of Christ; and, in my life,
   Would practise what he taught. The Son of God
   Came not to you in power: humble in mien,
   Lowly in heart, the man of Nazareth
   Preach'd mercy, justice, love: 'Woe unto ye,
   Ye that are rich: if that ye would be saved
   Sell that ye have, and give unto the poor.'
   So taught the Saviour: Oh, my honest friends,
   Have ye not felt the strong indignant throb
   Of justice in your bosoms, to behold
   The lordly Baron feasting on your spoils?
   Have you not in your hearts arraign'd the lot
   That gave him on the couch of luxury
   To pillow his head, and pass the festive day
   In sportive feasts, and ease, and revelry?

Have you not often in your conscience ask'd,
Why is the difference; wherefore should that man,
No worthier than myself, thus lord it over me,
And bid me labour, and enjoy the fruits?
The God within your breasts has argued thus:
The voice of truth has murmur'd. Came ye not
As helpless to the world? Shines not the sun
With equal ray on both? Do ye not feel
The self-same winds of heaven as keenly parch ye?
Abundant is the earth—the Sire of all,
Saw and pronounced that it was very good.
Look round; the vernal fields smile with new flowers,
The budding orchard perfumes the sweet breeze,
And the green corn waves to the passing gale.
There is enough for all; but your proud Baron
Stands up, and, arrogant of strength, exclaims,
'I am a Lord—by nature I am noble:
These fields are mine, for I was born to them,
I was born in the castle—you, poor wretches,
Whelp'd in the cottage, are by birth my slaves.'
Almighty God! such blasphemies are utter'd:
Almighty God! such blasphemies believed!
Tom Miller This is something like a sermon.
Jack Straw   Where's the bishop
Would tell you truths like these?
. . .

John Ball My brethren, these are truths, and
    weighty ones,
Ye are all equal: nature made ye so.
Equality is your birthright.—When I gaze
On the proud palace, and behold one man
In the blood-purpled robes of royalty,
Feasting at ease, and lording over millions,
Then turn me to the hut of poverty,
And see the wretched labourer worn with toil,
Divide his scanty morsel with his infants,
I sicken, and indignant at the sight,
'Blush for the patience of humanity.'
Jack Straw We will assert our rights.

Tom Miller   We'll trample down
  These insolent oppressors.
John Ball   In good truth,
  Ye have cause for anger: but, my honest friends,
  Is it revenge or justice that ye seek?
  Mob   Justice! Justice!
John Ball Oh, then, remember mercy;
  And though your proud oppressors spare not you,
  Show you excel them in humanity.
  They will use every art to disunite you;
  To conquer separately, by stratagem,
  Whom in a mass they fear;—but be ye firm;
  Boldly demand your long-forgotten rights,
  Your sacred, your inalienable freedom.
  Be bold—be resolute—be merciful:
  And while you spurn the hated name of slaves,
  Show you are men.
Mob   Long live our honest priest.
Jack Straw He shall be made archbishop.
John Ball My brethren, I am plain John Ball,
    your friend,
  Your equal: by the law of Christ enjoin'd
  To serve you, not command.
Jack Straw   March we for London.
Tyler Mark me, my friends—we rise for Liberty—
  Justice shall be our guide: let no man dare
  To plunder in the tumult.
Mob Lead us on. Liberty! Justice!
  [Exeunt, with cries of Liberty! No Poll-tax! No war.

Act III Scene II

  John Ball, a prisoner, is questioned by Sir John Tresilian
  . . . .
Sir John Tr. Did you not tell the mob they were
    oppress'd;
  And preach upon the equality of man;
  With evil intent thereby to stir them up
  To tumult and rebellion?

John Ball   That I told them
    That all mankind are equal, is most true:
    Ye came as helpless infants to the world;
    Ye feel alike the infirmities of nature;
    And at last moulder into common clay.
    Why then these vain distinctions?—bears not the earth
    Food in abundance?—must your granaries
    O'erflow with plenty, while the poor man starves?
    Sir Judge, why sit you there, clad in your furs,
    Why are your cellars stored with choicest wines?
    Your larders hung with dainties, while your vassal,
    As virtuous, and as able too by nature,
    Though by your selfish tyranny deprived
    Of mind's improvement, shivers in his rags,
    And starves amid the plenty he creates.
    I have said this is wrong, and I repeat it—
    And there will be a time when this great truth
    Shall be confess'd—be felt by all mankind.
    The electric truth shall run from man to man,
    And the blood-cemented pyramid of greatness
    Shall fall before the flash.
Sir John Tr.   Audacious rebel:
    How darest thou insult this sacred court,
    Blaspheming all the dignities of rank?
    How could the Government be carried on
    Without the sacred orders of the King
    And the nobility?
John Ball   Tell me, Sir Judge,
    What does the Government avail the peasant?
    Would not he plough his field, and sow the corn,
    Ay, and in peace enjoy the harvest too?
    Would not the sun shine and the dews descend,
    Though neither King nor Parliament existed?
    Do your court politics aught matter him?
    Would he be warring even unto death
    With his French neighbours? Charles and Richard
       contend,
    The people fight and suffer:—think ye, Sirs,
    If neither country had been cursed with a chief,

The peasants would have quarrell'd?
King   This is treason!
The patience of the court has been insulted—
Condemn the foul-mouth'd contumacious rebel.

. . .

51 Samuel Taylor Coleridge: The Plot Discovered; or an Address to the People, against Ministerial Treason (1795)

[A political lecture delivered at Bristol, attacking the Treason bill and the Convention or Seditious Meetings bill introduced by Pitt's ministry in 1795. pp. 3–45. Printed in *The Collected Works of Samuel Taylor Coleridge*, ed. L. Patton and P. Mann (1971), i, 285–313. Extract 53 however shows that by 1798 he was disenchanted with the French Revolution and was becoming more conservatively inclined.]

. . . 'THE MASS OF THE PEOPLE HAVE NOTHING TO DO WITH THE LAWS, BUT TO OBEY THEM!'—Ere yet this foul treason against the majesty of man, ere yet this blasphemy against the goodness of God be registered among our statutes, I enter my protest! Ere yet our laws as well as our religion be muffled up in mysteries, as a CHRISTIAN I protest against this worse than Pagan darkness! Ere yet the sword descends, the two-edged sword that is now waving over the head of Freedom, as a BRITON, I protest against slavery! Ere yet it be made legal for Ministers to act with vigour beyond law, as a CHILD OF PEACE, I protest against civil war! This is the brief moment, in which Freedom pleads on her knees: we will join her pleadings, ere yet she rises terrible to wrench the sword from the hand of her merciless enemy! We will join the still small voice of reason, ere yet it be overwhelmed in the great and strong wind, in the earthquake, and in the fire! These detestable Bills I shall examine in their undiminished proportions, as they first dared shew themselves to the light, disregarding and despising all subsequent palliatives and modifications. From their first state it is made evident beyond all power of doubt, what are the wishes and intentions of the present Ministers; and their wishes and intentions having been so evidenced, if the legislature authorize, if the people endure one sentence of such Bills from such manifest conspirators against the Constitution, that legislature will by degrees authorize the whole, and the people endure the whole, yea, that legislature will be capable of authorizing even worse, and the people will be unworthy of better.

The first of these Bills [the Treason bill] is an attempt to assassinate the Liberty of the Press, the second [the Convention bill], to smother the Liberty of Speech. . . . [They] were conceived and laid in the dunghill of despotism among the other yet unhatched eggs of the old Serpent. In due time and in fit opportunity they crawled into light. Genius of Britain! crush them!

. . . To promulgate what we believe to be truth is indeed a law beyond law; but now if any man should publish, nay, even in a friendly letter or in social conversation any should assert a Republic to be the most perfect form of government, and endeavour by all argument to prove it so, he is guilty of High Treason: for what he declares to be the more perfect, and the most productive of happiness, he recommends; and to recommend a Republic is to recommend an abolition of the kingly name. By the existing treason laws a man so accused would plead, It is the privilege of an Englishman to entertain what speculative opinions he pleases, provided he stir up to no present action. Let my reasonings have been monarchical or republican, whilst I act as a royalist, I am free from guilt. Soon, I fear, such excuse will be of no avail. . . . All political controversy is at an end. Those sudden breezes and noisy gusts, which purified the atmosphere they disturbed, are hushed to deathlike silence. The cadaverous tranquillity of despotism will succeed the generous order and graceful indiscretions of freedom—the black moveless pestilential vapour of slavery will be inhaled at every pore. . . .

We proceed to the second Bill, for more effectually preventing seditious meetings and assemblies. . . .

Where? when? and by whom have factious and seditious speeches been made, and the public peace endangered, by assembled petitioners? Unless these Questions are circumstantially answered, and the answers proved by legal evidence, an act for repealing the Constitution will have passed on the strength of a ministerial assertion. Where, when, and by whom? Within the last years in various parts of the kingdom heavy grievances have called together crowded meetings.

Which of these have endangered the public peace? As far as my information, as far as the newspaper accounts may be trusted, the more numerous the assembly, the more strict has been the good order. What were the factious and seditious speeches? Let them be specified. Are they such as Locke and Lord Somers would have disavowed? Or were they only bold and constitutional remonstrances against dark and ministerial iniquities? If not such, if they are truly factious and seditious (that is, exciting to violence) the existing laws are sufficient authority for apprehending the speakers; let them be brought forwards and examined; let them and the ministers be confronted! . . .

. . . These bills are levelled against all who excite hatred or contempt of the Constitution and Government: that is, all who endeavour to prove the Constitution and Government defective, corrupt, or fraudulent. (For it has been before observed, that all detection of weakness, imposture, or abuse, necessarily tend to excite hatred or contempt.) Now the Constitution and Government are defective and corrupt, or they are not. If the former, the Bills are iniquitous, since they would *kill off* all who promulge truths necessary to the progression of human happiness: if the latter, (that is, if the Constitution and Government are perfect) the Bills are still iniquitous, for they destroy the sole boundary which divides that Government from Despotism, and *change* that Constitution, from whose present perfectness they derive their only possible justification. In order to prove these assertions, we must briefly examine the British Constitution, or mode of Government.

Governments have assumed many different forms; but in their essence and properties, all possible modes of Government are reducible to these three: Government *by* the people, Government *over* the people, and Government *with* the people.

The Government is *by* the people, when the affairs of the whole are directed by all actually present; as among the American Tribes, and (perhaps) in Athens and some other of the ancient Grecian States, or by all *morally* present, that is, where every man is represented, and the representatives act according to instructions. Such, I trust, will be the Government of France. France! whose crimes and miseries posterity will impute to us. France! to whom posterity will impute their virtues and their happiness.

Government *over* the people is known by the name of Despotism, or arbitrary Government: which term does not necessarily imply that one man possesses exclusively the power and direction of the state, for this is no where the case. . . . Despotism is that Government, in which the people at large have no voice in the legislature, and possess no other safe or established mode of political interference: in few words, where the majority are always acted upon, never acting.

The *third* mode is Government *with* the people. This ought to be a *progressive* Government ascending from the *second* mode to the first: at least, it is bad or good according to its distance from, or proximity to, the first mode.

The Constitution and Government of Great Britain is evidently not the first mode, that is, a Government *by* the people. They who contend that it is the second mode, will detail from what the people at large are excluded: they, who would prove it to be the third or mixed mode, must point out to what the people are admitted. And for the honour of our country let these have the first hearing. We are astonished (these would say) at the audacity as well as the blindness of men who dare entertain a doubt on this subject. The English Constitution is the freest under heaven: our Liberty suffers restrictions only to acquire steadiness and security. The people by their proxies in the House of Commons, are a check on the nobility, and the nobility a check on the people: while the King is a check on both. The best disciplined people are subject to giddy moments, which will be most effectually resisted by the wisdom of men educated from their infancy for the senatorial office; whose privileges and even prejudices are an antidote against the epidemic disorders of discontent, and thirst of innovation. And what is the King, but the majestic guardian of Freedom, gifted with privileges that will incline, and prerogatives that enable him to prevent the legislative from assuming the executive power: the union of which is one distinguishing feature of tyranny? such is the Constitution, concerning which it is asked whether or not it be Despotism!!!

Their opponents reply, it is very possible to sketch out an

admirable theory of Government, and then *call* it the British Constitution. . . . We do not ask what a British Constitution might be, nor what the British Constitution has been, we enquire what it now is. We affirm, that a Government, under which the people at large neither directly or indirectly exercise any sovereignty, is a Despotism. . . . The people (you say) exercise a legislative power by proxies, that is, by the majority in the House of Commons. But in the House of Commons three hundred and six are nominated or caused to be returned by one hundred and sixty Peers and Commoners with the Treasury, and three hundred and six are more than a majority: the majority therefore of the House of Commons are the choice, and of course the proxies of the Treasury, and the one hundred and sixty two. Of the rest (that is, the minor number of the House of Commons) some are elected by corporate bodies, others through the undue practices of returning officers, and twenty eight have seats in parliament by *compromises*. And after that these are subtracted, with regard to the yet remaining members, it would be an insult to common sense to assert, they are elected by the people at large. . . . The right of election therefore, as it at present exists in England, must be considered not as an exception to Despotism, but as making it more operose and expensive from the increased necessity of corruption. The people at large exercise no sovereignty either personally, or by representation. Such would be the reply of those who might contend that the Government of England is Despotism. . . .

Hitherto nothing has been adduced that truly distinguishes our Government from Despotism: it seems to be a Government *over*, not *by*, or *with* the people. But this conclusion we disavow. The Liberty of the Press, (a power resident in the people) gives us an *influential* sovereignty. By books necessary information may be dispersed; and by information the public will may be formed; and by the right of petitioning that will may be expressed; first, perhaps, in low and distant tones such as beseem the children of peace; but if corruption deafen power, gradually increasing till they swell into a deep and awful thunder, the VOICE OF GOD, which his vicegerents must hear, and hearing dare not disobey. This unrestricted right of over-awing the Oligarchy of Parliament by constitutional expression of the general will forms our liberty: it is the sole boundary that divides us from Despotism. . . . By the almost winged communication of the Press, the whole nation becomes one grand Senate, fervent yet untumultuous. By the right of meeting together to petition (which, Milton says, is good old english for *requiring*) the determinations of this Senate are embodied into legal form, and conveyed to the *executive* branch of Government, the Parliament. The present Bills annihilate this right. The *forms* of it indeed will remain; (the *forms* of the Roman republic were preserved under Tiberius and Nero) but the reality will have flown. . . .

Does Haughty Gaul Invasion Threat
(1795)

[Burns sympathised with some of the ideals of the 'rights of man' school, but the threat of a French invasion brought out his conservative streak.]

Does haughty Gaul invasion threat?
　　Then let the louns beware, Sir;
There's wooden walls upon our seas,
　　And volunteers on shore, Sir:
The Nith shall run to Corsincorn,
　　And Criffel sink in Solway,
Ere we permit a Foreign Foe
　　On British ground to rally!
We'll ne'er permit a Foreign Foe
　　On British ground to rally!

O let us not, like snarling curs,
　　In wrangling be divided,
Till, slap! come in an unco loun,
　　And wi' a rung decide it!
Be Britain still to Britain true,
　　Among ourselves united;
For never but by British hands
　　Maun British wrangs be righted!
No! never but by British hands
　　Shall British wrangs be righted!

The kettle o' the Kirk and State,
　　Perhaps a clout may fall in't;
But deil a foreign tinkler loun
　　Shall ever ca' a nail in't.
Our fathers' blude the kettle bought,

And wha wad dare to spoil it,
By Heav'ns! the sacrilegious dog
  Shall fuel be to boil it!
By Heav'ns! the sacrilegious dog
  Shall fuel be to boil it!

The wretch that would a tyrant own,
  And wretch, his true-sworn brother,
Who would set the Mob above the Throne,
  May they be damn'd together!
Who will not sing, 'God save the King,'
  Shall hang as high's the steeple
But while we sing 'God save the King,'
  We'll ne'er forget THE PEOPLE!
But while we sing 'God save the King,'
  We'll ne'er forget THE PEOPLE!

53 Samuel Taylor Coleridge: France: An Ode (1798)

[Lines 22–42, 64–105]

II

When France in wrath her giant-limbs upreared,
  And with that oath, which smote air, earth, and sea,
  Stamped her strong foot and said she would be free,
Bear witness for me, how I hoped and feared!
With what a joy my lofty gratulation
  Unawed I sang, amid a slavish band:
And when to whelm the disenchanted nation,
  Like fiends embattled by a wizard's wand,
    The Monarchs marched in evil day,
    And Britain joined the dire array;
  Though dear her shores and circling ocean,
Though many friendships, many youthful loves
  Had swoln the patriot emotion
And flung a magic light o'er all her hills and groves;
Yet still my voice, unaltered, sang defeat
  To all that braved the tyrant-quelling lance,
And shame too long delayed and vain retreat!
For ne'er, O Liberty! with partial aim
I dimmed thy light or damped thy holy flame;
  But blessed the paeans of delivered France,
And hung my head and wept at Britain's name.

IV

Forgive me, Freedom! O forgive those dreams!
  I hear thy voice, I hear thy loud lament,
  From bleak Helvetia's icy caverns sent—
I hear thy groans upon her blood-stained streams!
  Heroes, that for your peaceful country perished,
And ye that, fleeing, spot your mountain-snows
  With bleeding wounds; forgive me, that I cherished
One thought that ever blessed your cruel foes!
  To scatter rage, and traitorous guilt,
  Where Peace her jealous home had built;
    A patriot-race to disinherit
Of all that made their stormy wilds so dear;
    And with inexpiable spirit
To taint the bloodless freedom of the mountaineer—
O France, that mockest Heaven, adulterous, blind,
  And patriot only in pernicious toils!
Are these thy boasts, Champion of human kind?
  To mix with Kings in the low lust of sway,
Yell in the hunt, and share the murderous prey;
To insult the shrine of Liberty with spoils
  From freemen torn; to tempt and to betray?

V

The Sensual and the Dark rebel in vain,
Slaves by their own compulsion! In mad game
  They burst their manacles and wear the name
    Of Freedom, graven on a heavier chain!
  O Liberty! with profitless endeavour
Have I pursued thee, many a weary hour;
  But thou nor swell'st the victor's strain, nor ever
Didst breathe thy soul in forms of human power.
  Alike from all, howe'er they praise thee,
    (Nor prayer, nor boastful name delays thee)
      Alike from Priestcraft's harpy minions,
And factious Blasphemy's obscener slaves,

Thou speedest on thy subtle pinions,
The guide of homeless winds, and playmate of the waves!
And there I felt thee!—on that sea-cliff's verge,
    Whose pines, scarce travelled by the breeze above,
Had made one murmur with the distant surge!
Yes, while I stood and gazed, my temples bare,
And shot my being through earth, sea and air,
    Possessing all things with intensest love,
    O Liberty! my spirit felt thee there.